Discourses on Prayer

Thomas Boston

Vintage Puritan
GLH Publishing
Louisville, KY

Sourced from *The Whole Works of Thomas Boston*. Vol. XI.
Edited by Samuel M'Millan. Aberdeen: George and Robert King, 1852.

Reprinted by GLH Publishing, 2022
Additional footnotes © GLH Publishing, 2022

ISBN:
Paperback 978-1-64863-105-4
Epub 978-1-64863-098-9

For information on new releases, weekly deals, and free ebooks visit
www.GLHpublishing.com

CONTENTS

I. Of the Nature of Prayer in General; with the Import of Praying without Ceasing 1

Pray without ceasing.
1 Thessalonians v. 17

II. Of the Spirit's Help in Prayer 12

Likewise the Spirit also helpeth our infirmities; for we know not what we should pray for as we ought; but the Spirit itself maketh intercession for us with groanings which cannot be uttered.
ROMANS viii. 26

III. Of Praying in the Name of Jesus Christ 79

Whatsoever ye shall ask the Father in my name, he will give it you.
JOHN xvi. 23

IV. Of God's Hearing of Prayer 96

O thou that hearest prayer, unto thee shall all flesh come.
PSALM lxv. 2

V. On Acceptance with God: The Doctrine of the Acceptance of Men's Works Explained, and a Practical Regard thereto in all the Duties of Life Inculcated 125

For if there be first a willing mind, it is accepted according to that a man hath, and not according to that he hath not.
2 CORINTHIANS viii. 12

VI. Jesus Christ the Beloved One, and Sinners Accepted of God Freely in Him 153

His grace, wherein he hath made us accepted in the Beloved.
EPHESIANS i. 6

I. Of the Nature of Prayer in General; with the Import of Praying without Ceasing[1]

Pray without ceasing.
1 Thessalonians v. 17

THESE words are an exhortation briefly delivered, as laws use to be; and therein we have, 1. A duty proposed, "Pray." 2. The manner of it, "without ceasing."

I. We have the duty itself, "Pray." It may be asked, What is prayer? I answer, It is "an offering up of our desires to God, for things agreeable to his will, in the name of Christ, with confession of our sins, and thankful acknowledgement of his mercies." Here I shall consider,

1. The object of prayer, or whom we are to pray to.
2. The parts of prayer.
3. The matter of it.
4. In whose name we are to pray.
5. The several kinds of prayer.

First, I am to consider the object of this duty, or whom we are to pray to; that is, God: not to saints and angels, as the Papists do; for prayer is a part of religious worship, and therefore due to God only, Matth. iv. 10; and he only knows all things, and is present everywhere to hear us, Isa. lxiii. 16. To all the three persons in the Trinity prayer is due. That it is so to the Father, nobody doubts. That it is due to Christ, the Son, appears from Stephen's calling upon him in his last moments, and saying, "Lord Jesus, receive my spirit," Acts vii. 59. Even Christ the Mediator is to be worshipped, though his divine nature is the reason why he is worshipped, Heb. i. 6, "And let all the angels of God worship him." The Holy Ghost

---

1 The substance of two Sermons preached at Etterick, in the year 1727.

also is to be worshipped, as appears from the apostolical benediction, 2 Cor. xiii. 14, "The communion of the Holy Ghost be with you all."

In respect of the object of worship, people would do well to satisfy themselves, in their addresses to God, with the belief of the Trinity of persons in the Godhead, who are but one object of worship, and not think to comprehend God, but to make use of the names and titles he has taken to himself in the word. Beware of imaginations of God or the three persons, and of dividing the object of worship, as if praying to the Father, you did not also pray to the Son and the Holy Ghost.

It is most necessary our prayers begin with such a description of God, as may both strike fear and dread in our hearts; and confidence of being heard; as, "Our Father which art in heaven"; "O, Lord, the great and dreadful God, keeping the covenant, and mercy," &c., Dan. ix. 4. And this will readily be the case, if we have due thoughts of his glorious majesty and infinite excellency.

Secondly, The parts of prayer are three, (1.) Confession, (2.) Thanksgiving, and (3.) Petition.

1. Confession, Dan. ix. 4, 5, "I prayed unto the Lord my God, and made my confession, and said, O Lord the great and dreadful God, keeping the covenant, and mercy to them that love him, and to them that keep his commandments: we have sinned, and have committed iniquity, and have done wickedly, and have rebelled," &c. It well becomes sinful dust and ashes, in addresses to God, to come with a blush in the countenance, and tears in the eye, and confession in the mouth. It is necessary to humble us in the sight of God, and it is the humble only that are heard, Psalm x. 17. Confession is the vomiting up of the sweet morsel, and God has joined pardon and confession together, 1 John i. 9, "If we confess our sins, he is faithful and just to forgive us our sins, and to cleanse us from all unrighteousness." God's ears are shut to those whose mouths are bound up from this. Some say they cannot pray: O can ye not confess what you are, have done, and daily are doing? How can ye want matter of prayer, while ye have so many sins to confess?

2. Thanksgiving, Phil. iv. 6, "In every thing by prayer and supplication with thanksgiving, let your requests be made known unto God." Every man is God's debtor for mercies, as well as sins; the least return ye can make, is to acknowledge debt. He that is unthankful for what he has got, cannot think to come speed in addresses for more.

3. Petition, wherein prayer properly consists. It is an offering up of our desires to God. Wherein we may note the act of prayer, "offering up our desires." The prayer that God makes account of is first in the heart, 1 Cor. xiv. 15, "I will pray with the spirit, and I will pray with the understanding also." It is a pouring out of the heart to God, Psalm lxii. 8. The Spirit of God moves on the waters of our affections, and then they are poured out before the Lord, as the water of the well of Bethlehem was by David. Many times our prayers come as mud out of a vessel; but as water they should flow freely. Then,

In prayer there are real desires of what we seek of God, which desires are offered to the Lord. The mouth must not speak out anything but what is the desire of the heart. It is dangerous to mock God, who knows the heart; to confess sin, and not have the heart affected with it; to seek supply of wants from him, and not have the heart impressed with a due sense of the want of them. There are two sorts of desires.

(1.) There are *natural* desires, which are the mere product of our own spirits, offered unto God, but not regarded as prayer (Hos. vii. 14.) by the Lord. These may be not only for temporal things but for spiritual also, as those who said to Christ, "Lord evermore give us this bread." A natural man, from a gift of prayer, may seek grace and glory, as a bridge to lead him over the waters of wrath; but coming only from their own spirits, such a prayer is not acceptable.

(2.) There are *spiritual* desires, Zech. xii. 10; which the saints breathe out unto God, having them first breathed into them by the Spirit, Rom. viii. 26. And these may be for temporal things, as well as spiritual, accepted, seeing they are put up in a spiritual manner. These are always sincere and fervent, so as the soul earnestly craves the things sought.

Thirdly, The matter of prayer, or what we are to petition and seek for. These are, the things that are agreeable to God's will. To pray for the fulfilling of unlawful desires, is horrid, Jam. iv. 3. But the will of God is the rule of our prayers, 1 John v. 14, "This is the confidence that we have in him, that if we ask anything according to his will, he heareth us." We find the will of God in his commands and promises. Whatever God has commanded us to seek, whatever he has promised, that we may and ought to pray for. These are, (1.) Spiritual mercies, grace, glory, the increase of grace, comforts, &c. (2.) Temporal mercies, health, strength, &c., mercies relating to our bodies and temporal estate in the world.

Some have no freedom to bring their temporal concerns to their prayers. ANS. That we may and ought to do it, is plain.

1. In that God has given them a place in his covenant; they are promised as well as spiritual mercies, 1 Tim. iv. 8, "Godliness is profitable unto all things, having promise of the life that now is, and of that which is to come." Isa. xxxiii. 16, "Bread shall be given him, his water shall be sure." Psalm i. 3, "Whatsoever he doth shall prosper."

2. It has been the practice of the saints in all ages. Memorable is Agur's prayer, Prov. xxx. 8, "Give me neither poverty, nor riches, feed me with food convenient for me."

3. Christ teaches us so to do in that pattern of prayer, Matth. vi. 9, &c., "Give us this day our daily bread," where we may observe, that they ought to have a place in our prayers daily.

4. God has commanded it, Phil. iv. 6, "Be careful for nothing: but in every thing by prayer and supplication with thanksgiving, let your requests be made known unto God." Ezek. xxxvi. 37, "Thus saith the Lord God, I will yet for this be inquired of by the house of Israel, to do it for them." Compare vers. 30, 33, &c., "I will multiply the fruit of the tree," &c. It is a general command, "In all thy ways acknowledge him," Prov. iii. 6.

5. Sin and duty are very large. Men are under a law as to their management of temporal concerns, and light and wisdom should be sought for the same from the Lord, Psalm cxii. 5, "A good man will guide his affairs with discretion." No doubt many things go the worse with us, that God is so little owned in them. If that be true, that "God doth instruct the plowman to discretion, and doth teach him," Isa. xxviii. 26, there is a good reason we pray, that "God may establish the work of our hands upon us," Psalm xc. ult. Surely those Christians that neglect it, deprive themselves of many experiences of the Lord's kindness. For the temporal mercies they meet with, were they answers of prayer, would be so many experiences of the Lord's love, Isa. xli. 11. Nay, I think it were a piece of Christian prudence, for the child of God, when he finds his heart not so affected as he would have it for spiritual mercies, to make an errand to God of a temporal mercy, whereby his heart may be the more fitted for asking spiritual blessings; as we have instances often in the Psalms, and also in the famous wrestling of Jacob. Only,

(1.) Pray for temporal mercies for the sake of spiritual, not contrariwise, Matth. vi. 33, "Seek ye first the kingdom of

God, and his righteousnesss, and all these things shall be added unto you." Prov. xxx. 8-9, "Give me neither poverty, nor riches, feed me with food convenient for me: lest I be full, and deny thee, and say, Who is the Lord? or lest I be poor, and steal, and take the name of my God in vain."

(2.) Keep within the bounds of the promise. Now, all promises of temporal things have this condition, if they be for God's glory and his children's good. Pray so as you may be content to want them, if God see it meet. But as for grace, the favour of God, and communion with him here and hereafter, it can never be our duty to be content to want them, 1 Thess. iv. 3, "For this is the will of God, even your sanctification."

Fourthly, In whose name are we to pray? In the name of Christ, John xiv. 13, 14, "Whatsover ye shall ask in my name, that will I do, that the Father may be glorified in the Son. If ye shall ask any thing in my name, I will do it." This is to plead the merits of Jesus Christ. We must come to God in the name of Christ, laying all the stress upon his merits. All things go by favour in the court of heaven; the Father hears us for the Son's sake. This implies that we must be in Christ, before we can pray acceptably. But I shall consider this particular more fully, when I come, in course, to speak of praying in the name of Christ.

Fifthly, There are several kinds of prayer. I shall speak a word to these three, ejaculatory, secret, and family.

1. Ejaculatory prayer, which is a sudden dispatch of the desires of the soul to heaven, upon any emergent occasion; sometimes with the voice, and sometimes without it. I will say of it,

(1.) It has been the practice of the saints. Thus Jacob, when making his testament, says, Gen. xlix. 18, "I have waited for thy salvation, O Lord." And when giving charge to his sons concerning Benjamin, chap. xliii. 14, "God Almighty give you mercy be fore the man," &c. Moses, when brought into a great strait at the approach of the Egyptians, Exod. xiv. 15, "The Lord said unto Moses, Wherefore criest thou unto me? Speak unto the children of Israel, that they go forward." David, when told of Ahithophel's being among the conspirators with Absalom, says, 2 Sam. xv. 31, "O Lord, I pray thee, turn the counsel of Ahithophel into foolishness." And Nehemiah, when in the king's presence, and asked by him his request, says, chap. ii. 4, "I pray to the God of heaven."

(2.) Such prayers are very necessary. Light and strength for duty, against temptation, &c., are often needed, when we cannot get to our knees.

(3.) They are very useful for present help, and are notable means to keep the soul habitually heavenly and in a proper frame, when we make more solemn approaches to God.

(4.) It is no small mercy, that God's door stands always open, and that our prayers may be at heaven, before we can be at a secret place.

2. Secret prayer, wherein the man or woman goes alone to a secret place, and they pour out their souls before the Lord.

(1.) It is commanded expressly by our Lord, Matth. vi. 6, "When thou prayest, enter into thy closet, and when thou hast shut thy door, pray to thy Father which is in secret," &c.

(2.) They will have much ado to evidence their sincerity, whose prayers are all before men, Matth. vi. 5, 6, "When thou prayest, thou shalt not be as the hypocrites are: for they love to pray, standing in the synagogues, and in the corners of the streets, that they may be seen of men," &c. A hypocrite may pray in secret; but a sincere soul will be loath to neglect it.

(3.) As no man knows our case so well as ourselves, so it is a sign of little acquaintance with our own hearts, if we have not something to tell Christ, which we cannot tell before others, Cant. vii. 11, 12, "Come, my Beloved, let us go forth into the field: let us lodge in the villages. Let us get up early to the vineyards, let us see if the vine flourish, whether the tender grape appear, and the pomegranates bud forth: there will I give thee my loves."

(4.) The greatest enjoyments of the people of God have been in secret prayer; as in the case of Jacob, Daniel, &c.

3. Family prayer. God must be worshipped in our families, as well as in our closets.

(1.) God commands it, in so far as he requires every kind of prayer, Eph. vi. 18, "Praying always with all prayer." The scripture speaks of a church in Aquila's house, Rom. xvi. 5. Surely the family was not such a one that shut God out of doors. The family sacrifice was God's ordinance, Exod. xii. 21, "Draw out, and take you a lamb, according to your families, and kill the passover."

(2.) It was the practice of Christ, Matth. xxvi. 30, John xvii. and of the saints, as Job, chap. i. 5, Joshua, chap. xxiv. 15, and Cornelius, Acts x. 2. Elisha prayed with his servant, 2 Kings iv. 33.

(3.) The master of the family has the charge of the souls under his roof; and surely the case of a family requires family prayer. Are there not family wants, sins, and mercies, that require such an exercise?

O what a heavy vengeance abides families that are without the worship of God! Jer. x. 25, "Pour out thy fury upon the heathen that know thee not, and upon the families that call not on thy name." That house that is not sanctified by prayer, is like to be the house of the wicked, where God's curse is. How will ye answer for the souls committed to your charge, who do not pray in your families? No wonder godly persons should scare at your family; though indeed it is to be lamented, that many professors like Jonah will flee from the presence of the Lord, out of a praying family to a prayerless one; whom a storm sometimes pursues.

Before proceeding to the other head, the manner of praying, permit me to make a very brief improvement of what has been said.

1. Let me address myself to those that live in the total neglect of this duty of prayer. O repent and amend, and set about this necessary duty. Consider,

(1.) A prayerless person is a graceless person, in a state of wrath, in the gall of bitterness and the bond of iniquity. No sooner is Paul converted, but, "behold, he prayeth." Still-born children cannot be heirs. The Spirit of grace is the Spirit of supplication. The Spirit makes us to cry, "Abba, Father."

(2.) A prayerless person is a thief and a robber of what he possesses in the world. How darest thou use God's creatures, and not ask his leave? 1 Tim. iv. 4, 5, "For every creature of God is good, and nothing to be refused, if it be received with thanksgiving: for it is sanctified by the word of God and prayer." Surely, thou prayerless one, a curse is on thy house, thy basket, and thy store. But, alas! many live like swine; they never look up to heaven, nor cry till the knife of death be at their throat.

(3.) It is a privilege that God will allow us to come so near him, and to pour out our hearts before him, a privilege bought by the blood of Christ. The prayless person undervalues this rich privilege, trampling on that blood that bought it, which will be a worm in his conscience in hell that will gnaw it for ever.

(4.) Thy soul lies at stake. That dumb devil that possesses thee, must be cast out of thee, or thou art undone for ever. Thou art lost by nature; wilt thou not cry for the life of thy poor soul? God says to thee, as Pilate to Christ, John xix. 10, "Speakest thou not unto me? knowest thou not, that I have power to *damn* thee, and have power to save thee?" Thou canst not be saved, without calling on the Lord by prayer.

But perhaps one may say, I will pray on a deathbed. ANSW. What if God cut thee off in a moment? what if thou die in the rage of a fever? how knowest thou that God will then hear thee? Ponder and seriously consider what the Lord says, Prov. i. 24–31, "Because I have called, and ye refused, I have stretched out my hand, and no man regarded; but ye have set at nought all my counsel, and would none of my reproof: I also will laugh at your calamity, I will mock when your fear cometh; when your fear cometh as desolation, and your destruction cometh as a whirlwind; when distress and anguish cometh upon you. Then shall they call upon me, but I will not answer; they shall seek me early, but they shall not find me: for that they hated knowledge, and did not choose the fear of the Lord. They would none of my counsel: they despised all my reproof. Therefore shall they eat of the fruit of their own way, and be filled with their own devices." And remember that such a conduct will bring you to that miserable pass described, Isa. viii. 21, 22, "And they shall pass through it, hardly bestead and hungry: and it shall come to pass, that when they shall be hungry, they shall fret themselves, and curse their king, and their God, and look upward. And they shall look unto the earth: and behold trouble and darkness, dimness of anguish; and they shall be driven to darkness."

Another may say, I cannot pray. ANSW. Will ye try, for God calls thee; thou mayst expect assistance, Exod. iv. 11, "Who hath made man's mouth? or who maketh the dumb, or deaf, or the seeing, or the blind? have not I the Lord?" Seriously consider thy state and sins, and thou shalt have matter for confession; consider thy mercies, and thou shalt have matter for thanksgiving; consider thy wants, and thou shalt have matter for petition. Though thou canst not express thyself as some others, yet be sincere. Parents love to hear their babes that are learning to speak; and God will never refuse to hear the sincere language of a heart, though it is not expressed in the most proper words.

2. To praying persons I would say, Continue constantly in this duty of prayer, and never give it over as long as you live. Consider,

(1.) Your need, wants, temptations, snares, &c. never cease, nor will cease while ye are here; and why should ye cease to pray? God will have his people live from hand to mouth, because he loves to have them always about his hand.

(2) Praying is a soul-enriching trade. It is a trade with heaven, and brings down temporal and spiritual mercies. He that drives this trade most diligently, will be found the most thriving Christian. Surely the leanness among professors is owing to this neglect in a great measure.

(3.) If ever a time called for prayer, this time does, while the ark of God is in hazard, and damnable errors are spreading. O then pray, and pray frequently, and ere long your prayers shall be turned to praises.

II. I proceed to consider the manner of praying, or to shew, in what respects we are to "pray without ceasing." This is not to be understood as if we should spend our whole time in the exercise of prayer: for there are many other duties, both of our station in life and as Christians, that we are bound to perform; and these must have their time; and God does not bind us to inconsistencies. But we must,

1. Pray frequently, as David did, Psalm cxix. 164, "Seven times a-day do I praise thee: because of thy righteous judgments." The Christian should be no stranger to, but often at that work. It is a piece of walking with God, wherein the soul seeks communion with Heaven, and wherein he should abound, Col. ii. 6, 7. We find Daniel frequently at it, when it was death to pray, Dan. vi. 10. See Psalm lv. 17, "Evening and morning, and at noon will I pray, and cry aloud: and he shall hear my voice." Hereby may be known what case the soul is in; the more diligent one is in this duty, he will be the more thriving.

2. Pray statedly, without ceasing from the set times of prayer. These are evening and morning. The morning and evening sacrifice were called "the continual burnt-offering," Exod. xxix. 39, 41, 42, as being offered continually at these times. And these times were the times of prayer, Acts iii. 1. The light of nature itself teaches us to begin and end the day with the worship of God. And they should be reckoned lost days that are not so begun and ended.

3. Pray occasionally, without ceasing from embracing occasions of praying which the Lord puts in your hand. Do as David did, Psalm xxvii. 8, "When thou saidst, Seek ye my face; my heart said unto thee, Thy face, Lord, will I seek." An observing Christian will sometimes find himself called to pray between hands; and it is dangerous to sit the motion of an occasional tryst that God sometimes sets a person. To such

a tryst there concurs, (1.) An inward moving of the soul to converse with God by prayer, Psalm xxvii. 8, just cited; the Spirit of the Lord exciting to duty, by representing a particular need, or fit occasion of converse with God, and so pressing a man forward to the throne to supplicate. (2.) A fair opportunity for it, Gal. vi. 10. And forasmuch as there may be motions to prayer, that are not from the Spirit of God, they may thus be discerned by the unseasonableness of them; for the Spirit of God puts people to duty seasonably, Psalm i. 3.

4. Pray constantly, Eph. vi. 18, "Praying always with all prayer and supplication in the Spirit, and watching thereunto with all perseverance." There must be a persevering in this duty, in the several kinds thereof, as the Lord gives opportunity. And this imports a continuing the course of praying, never giving up with it while breath remains, nor giving it over for a time, Psalm cxix. 112. The latter makes way for the former, as swooning does for dying for good and all.

5. Pray "importunately," not fainting nor giving over your tabled petitions as long as your needs remain, but resolutely pursuing them before the throne; Luke xviii. 1, "And he spake a parable unto them, to this end, that men ought always to pray, and not to faint." Pray till you get the answer of your prayers, if it should be never so long delayed. God loves to have such petitioners about him as are resolute, and will not take a nay-say, as in the woman of Canaan's case; Matth. xv. 22–28.

6. Be *habitual* in the use of ejaculatory prayer; for this is a kind of prayer that can be mixed with whatever other good thing ye are about. There is an occasion for lifting up the heart to the Lord in an ejaculatory petition, in every business that is lawful, and in every company; and there is always an opportunity for it too. All our actions should be seasoned with it.

7. *Lastly*, Keep your hearts always in a praying frame; that whenever God calls you, you may be ready as the soldier at the sound of the trumpet; Eph. vi. 18. Hereto two things are necessary. (1.) That ye keep a clean conscience, watching against sin, having habitually recourse to the blood of sprinkling; Heb. ix. 14. (2.) That ye use moderation in all things, Phil. iv. 5. That joy or sorrow, eating or drinking, working or diversion, that unfits a man for prayer, is too much; for glorifying God is our chief end, to which all other ends must be subordinated; 1 Cor. x. 31, "Whether ye eat or drink, or whatsoever ye do, do all to the glory of God."

Use I. Of reproof to those that, being come to years of discretion,

1. Have not yet begun to pray; but live like beasts, eating, working, or playing, and sleeping, but have not begun to pray to the God that made them. Ah! know ye not that ye must die, and live eternally in another world? that ye are criminals, and have forfeited your life by your sin? that ye must be pardoned, or perish? And ye that have not set up God's worship in your families, will ye not give God house-room with you? Know your danger, and flee from the fury which the Lord will pour out on those who call not on his name.

2. Those that have left off praying. Sometimes they have prayed, but have given it over now; some in secret, and some in their families. Remember that this makes you apostates, and that apostasy is very dangerous. Consider the two following scripture-passages; 2 Pet. ii. 21, "It had been better for them not to have known the way of righteousness, than after they have known it, to turn from the holy commandment delivered unto them." Heb. x. 38, "If any man draw back, my soul shall have no pleasure in him."

3. Those that pray now and then only, as it suits with their conveniency. Some will pray on the Sabbath-day, when they have no other thing to do. Sometimes they are in a good mood, and take a start of praying; at other times they will rise from bed, and go to it, without ever bowing a knee to God. They will pray at even, but not at morn. Some cannot be got to set up the worship of God in their families in the morning, others for several days in a week have no family worship, sometimes in the year in the throng of business. Let conscience say, if that be "praying without ceasing." Is it not a contempt of God in his worship, and like the hypocrite; Job xxvii. 10, of whom it is said, "Will he always call upon God?"

Use II. Pray without ceasing. For, (1.) Satan never ceases to seek your destruction, 1 Pet. v. 8. (2.) Your need of the Lord's help never ceaseth; ye need direction, protection, life, strength, mercies of all kinds, spiritual and temporal. (3.) *Lastly*, Time never ceases to run, and ye know not when it may run out. There is good reason we pray always, since we know no time wherein death may not overtake us.

II. Of the Spirit's Help in Prayer[2]

Likewise the Spirit also helpeth our infirmities; for we know not what we should pray for as we ought; but the Spirit itself maketh intercession for us with groanings which cannot be uttered.
Romans viii. 26

Somewhat of the nature of prayer in general, with the import of praying without ceasing, has been explained to you; but it is not every kind of prayer that is acceptable to God. Among praying people there is a twofold cry that goes to heaven, (1.) The cry of strangers, not known and approved there. That is prayer wrought out by ourselves, in virtue of a natural sense of want, by a gift of knowledge and utterance. (2.) The cry of children; that is prayer wrought in us by the help of the Holy Spirit dwelling and acting in us, and is accepted of God. Of this our text speaks. In which,

1. The connection is to be noticed, "likewise." This chapter is an inventory of the privileges of believers. (1.) Freedom from condemnation, ver. 1, "There is therefore now no condemnation to them which are in Christ Jesus." (2.) Sanctification, ver. 5, "They that are after the Spirit, do mind the things of the Spirit." (3.) Comfort against death, ver. 10, "If Christ be in you, the body is dead, because of sin; but the Spirit is life, because of righteousness." (4.) Sonship to God, ver. 14, "As many as are led by the Spirit of God, they are the sons of God." (5.) Glorification abiding them, ver. 18, "For I reckon, that the sufferings of this present time, are not worthy to be compared with the glory which shall be revealed in us." From this high privilege the apostle looks down on the cross and afflictions here laid on believers, and shews there is no

---

[2] Several Sermons preached at Etterick, in the year 1727.

comparison betwixt these afflictions and that glory, they being but like a prick with a pin received by one in his way to a crown. And this is a first grand consolation against the cross laid on believers. (6.) The help of the Spirit for the present, in the text. And this is the second grand consolation of believers under the cross. They have not only, under all their afflictions, eternal glory made sure to them in end; but for the present time, while they are going under their burden, they have the Spirit of the Lord helping them, and particularly in prayer, the noted relief of the distressed, "Like-wise the Spirit also helpeth our infirmities," &c. And that is a great consolation under the cross.

2. The words themselves, in which we may observe two things:—

1*st*, A general assertion of the Spirit's assisting of believers in the midst of their infirmities. And here, (1.) There is something supposed, namely, That they are compassed with infirmities while here. They are recovered of their deadly sickness of sin, but they are still weak; they are restored to life, but they have as yet little strength, and are much bowed down with pressures on them. (2.) Something expressed, namely, the Spirit's helping of them in that case. Weak people need help, especially under heavy burdens. And believers want not help under theirs; they have the best of help, the help of God himself, the eternal Spirit of the Father and the Son, the third person of the glorious Trinity, by whom the Father and the Son do act in them. He "helps our infirmities," *i. e.* helps us in our infirmities, to whatsoever we have to do or bear.

This help of the Spirit is a joint action, as the word imports. *Q. d.* He "together over-against" takes a lift of our burden. Where the Spirit helps, the man is not idle; but while the believer is going under his burden, he lifts the heavy end of it, and makes it the lighter to us; he does as the nurse with the child learning to go; the child moves his feet, but she holds him up and helps him, holding it by the arms.

2*dly*, A particular condescension, namely, his helping them in prayer, which brings great relief under the cross. And here,

(1.) We have a general infirmity that believers labour under, and that is little skill of praying. Whenever the grace of God touches their hearts, they are set a-praying; however, they are in it but like children beginning to speak; while unbelievers meanwhile are but like dumb people making a roar. Their weakness and unskilfulness in praying lies in two things.

[1.] In the matter of prayer, "We know not what we should pray for." We are apt, instead of bread, to ask a stone; instead of a fish, a scorpion; to pray for what would do us ill, and against what is for our good.

[2.] In the manner of prayer, "We know not what we should pray for as we ought." We cannot put our prayers in right shape, even when we are right as to the matter of them. We cannot put our petitions in form, in the style of the court of heaven.

(2.) The Spirit's help afforded them in this case: "But the Spirit itself maketh intercession for us," &c. Where we may notice,

[1.] The agent in this help, "the Spirit itself," rather "the Spirit himself"; the meaning certainly is so, for the Spirit here spoken of is a person, not a thing; though, by reason of the language the apostle wrote in, it is expressed neutrally.

[2.] The help itself, He "maketh intercession for us." Christ intercedes for us in heaven; the Spirit intercedes in us, by his effectual working in us, helping us to pray aright, and make intercession for ourselves. He forms our petitions for the court of heaven. No gifts could avail to this end. If the best gift without the Spirit were bestowed on a man, he could not make a prayer that would be acceptable to God, though it might be much admired of men.

[3.] An instance of a particular, whereto the Spirit helps in prayer "with groanings." Not that the Spirit's help in prayer appears in these only; but that even these groanings for divine aid, which believers have in their prayer, though they may be reckoned small things, yet are really great and prevalent with God, as proceeding from and produced in them by his own Spirit; and they are more forcible and expressive of the desires of the soul than any words; so they are "groanings which cannot be uttered." It is evident, that the Spirit of God in himself doth not groan; but groanings are attributed to him, so far as he causes us to groan, by exciting our affections. Therefore his intercession is to be understood of his causing and helping us to intercede in prayer for ourselves.

The following doctrines may be observed from the words thus explained.

DOCTRINE I. It is a comfortable case under affliction, where the party is helped from heaven to pray under their burden.

DOCTRINE II. It is the privilege of believers to have the help of the Holy Spirit, under the infirmities with which they are compassed while here.

DOCTRINE III. Such is the weakness of God's own children, that they have not skill to manage even their addresses to God by prayer aright, without the Spirit.

DOCTRINE IV. All our praying aright is so far done by the help of the Spirit, that it is justly reckoned his work, his making intercession for us.

DOCTRINE V. ult. The Spirit helps believers to pray, particularly causing in them gracious groanings, which cannot be uttered.

DOCT. I. It is a comfortable case under affliction, where the party is helped from heaven to pray under their burden. This doctrine arises from the connection and scope of the words.

In discoursing from it, I shall consider,
I. What is the help from heaven to pray under a burden.
II. The comfort that is in this case.
III. Make improvement.

I. What is the help from heaven to pray under a burden. I take it up in these two particulars.

1. Help to lay the case before the Lord, and to table petitions before the throne of grace upon the case. If any are thus helped it is a token for good, they may take comfort of it; Psalm lxvi. 16, 17, "Come and hear, all ye that fear God, and I will declare what he hath done for my soul. I cried unto him with my mouth, and he was extolled with my tongue." Little do we know how to table petitions on our case at the court of heaven; but if a shower of trouble should fall on us, and withal the spirit of prayer be poured on us, we would have no cause to complain. Though the Lord press down a person with the one hand, and stir him up to the exercise of prayer with the other, it is a hopeful case, as was that of Jonah, chap. ii. 1.

2. Help to insist and resolutely to hang on and not faint, however longsome the hearing may be, Col. i. 11. Thus the Spirit helps the children of God in prayer; Psalm cxxxviii. 3, "In the day when I cried thou answeredst me; and strengthenedst me with strength in my soul"; 2 Cor. xii. 9, "And he said unto me, My grace is sufficient for thee; for my strength is made perfect in weakness." The patience of others in ap-

plications to the throne of grace will soon be tired out; they cannot wait, so they drop the matter, Job xxvii. 10, and go to another door. But those in whom the Spirit dwells see no other door, John vi. 68, and the Spirit is a spring of living water in them, which causes them to hold on.

II. What is the comfort that is in this case. It is manifold. I instance in the following particulars.

1. That is comfortable in it, that the native effect of affliction is stopped in such a person by influence from heaven. Affliction in its own nature is a whip, a brier, a thorn; and the native effect of it is, to drive the sinner away from God, to harden his heart, irritate his corruption, and make his heart a hell; Job xxxvi. 13, "The hypocrites in heart heap up wrath; they cry not when he bindeth them." But, by divine institution, it is a medicine, having a promise annexed to it; Isa. xxvi. 9, "When thy judgments are in the earth, the inhabitants of the world will learn righteousness"; and so it brings the believing sinner to God, as the bitter potion causes the sick man turn to his physician, who would all he could keep himself out of the way of an enemy that had given him such a bitter draught, Rom. x. 14.

2. It is comfortable, even that the party gets a vent to his full heart. Those in a trouble find a kind of relief in pouring out their heart into the bosom of a sympathising friend; and it is an aggravation of affliction, when the fire must burn in the bosom, and there is no access to give it a vent. How much more is it a solid comfort, to be helped to pour out one's heart unto a gracious God, able and willing to help in due time? Micah resolved to take comfort this way; Micah vii. 7, "I will look unto the Lord; I will wait for the God of my salvation; my God will hear me." And Hannah got it; 1 Sam. i. 15, 16, "And Hannah answered and said, No, my lord, I am a woman of a sorrowful spirit; I have drunk neither wine nor strong drink, but have poured out my soul before the Lord. Count not thine handmaid for a daughter of Belial; for out of the abundance of my complaint and grief have I spoken hitherto." Ver. 18, "And she said, Let thine handmaid find grace in thy sight. So the woman went her way, and did eat, and her countenance was no more sad."

3. It is comfortable that the Lord takes that way to draw the sinner to him, and keep him about his hand, and it is effectual; Hos. v. ult., "I will go and return to my place, till they acknowledge their offence, and seek my face; in their affliction they will seek me early." We reckon in the world, that

they are in the best case that hold all within themselves; but in respect of spiritual thriving, they are fairest for that who are kept from hand to mouth, and never want a new errand to God's door. The Lord loves to have his children always about his hand, but they would be like children at their play about meal-time, that would never mind home if hunger did not bite them; and so in effect it fares with many.

4. That is comfortable in it, that it is a sign of eternal good-will and everlasting love to such persons; Luke xviii. 7, "And shall not God avenge his own elect, which cry day and night unto him, though he bear long with them?" They would be tired out, if they were not God's chosen, possessed by his Spirit. Do ye see a place which is always fall of water, summer and winter, in the greatest drought? ye may be sure that is no pool, but a spring, John iv. 14. The man prays and wrestles against a body of death, cries and goes on under a weight of trials; he holds on notwithstanding of seeming fruitlessness. See the verdict; Matth. xxiv. 13, "He that shall endure unto the end the same shall be saved."

5. That is comfortable in it, that his prayers shall be heard at length to his heart's content, if it should not be till he get into heaven; Luke xviii. 8," I tell you that he will avenge them speedily."

The help of the Spirit in prayer is a certain pledge of the hearing of prayer, Jam. v. 18. If a poor man were to petition the king, but had no skill to draw his petition; and the king should send one from about his hand to help that poor man, and draw his petition for him; would not that be a sign that the king had a good mind to grant it? So it is equally a certain sign of God's good-will to the praying person, and a certain token that his prayers shall be heard to his full satisfaction at length, that the Spirit now helps him in prayer, and, as it were, draws his petitions for him.

6. It is comfortable, that the party is now and then getting some off-fallings about the Lord's hand; otherwise he would give over. In the way of duty, wherein people are not formal, but truly serious, there is a concomitant reward; Psalm xix. 11, "In keeping of them there is great reward"; and particularly in prayer; Isa. xlv. 19, "I said not unto the seed of Jacob, seek ye me in vain." Though the Lord does not give the main request for the time, yet be gives something that keeps the heart from fainting; Lam. iii. 57, "Thou drewest near in the day that I called upon thee; thou saidst, Fear not." So we find it happened to Paul; 2 Cor. xii. 8, 9, "For this thing I besought the

Lord thrice that it might depart from me. And he said unto me my grace is sufficient for thee; for my strength is made perfect in weakness. Most gladly, therefore, will I rather glory in my infirmities, that the power of Christ may rest upon me."

From what is said on this doctrine, the following things may be shortly observed for improvement.

1. The Lord's cross on his people's back, is better than the world's crown on the head of his enemies. For there is more comfort in the one's being helped from heaven to commit their case to the Lord, and depend on him for it, than in all the prosperity of the wicked. For all is well that ends well; and the former will have a joyful end, the latter a sad one, Prov. i. 32, 33.

2. They are doubly to be pitied, who are under an afflicted lot, and withal strangers to the duty and comfort of prayer. This world is a place wherein neither good nor bad will miss their share of crosses. But to see this world frowning on a man, and in the meantime him not seeking his comfort from heaven; to see a person full of matter of complaints, and yet having no heart to pour them out into the bosom of our heavenly Father, is a sad sight.

3. Let praying people beware of afflictions deadening them, and taking heart and hand from them in prayer. Satan will do his utmost to work up afflictions to this pitch; and when he has got it done, he has what he would wish, he has an envenomed arrow sticking in their flesh. Let them haste to get it away, as ever they would cast a coal of hell out of their bosom; and remember that "God is love; and he that dwelleth in love, dwelleth in God, and God in him," 1 John iv. 16; that "the Lord doth not afflict willingly, nor grieve the children of men," Lam. iii. 33; and that "all things work together for good, to them that love God, to them who are the called according to his purpose," Rom. viii. 28.

4. *Lastly*, Let those who are helped to pray under their affliction be thankful, and acknowledge God has not forgotten them. When the Lord's people have plied the throne of grace long for a mercy, and yet it comes not, they are ready to think that the Lord regards them not. But if ye be helped still to hang on, that very thing is an evidence that it is not true; and is a token for good in your case.

DOCTRINE II. It is the privilege of believers to have the help of the Holy Spirit, under the infirmities with which they are compassed while here.

Here I shall shew,

I. What are the infirmities believers are compassed with here.

II. Why in the depth of sovereign wisdom, believers are left compassed so with infirmities while here.

III. Consider the Spirit's helping believers under these infirmities.

IV. Make some practical improvement.

I. I am to show what are the infirmities believers are compassed with here.

First, They are always compassed with natural infirmities.

1. Pure natural infirmities, which though they be their weights and burdens, yet are not their sins. There is a natural weakness inwrought with human flesh, though at its prime of vigour, Isa. xl. 6, so that it was found even in the man Christ, 2 Cor. xiii. 4. This makes God's children objects of their Father's pity, Psalm ciii. 13, 14, "Like as a Father pitieth his children: so the Lord pitieth them that fear him. For he knoweth our frame: he remembereth that we are dust." Such are the need of meat, drink, sleep, &c., whereby the tabernacle must be daily underpropped, Matth. xxvi. 41. Even Samson was sore pressed with such infirmity, Judges xv. 18, "He was sore athirst."

2. Sinful natural infirmities, which are both pressures on them, and defilements of them, wounding and polluting.

(1.) Common to them all, namely, the remains of the corruption of nature, which makes them all a company of poor weaklings, groaning under their infirmities, Rom. vii. 24. Their sanctification is imperfect; every grace in them has the contrary weed of corruption growing by the side of it. Grace indeed has got the house, but dwells not alone in it; the Canaanites are left in the land, and they cannot quite drive them out. Hence is the struggle not only with those without, but those within.

(2.) Peculiar to every one of them, namely, the particular bias of corrupt nature in each of them, arising from their natural constitution and temper; and this is a cast of disposition to some particular evil, commonly called "the predominant sin, the sin which doth so easily beset us," Heb. xii. 1. Thus the peculiar infirmity of some is passion, of others vanity, worldliness, &c. Every one will know their own, for it will be that which costs more struggle than anything else, and in which they will find need of the peculiar help of the Spirit.

Secondly, They are often compassed with accidental infirmities.

1. Sinless ones. Such are afflictions, trials, and temptations, which though not their sins, yet are heavy weights to them, causing them much need of help, as in Paul's case, 2 Cor. xii. 7, 8, 9. Thus diseases and ailments of whatsoever nature go under the name of infirmities, as weakening body or spirit, Luke v. 15. Timothy had frequent attacks by them, 1 Tim. v. 23. And in the road to heaven such weights and pressures one way or other will not be missed, Acts xiv. 22.

2. Sinful ones, being wrong casts of spirit, arising from education or other circumstances, giving them as it were a second nature. Such was the infirmity of the disciples, whereby they were ready on all occasions to mind a temporal kingdom of Christ, and to be stumbled at his sufferings; and the bias towards the ceremonial law, which the believing Jews had remaining with them; Rom. xv. 1.

Hence the infirmities of believers may be taken up in the following particulars:—

1. They have weak heads for discerning and understanding sin and duty, snares, temptations, and proper means for eviting the one, and compassing the other, Jer. x. 23, "It is not in man that walketh to direct his steps." The subtle enemy is ready to outwit them, and by his devices to triumph over their weakness. Therefore we are warned not to trust our own understanding, Prov. iii. 5.

2. They have weak hearts for venturing on difficulties, which make them ready to faint at the appearance of them, Isa. xxxv. 4. And the formidable enemy is ready to damp them, and discourage them. They know themselves how little strength they have; and their faith being weak withal, they are apt to sink in their courage for doing and suffering.

3. They have weak hands fore doing of duties in the right manner, Isa. xxxv. 3. They are not in themselves man enough for the most ordinary duties of religion, and therefore being left to themselves, they quite mismanage them, John xv. 5, 2 Cor. iii. 5. And sometimes the Lord calls them to extraordinary duties.

4. *Lastly*, They have weak backs for bearing burdens, so that they are easily bowed down, yea and foundered under them, 2 Cor. ii. 16. Their suffering strength is small, considering the weak frame of their bodies, and the remaining distempers in their souls.

II. I come now to show why, in the depth of sovereign wisdom, believers are left compassed so with infirmities while here. Surely it is not for want of power in their Father to deliver them: for he is almighty, and in the moment he gave them grace, could have perfected them in soul and body. Neither is it for want of love to and concern for them; for he has the bowels of a Father, and gave them his own Son, which was more than all that. But so it is ordered,

1. That the members may be conformed to the head, Rom. viii. 29. Our Lord Jesus did not enter to his glory, but after a long track of sufferings, Heb. ii. 10. This was necessary in the case of Christ the head, for the purchasing of our salvation, Matth. viii. 17; Luke xxiv. 26. And it is necessary in the case of believers, that they may be conformed to him, bearing the image of his sufferings, for his glory.

2. That the emptiness of the creature may be discovered, and the pride of all created glory stained, and that the crown may be put on the head of free grace only; so that we may say, "The Lord of hosts hath purposed it, to stain the pride of all glory, and to bring into contempt all the honourable of the earth," Isa. xxiii. 9. There in a scene is opened, wherein there is a full display of the nothingness of the creature, that heaven may appear to be peopled with those that could have no pretensions to it, but on the score of mere free grace.

3. That all the graces of the Spirit in believers may be brought forth into the field of battle, and exert themselves, 1 Pet. i. 6, 7. There are some graces whose exercise is to be eternal, as love, reverential fear, &c. these will be exerted in heaven as well as here. But there are others that are occasional in their exercise, such as faith, hope, patience, watchfulness, &c. which agree only to a state of imperfection: and there they have occasion to show themselves. So, for the exercise of these, and trial of both sorts, the Canaanites are left in the land. And therefore some are loaded with peculiar infirmities.

4. That the power of the grace of Christ may be magnified. The infirmities wherewith believers are compassed, make a scene wherein the power of Christ is signally displayed, as, says the apostle, 2 Cor. xii. 9, "Most gladly therefore will I rather glory in my infirmities, that the power of Christ may rest upon me." God could have seated Israel in Canaan, without stroke of sword; but then Joshua's valour, which appeared in the conquest of that land, had lain hid. Believers are committed into Christ's hand, as the great Pilot, to guide them through the sea of this world, to the shore of

Immanuel's land: and it will magnify the power of his grace, that by his conduct so many broken ships are brought safe ashore, through so many rocks and shelves, and suffering so many storms.

5. That the bruised serpent may be beat the more shamefully, and Christ's victory and triumph over him may be the more signal. He encountered Christ in person on the cross; and there he was over come, the Son of God being an overmatch for all the powers of hell. But that his defeat may be more shameful, he is yoked with poor believers with a heap of infirmities about them; and by them too, after he has done his worst, he is baffled at length, Rom. xvi. 20. "The God of peace shall bruise Satan under your feet shortly."

And here it is worth observing, that our Lord Jesus singles out some of his people to combat with Satan, loaded with some uncommon infirmity, whereby he has a peculiar advantage against them, that he has not against others: and all to make that malicious spirit's defeat yet more shameful. As if one, to pour contempt on his enemy, should say, I will take such an one of my children that are not quite recovered out of their sickness, and I will bind one of his arms behind his back, and yet make him throw you down, and tread on you. Thus Job was stript of all his comforts, his children, wealth, and health; nothing left him but his life, and his unkind wife that Satan had use for; and Satan makes a furious attack on him to blaspheme, when he had him at all this disadvantage. And yet he was baffled in the end, Jam. v. 11, "Ye have heard of the patience of Job, and have seen the end of the Lord; that the Lord is very pitiful and of tender mercy." And when the gospel was to be spread in the world, Satan had the power of the sword and the learning in the world engaged in the defence of his kingdom; and Christ singles out a few fishermen, neither swordsmen nor bookmen, Paul excepted, and they pull it down; notwithstanding all the magistrates could do by their force, and they learned by their subtilty to support it.

6. *Lastly*, To screw up the glory of the exceeding riches of grace to a height, Eph. ii. 7, "That in the ages to come he might show the exceeding riches of his grace, in his kindness towards us, through Christ Jesus." According to this dispensation, believers are drowned deeper in the debt of free grace, than otherwise they would have been, Rom. v. 20. By these infirmities wherewith they are compassed, it comes to pass that their accounts of pardoning and supporting grace are swelled with many items; the view of which will make them

sing the praises of God in heaven, on a higher key than innocent Adam would have done.

III. We shall consider the Spirit's helping believers under those infirmities they are compassed with. And here I shall shew,

1. The import of this.
2. How the Spirit helps them under their infirmities.

First, I am to show the import of the Spirit's helping believers under their infirmities. It imports in it,

1. A bent of heart in the believer toward his work and duty, set him by the great Master, Rom. vii. 22; for what people have no mind to, they need no help for. The heart of every child of God is reconciled to the whole law, Heb. viii. 10. And what God carves out for him either to do or suffer, he would fain come up to, Matth. xxvi. 41. Even when there is a felt averseness to it, this bent in the renewed part remains with him, to which that averseness is a burden, Rom. vii. 22, 23.

2. The infirmities hanging about the believer, make duty difficult to him: if it were not so, what need would he have of help? Matth. xxvi. 40, 41. These hang like weights on him, and draw him down, when he would mount upwards; so his executive powers cannot answer his will. He is at best like a bird flying with a stone tied to its foot; whereby it comes to pass, that it cannot fly far till it light, and the short way it flies is with difficulty.

3. The believer is sensible of his infirmities, for it is supposed that he is wrestling under them, Rom. vii. 23, 24, He sees, he feels, that he is not man enough for his work; that his own hands are not sufficient for him, nor his own back for his burden; this is what drives him out of himself to the grace that is in Christ Jesus, 2 Cor. iii. 5. And thus he lies open to the help of the Spirit, while proud nature in unbelievers is left helpless, 1 Pet. v. 5, "God resisteth the proud, and giveth grace to the humble." Isa. xl. 4, "Every valley shall be exalted, and every mountain and hill shall be made low."

4. The believer aims at and attempts to do his duty, over the belly of his infirmities. For helping is a joint action, Phil. iii. 14, "I press towards the mark." Many feel a difficulty in the weightiest parts of religion, that makes them at length to give them over. They neither have ability in themselves to master such a lust, nor have the grace to betake themselves to Christ for the help of his Spirit. But they sit down contented under it, soothing themselves with this, that every one has his infirmity, and that is theirs; and so they discover their hypocrisy.

But real saints wrestle with their infirmities, sit not down, but go on though they go halting.

5. *Lastly*, The spirit of the Lord comes in to the believer's help in this case, so as the work and duty is got done. "For the Spirit helpeth our infirmities." As the nurse helps the child attempting to go, or one helps a man attempting to lift up a weighty burden; so the Spirit helps the weak believer essaying his duty, to perform it. He stretches out the withered hand, and with the aiming to stretch it out, power is sent in from above.

Secondly, I am next to show how the Spirit helps believers under their infirmities.

1. He helps them by his influence in gifts. Here he does two things.

1*st*, He bestows on them gifts necessary for the performance of what the Lord calls them to, of whatever nature that be, temporal or spiritual, 1 Cor. xii. 8-11, "To one is given by the Spirit, the word of wisdom; to another the word of knowledge by the same Spirit; to another faith by the same Spirit; to another the gifts of healing by the same Spirit; to another the working of miracles; to another prophecy; to another discerning of spirits; to another divers kinds of tongues; to another the interpretation of tongues. But all these worketh that one and the self-same Spirit, dividing to every man severally as he will." The gifts of believers are various, according to the variety of their stations in life, and the respective particular duties required of them in their stations. Every one has not all, nor will ever have all; because there are many of them which they have no necessity for, in respect of what God calls them to. But there are two things I would have you advert to.

(1.) Whatever good gift a child of God has, he will get use for it, for God, soon or late, 1 Cor. xii. 7; though for a time he may have little or none for it. For in that case the Spirit lays in aforehand for their help. David had the gift of music in his younger years; the use of it for God appeared afterwards, when on that account he was sent for to Saul's court, and afterwards he ordered the temple service in that point. Paul had a gift of human learning; he got use for it afterwards, when he fought those at Athens with their own weapons, Acts xvii. 28. Moses had a gift of extraordinary meekness of temper, and Job of extraordinary patience; each got as much ado with them for God.

An unbeliever indeed may have a gift, which he never has any use for, for God. For he always does one of two things with it; either he hides it in the earth, and makes no use of it all, Matth. xxv. 25; or else he uses it to the service of his own lusts, Jam. iv. 3, 4. But God will not let any good gift in his own people lie by useless.

(2.) Whatever duty, in temporal or spiritual things, God calls a believer to, he will, in a way of believing, get the gift from God necessary for it, Prov. x. 29, "The way of the Lord is strength to the upright": and iii. 6, "In all thy ways acknowledge him, and he shall direct thy paths." For it is the office of the Spirit to help his people's infirmities. And so a call from the Lord to any piece of work, imports a promise of a gift of ability for it, the sap of which promise is to be sucked by believing it; and it is withal a call to look to the Lord for the help of his Spirit. For the Lord treats not his children as the Egyptian taskmasters did, who would have the Israelites make brick without giving them straw. Moses is called to go Jehovah's ambassador to the court of Egypt; he is sensible of an infirmity, but the Spirit's help is secured to him, Exod. iv. 10, 12. Bezaleel and Aholiab must work the curious work of the tabernacle. Where should they have learned it, when they were slaves in Egypt at the brick-kilns? But the Spirit helps their infirmity, bestowing on them necessary gifts, Exod. xxxi. 2, &c.

But in case the believer do not go to God for the gift, in the way of believing, no wonder he want it. For is it anything strange that the help of the Spirit is not given a man, in a particular, wherein he does not look for it? as he is commanded to do, Prov. iii. 6.

2*dly*, He influences them to the exercise of these gifts, Matth. x. 19, 20, "But when they deliver you up, take no thought how or what ye shall speak, for it shall be given you in that same hour what ye shall speak. For it is not ye that speak, but the Spirit of your Father which speaketh in you." As every good gift is from the Spirit, so the same Spirit has not given them away so to any, but that he has still lock and key on them, opening them out, and shutting them up as he will, Isa. xxix. 14. Therefore there ought to be a dependance on the Lord, for the help of his Spirit, to the exercise of any gift necessary for what the Lord calls one to. That unbelievers have a common influence of the Spirit, in the way of common providence, to the exercise of their gifts, though they look not to the hand it comes from, is for the benefit of human society; but even the Spirit's influence on gifts, coming to believers in the channel of the covenant, their blunders and mismanagements in the exercise of their gifts, are rebukes to them for their not looking more to the help of the Spirit therein, and to bring them to their duty.

2. He helps them by his influence in grace. Here he helps their infirmities three ways.

1st, He preserves the grace he has planted in believers, so as it never dies out; 1 John ii. 27, "The anointing which ye have received of him, abideth in you; and ye need not that any man teach you; but, as the same anointing teacheth you of all things, and is truth, and is no lie; and even as it hath taught you, ye shall abide in him." The quickening spirit of Christ being communicated to the dead elect in the time of loves, they are made to live and believe in Christ, and so are united to him; upon which union the same Spirit takes of the treasure of grace in Christ, and plants in the believer grace for grace in Christ Jesus, Eph. i. 13, with John i. 16. And this for all time after he preserves; 2 Tim. i. 14, "That good thing which was committed unto thee, keep by the Holy Ghost which dwelleth in us." John x. 28, "I give unto them eternal life, and they shall never perish, neither shall any pluck them out of my hand." Deut. xxxiii. 3, "All his saints are in thy hand; and they sat down at thy feet; every one shall receive of thy words," *i.e.* thy Spirit. Luke xi. 20; with Matth. xii. 28. Now, this is a great helping of their infirmities, if ye consider jointly these four things.

(1.) That holy quality called grace, is in its own nature a thing liable to be lost. Adam at his creation was endowed with a far greater measure of it than any believer has in this world; yet that holy fire in him was quite extinguished; that heavenly plant, by one bite of the venomous teeth of the old serpent, died out quite, and withered away. How then is it preserved in believers compassed with infirmities, but by the help of the Spirit? Free-will in Adam lost it, but the free grace of the free Spirit preserves it in weak ones of his family.

(2.) It dwells with an ill neighbour, even the corruption of nature, that is quite opposite to it. The old man of sin had the first possession, the new man of grace is brought in upon him, and meets with a continual resistance, yet is preserved. There is the weight of a body of sin and death pressing grace in the believer, yet is it not crushed to death. Whoso looks into his own heart, and sees what powerful lusts are there, must needs wonder to see the pearl kept in such a dung-hill, and the spark of holy fire kept in the midst of an ocean of corruption; and must own it to be entirely owing to the help of the

Spirit; Gal. v. 17, "The flesh lusteth against the Spirit, and the Spirit against the flesh, and these are contrary the one to the other, so that ye cannot do the things that ye would."

(3.) The whole force of hell is bent for its extinction; 1 Pet. v. 8, "Your adversary the devil, as a roaring lion, walketh about seeking whom he may devour." The image of God repaired in a believer, though but in part, is an eye-sore to Satan, he cannot endure to look at it. Therefore he uses all his subtilty, power, and unwearied diligence to rase it. He works against it incessantly, turns himself into all shapes that he may overturn it; employs his friends within and his friends without to the same purpose, yet it is preserved. How? but by the help of the Spirit; 1 John iv. 4, "Ye are of God, little children, and have overcome them; because greater is he that is in you than he that is in the world."

(4.) *Lastly*, The believer in himself is but a weak creature; he has a weak head, heart, hands, and back; is easily outwitted by a subtle enemy, discouraged, overthrown, and bowed down. Innocent Adam's strength and skill failed in preserving the grace received in his creation; yet the believer's grace received in his new creation is never lost; though of itself it is a perishing quality, is surrounded with corruption, and the whole force of hell is employed to extinguish it. For why? the almighty Spirit helps their infirmities.

2dly, He excites grace in them, and brings it forth into exercise; Phil. ii. 13, "For it is God which worketh in you, both to will and to do of his good pleasure." If the exercise of gifts depends on a common operation of the Spirit, surely the exercise of grace on a special operation of the same Spirit. As the fire buried under the ashes will not serve the purposes of the family's provision, nor the tree with its sap retired into the heart and root bring forth fruit; so grace in the habit only is not sufficient for duty. The holy fire must be blown up, and through the return of the sap to the branches they must bud and blossom. And this is the work of the Spirit, Cant. iv. ult., "Awake, O north wind, and come, thou south, blow upon my garden, that the spices thereof may flow out; let my Beloved come into his garden, and eat his pleasant fruits." Now the Spirit excites grace in believers,

(1.) Presenting objects to their minds fit to rouse it up; and so he acts as a teaching Spirit; John xiv. 26, "He shall teach you all things, and bring all things to your remembrance, whatsoever I have said unto you." Corruption thrives most in darkness, because it belongs to the kingdom of darkness. But light let into the soul stirs up grace, therefore it is called the light of life, John viii. 12. Thus the Spirit presenting a man's sin to him in its ugly colours, stirs up the grace of repentance, Psalm li. 3; discovering the glory of God in the face of Jesus Christ, it excites love; and discovering the creature in its emptiness, excites contempt of the world. And this is a great help, for,

(1.) We are apt to forget these things when we have most need to mind them; as to forget human frailty and divine might, when there is greatest need of confidence in the Lord, against the terror of man; and the Spirit in that case is the believer's remembrancer, and so excites grace; Isa. li. 12, 13, "I, even I, am he that comforteth you; who art thou, that thou shouldst be afraid of a man that shall die, and of the son of man which shall be made as grass? and forgettest the Lord thy maker, that hath stretched forth the heavens and laid the foundations of the earth? and hast feared continually every day, because of the fury of the oppressor as if he were ready to destroy? And where is the fury of the oppressor?" Our weakness in such points makes us need a monitor, being often like Hagar, whose eyes saw not the well, though it was very near by, until God opened them, Gen. xxi. 19. So that when such a thing is suggested, one is often made to wonder how they saw it not.

(2.) When we do mind them, we cannot command a lively sight of them, without the blowing of the Spirit, Hos. viii. 12. They lie before our eyes as so many dry bones, till the Spirit set them in motion, by setting them in a due light. Joseph's brethren could not forget that they had been guilty concerning him, nor David that he had sinned in the matter of Uriah; but till the Spirit set these things in another light to them, they were not moved to repent.

(2.) By touching their hearts and affections, and immediately bringing them forth into exercise. Thus the sleeping spouse was awakened; Cant. v. 4, "My Beloved put in his hand by the hole of the door, and my bowels were moved for him." And so he acts as a quickening Spirit. The hearts of men are in the hand of the Lord, to turn them what way he will; and so he moves them by a touch in common things, as he did the band of men that went with Saul to Gibeah, "whose hearts God had touched," 1 Sam. x. 26; and he also moves them by a touch in gracious actions, as the spouse found; Cant. vi. 12, "Or ever I was aware, my soul made me like the chariots of Ammi-nadib." As the thaw wind makes the frozen waters to flow amain, and the air in the bellows blows up the fire; so there is an influence of the Spirit on the hearts of believers, opening them in the exercise of grace, Phil. ii. 13. This is a great help to believers; for,

(1.) Their hearts are oft-times very dead within them, when called to duty, either doing or suffering, Cant. v. 2, 3, "I sleep, but my heart waketh: it is the voice of my Beloved that knocketh, saying, Open to me, my sister, my love, my dove, my undefiled: for my head is filled with dew, and my locks with the drops of the night. I have put off my coat, how shall I put it on! I have washed my feet, how shall I defile them?" Their affections are flat, and their souls indisposed for spiritual action. But when the Spirit touches their hearts, they are fitted for duty; their spiritual life is brought forth into liveliness and activity, Psalm lxxx. 18, "Quicken us, and we will call upon thy name."

[2.] They can by no art of theirs remove their deadness of heart and affections, 2 Cor. iii. 5, but they will lie windbound in the harbour, till the Spirit blow. They may be long toiling in rowing in the use of means, and yet be still but where they were, for all they can do. But the influences of the Spirit rising and filling their sails, they will presently make way, Cant. vi. 12.

Now, this double action of presenting to their minds, and touching their hearts, whereby the Spirit excites grace, is signified to us by comparing the Spirit to fire, which has both light and heat with it, Matth. iii. 11. And there is a twofold mean the Spirit makes use of for that purpose, viz. the word and providence, of which afterwards.

3*dly*, He strengthens and increases grace in them, Eph. iii. 16, "That he would grant you, according to the riches of his glory, to be strengthened with might, by his Spirit in the inner man." Grace is a heavenly seed capable of growth, 2 Pet. iii. ult., and so admits of various degrees of strength, not only in different persons, in respect of which some are little children, others youths, others fathers, 1 John ii. but in the same person at different times, Is. xl. ult, "They that wait upon the Lord shall renew their strength." And indeed of its own nature it is a growing thing, as a seed; grace hath a seminal virtue in it, that fits it for growing and receiving more strength, John iv. 14. Meanwhile the seed will not grow unless it be watered from above; so grace grows not, but by the influence of the Spirit, Hos. xiv. 5, "I will be as the dew unto Israel: he shall grow as the lily, and cast forth his roots as Lebanon." Now the Spirit doth strengthen and increase grace,

(1.) By frequent exciting it into action. The habits of grace, as well as others, are strengthened by the repeated exercise of them. The more it shines, it shines the brighter, Prov. iv. 18. It is for this cause that God has bound converts also to the hearing of the word, whereby their graces are brought forth into one act after another, as the object is still anew proposed; and for this cause he trysts his people with a variety of incidents, afflictions, and trials, which bring their graces into frequent exercise, whereby at length they become strong.

(2.) By bringing forth into exercise one grace, he strengthens the rest, 2 Pet. i. 5, 8, "And besides this, giving all diligence, add to your faith, virtue; and to virtue, knowledge; and to knowledge, temperance: and to temperance, patience; and to patience, godliness; and to godliness, brotherly kindness; and to brotherly kindness, charity. For if these things be in you, and abound, they make you that ye shall neither be barren, nor unfruitful in the knowledge of our Lord Jesus Christ." As a mason by laying on a new stone in his wall, fastens the rest under it; or the sheaves of corn stand the more firmly, that one is set at the side of another; so one grace is still the better of another joined to it in the exercise thereof. So humility strengthens meekness and patience, love strengthens obedience in all points, and faith strengthens altogether; like a band or keystone in an arch, the more firm it is, the firmer is the whole arch; so the Spirit, by bringing forth one grace in the believer's heart after another, strengthens the whole collection, and makes it the more firm and steady.

(3.) By affording them Christian experiences, whereby they find the truth and reality of what they have believed, and the blessed sensible advantage of the exercise of grace, Rom. v. 3, 4, 5, "We glory in tribulations also, knowing that tribulation worketh patience; and patience, experience; and experience, hope; and hope maketh not ashamed, because the love of God is shed abroad in our hearts, by the Holy Ghost which is given unto us." Experienced Christians are therefore always the strongest Christians, even as the spoil got in one battle helps the soldier to fight the more stoutly in the next, 1 Sam. xvii. 36, 2 Tim. iv. 17, 18. Former experiences are the traveller to Zion's way-marks in dark steps, and his cordials in difficult ascents. Every taste of divine goodness and grace refreshes and strengthens. Now it is the Spirit that gives these experiences, John xvi. 14, "He shall receive of mine, and shall show it unto you."

(4.) By immediate supplies of grace, Phil. i. 19, "I know that this shall turn to my salvation through your prayer, and the supply of the Spirit of Jesus Christ." As the lamp is preserved from going out, and is caused to burn more vigorously, by new oil poured in; so grace is strengthened by the Spirit giving new supplies thereof, Isa. xliv. 3, 4. Hence the Spirit is said to "build us for an habitation to God," Eph. ii. ult. He works the first grace; and all the intermediate supplies of it, and the perfecting of it, are his, Psalm cxxxviii. ult, "The Lord will perfect that which concerneth me." Now, this is a great help; for,

[1.] Weighty is the work that lies to the believer's hand; doing work, suffering work. The Christian life is no easy life, however men that go no further than the outside of it, may make it so to themselves. It is a striving, taking by force, running, labouring, fighting, &c. How could it be managed, without the helps of the Spirit?

[2.] Great is the opposition that they must work against, Eph. vi. 12, "For we wrestle not against flesh and blood, but against principalities, against powers, against the rulers of the darkness of this world, against spiritual wickedness in high places." The wind will be blowing in their face from hell at all times; and sometimes they will meet with violent storms. How could they stand against it, if the Spirit did not help?

[3.] Weak are the hands that work is put into, that has all that opposition. There is a feebleness natural to them, that makes them oft bang down. How could they ever do that work maugre so much opposition, without the helps of the Spirit?

The means which the Spirit of God makes use of to preserve, excite, and strengthen grace in believers, and so to help them, are two.

1. Providences; Psalm xcii. 4, "For thou, Lord, hast made me glad through thy work; I will triumph in the works of thy hands." The kingdom of providence is put into the hand of the Mediator, for the behoof of the kingdom of grace; and he guides it by his Spirit. The wheels of providence are managed by the Spirit; Ezek. i. 20, and so managed as to help believers in their infirmities. And here two things are especially to be noticed,

(1.) Seasonable turns of the wheel of providence, whereby the believer's wain[3] is often kept up when it is at the over-

---

3 Wagon, cart.

setting;[4] 1 Cor. x. 13, "God is faithful, who will not suffer you to be tempted above that ye are able; but will with the temptation also make a way to escape, that ye may be able to bear it." Psalm xciv. 18, "When I said, My foot slippeth; thy mercy, O Lord, held me up." Thus many times the believer is brought to an extremity, as Isaac when the knife was at his throat, when providence seasonably interposes for his relief and outgate; Psalm cxxv. 3.

(2.) Seasonable intermixtures of providence. Thus the Spirit intermixes encouraging dispensations with difficult duties, Judg. vii. 13, 14., merciful incidents with their sharp afflictions; and, on the other hand, afflicting incidents with their prosperity; and all that they may neither be swallowed op with adversity, nor destroyed with prosperity.

2. Ordinances, Isa. xii. 3, "Therefore with joy shall ye draw water out of the wells of salvation." These are instituted by the King of Zion, for the special means of grace, whereby his Spirit is to work, and to render them effectual. And the experience believers have of the Spirit's helping their infirmities by these, makes them very precious in their sight. And among these there are two especially used for this end.

1*st*, The sacraments. They are exciting and strengthening ordinances particularly, and consequently preservative of grace. The eunuch's experience witnesseth this as to baptism, Acts viii. 39, he "went on his way rejoicing." And the Lord's supper is "the communion of the body and blood of Christ," 1 Cor. x. 16., which, by the Spirit's working, has been to the experience of many a great help.

2*dly*, The word. This is the most special mean. Providence has its efficacy from the word, and so have the sacraments. It is their continual mean of help, their every-day's meal, which they can go to when providence is most lowring,[5] and sacramental occasions offer not. And the Spirit uses it for their help three ways.

(1.) Preached, 1 Cor. i. 21, "It pleased God by the foolishness of preaching to save them that believe." This affords to the attentive believer a continued occasion of the exercise of his faith and love, while a variety of spiritual truths and objects are represented to him, in their turn; which the Spirit makes use of to draw forth his graces into exercise. Whence

---

4 To put in a disturbed state.

5 Gloomy, somber.

believers go away instructed, warmed, strengthened, in a word, edified, by reason of so many actings of grace, during their hearing, like the two disciples going to Emmaus, when they said, "Did not our heart burn within us, while he talked with us by the way, and while he opened to us the scriptures?" Luke xxiv. 32.

(2.) Read, 1 Tim. iv. 13, "Till I come, give attendance to reading." This has the same advantages attending it. Thereby the Spirit of God speaks immediately to the believer by his own word in his own express terms. And the experience of the usefulness of this mean has made saints prize their Bibles as their life.

(3.) Suggested, John xiv. 26, "He shall bring all things to your remembrance, whatsoever I have said unto you." The bringing of the word to mind with a man is the office of the Spirit; and by that means he helps believers' infirmities, bringing a word suitable to their case, into their remembrance, whether to clear them in doubts, comfort them under pressures, direct them in difficulties, or check them for their debordings, &c. And herein he uses often the very words of the Bible, always what is the sense and doctrine of the Bible. And,

[1.] Sometimes the Spirit barely suggests the word to the mind without any peculiar light about it, or power impressing it, John xiv. 26, just cited. Thus it is presented as an object for the believer to act faith on, and is a call to look up to the Spirit to enlighten it and help to believe it, Acts viii. 30–31. And thus a word at first coming in this way, comes afterwards to be illuminated by the Spirit's shining on it to the man.

[2.] Sometimes there is a peculiar light and power that comes along with it at the very first, clearly holding out the meaning of it, and impressing it so on their hearts, that they must needs believe and embrace it, John ii. 17, "And his disciples remembered that it was written, The zeal of thine house hath eaten me up." There were many Old Testament passages speaking more clearly of Christ which they understood not, but the Spirit thus suggested this to them.

Meanwhile it is to be observed, that all suggestions of the word are not from the Spirit of God. That Satan may suggest scripture to a man, is evident from Matth. iv. 6. Therefore is that warning, 1 John iv. 1, "Beloved, believe not every spirit, but try the spirits whether they are of God; because many false prophets are gone out into the world." But the cloven foot may be discerned in such cases two ways.

[1.] They are always of a tendency to drive sinners away from Christ, 1 John iv. 2, 3, "Hereby know ye the Spirit of God: every spirit that confesseth that Jesus Christ is come in the flesh, is of God. And every spirit that confesseth not that Jesus Christ is come in the flesh, is not of God." And they tend to drive out of the road of duty, Matth. iv. 6, "And saith unto him, If thou be the Son of God, cast thyself down: for it is written, He shall give his angels charge concerning thee, and in their hands they shall bear thee up, lest at any time thou dash thy foot against a stone." This was the design of the testimony he gave to Christ, and to his apostles; while the testimony was indeed true in itself, he gave it maliciously for an ill end. Therefore mark the tendency of suggestions of the word. Whatever tends to carry off from faith in Christ, or from any point of commanded duty, is not from the Spirit. For his work tends to faith and sanctification. Hence,

[2.] They are always applied by him contrary to their true sense and scope, forasmuch as the Lord's word cannot serve an ill purpose, unless it is wrested; as is evident from what the devil says to Christ, Matth. iv. 6, above cited, compared with Psalm xci. 11, 12, "For he shall give his angels charge over thee, to keep thee in all thy ways. They shall bear thee up in their hands, lest thou dash thy foot against a stone." And therefore the scripture-passage is to be considered, and how it agrees with other scriptures as to the sense and scope in which it is suggested, Matth. iv. 7, "Jesus said unto him, It is written again, Thou shalt not tempt the Lord thy God." The Holy Spirit is the Spirit of truth, and leads to the true sense and scope of scripture, John xvi. 13.

I add one observe more on the means, namely, that sometimes the Spirit helps believers' infirmities, by a particular providence trysting the word to their case. This often comes to pass in hearing the word preached, while the word in its ordinary course is brought directly to what is their case in the time; so that it is like the Midianite's telling his dream, Judg. vii. 13, while Gideon, unknown to him, was overhearing; or they are providentially led to such a place, where such a word suitable to their case is handled, Cant. iii. 3. The same particular providence appears often in the reading of the word, whether at family worship, or in secret, or by some providential casting of it in one's way.[6] I think it dangerous to make

---

6 Many instances of this are to be found in the author's own experience, in his Memoirs.

a fortune-book of the Bible, as some under temptation have opened the Bible, to know their case by the first word that should cast up to them. This is an unwarrantable and dangerous practice, though a merciful God may sometimes condescend to outshoot the devil in his own bow as in the case of her who threw the glass at the wall, and it broke not. But when people are thus met in the way of their duty, or surprised, with a word suited to their case, the work of the Spirit is to be owned in it, as an accomplishment of the promise, Isa. xxx. 21, "Thine ear shall hear a word behind thee, saying, This is the way, walk ye in it, when ye turn to the right hand, and when ye turn to the left." Certainly the Spirit gives instruction, reproof, invitations, to unbelievers this way; and much more helps the infirmities of his people the same way, for so the word is in its true use, 2 Tim. iii. 16, 17, "All scripture is given by inspiration of God, and is profitable for doctrine, for reproof, for correction, for instruction in righteousness: that the man of God may be perfect, throughly furnished unto all good works." And this should recommend the reading of the word of God in an ordinary.

I shall now make some short improvement of this doctrine.

USE 1. Of information. This teaches us and shews,

1. That believers owe their spiritual strength and comfort to the same hand that they owe their spiritual life to. As the mother who brought forth the child nurses it with her own breasts; so the Spirit, who is to the elect the Spirit of life to quicken them lying dead in sin, is likewise the Comforter to strengthen them under their infirmities when spiritually alive, John vi. 63, and xvi. 13; compare Psalm cxxxviii. ult.

2. The Lord calls none of his people to any duty, but they may get it done acceptably, however difficult it is. For the help of his own Spirit is their allowance; Phil. iv. 13, "I can do all things through Christ which strengtheneth me." Here is the great difference betwixt those under the law and under grace. The law or covenant of works exacts duty rigidly, but affords no help; the covenant of grace affords the promise of help with the command; for the latter is, but the former is not, the ministration of the Spirit, 2 Cor. iii. 8.

3. How that gospel-paradox; 2 Cor. xii. 10, "When I am weak, then am I strong," is so often verified in the experience of the saints. Many a time when they are strong and well buckled in all appearance for a work, it miscarries; why, they do not go out of themselves in a way of believing, and so the

Spirit withdraws. At other times they see themselves quite out of case and ability to manage such a work, and yet it succeeds; why, the Spirit comes in to their help, while they are sensible of need.

Use II. Of reproof. It may reach a reproof,

1. To believers sometimes venturing on duties, more in confidence of their own abilities, than of the Spirit's help, as Peter did when he said, "Though all men shall be offended because of thee, yet will I never be offended," Matth. xxvi. 33. This is the cause that the duty is marred; the bow so bended cannot miss to break. It is sometimes marred as to the very getting it done, and always as to its acceptance with God.

2. To unbelievers, who neither have the Spirit, nor are careful to have him dwelling in them, and influencing them. Their best works are dead works, having nothing of the quickening and sanctifying Spirit in them; and they themselves are but natural men spiritually dead, Jude 19. Whatever flourish they make with their gifts in duties, their best duties will no more be accepted of God than carrion, or a beast that died of itself would have been accepted on the altar.

3. To those who press on men still this and the other duty, without leading them to Jesus Christ for his Spirit and grace. This is another gospel, that will never make men holy, Gal. iii. 2, for it is not the ministration of the Spirit. And the same veil they cast over the Spirit and grace of Christ, they will always be found to cast over the corruption of man's nature too, that they may with some decency say to every man, Physician, heal thyself.

Use III. Of exhortation. And, 1. To natural men void of the Spirit. Be concerned to get the Spirit first to quicken you, and then to assist and help you. Ye can do nothing acceptable to God in that state; and no wonder, for ye have not the gracious help of the Spirit, without which ye can have no access to God, Eph. ii. 18. So ye and your works are both dead carcases before him.

Therefore come to Christ in the way of believing; for the fulness of the Spirit is lodged in him to be communicated, Rev. iii. 1. So uniting with him, ye shall receive the Spirit. The fire that was set to the incense, was brought from the altar of burnt-offering. See John xx. 22, and Gen. ii. 7.

2. To believers. (1.) Let this comfort you under, and reconcile you to, the state of infirmities, wherewith ye are compassed; 2 Cor. xii. 9, 10. Though sinless infirmities are not to be desired, and sinful ones are much to be lamented; yet it is

matter of rejoicing, that in these the Spirit gives sweet experience of his help.

(2.) Learn to look habitually for the help of the Spirit under your infirmities. While ye consider what ye have to do or bear, it is reasonable you cast one eye on your infirmity, but another eye upward for the Spirit's help. And by this means you will get his help. Luke xi. 13, "If ye being evil, know how to give good gifts unto your children; how much more shall your heavenly Father give the Holy Spirit to them that ask him?"

DOCTRINE III. Such is the weakness of God's own children, that they have not skill to manage even their addresses to God by prayer aright, without the Spirit. For we know not what we should pray for as we ought; but the Spirit itself maketh intercession for us." They are like children putting their hand to a work, but with so little skill, that they must needs have one to stand over them, and direct them at every turn.

In discoursing from this point, I shall shew,

I. What is implied in this truth.

II. Wherein believers are ready, through their weakness, to mistake, go wrong, and mismanage in their prayers.

III. *Lastly*, Apply.

I. I shall show what is implied in this truth. It implies,

1. That they are not of themselves able for what is to be done and borne in the Christian life; 2 Cor. iii. 5. So far from it, that they do not well know what is necessary for their help, what to seek of God for that end, and how to seek it. If a duty is to be done, a cross to be borne, they are at a loss there through weakness and infirmity; that sets them to their prayers: but then they are at a loss there again, they know not what, and how to ask.

2. That the children of God are all praying persons; Zech. xii. 10. If they can speak at all, they will speak to God by prayer; and even when they either cannot speak, or have no access to speak, if they have the exercise of judgment, they will pray in their hearts; 1 Cor. xiv. 15. So the habitual neglect of prayer is none of the spots of God's people. There is no child so unnatural, as to be still in his father's presence, and never to converse with him.

3. A gift of prayer, without the Spirit of prayer, cannot be sufficient to make one right prayer, that will be acceptable to

God; John iv. 24. Gifts of prayer are bestowed on believers, as well as others; but still they know not what to pray for as they ought, without the Spirit prompting them. The prayer that is the mere exercise of a gift, may indeed be edifying to the hearers, but cannot be acceptable to God.

4. Nay, habitual grace is not sufficient for praying aright; for still there is a necessity of actual assistance from the Spirit; Psalm lxxx. 18, "Quicken us, and we will call upon thy name." Life is not sufficient for making a discourse to our prince; a man may have life, and yet not be able to speak a word; but some vigour and liveliness is necessary to such a purpose. So spiritual life never departs wholly from the believer; 1 John iii. 9, but it must be breathed on anew to fit him for praying; Cant. iv. ult. New influences are still necessary; hence is the promise; Isa. xxvii. 3, "I will water it every moment."

5. *Lastly*, Prayers are marred so far as the Spirit of God does not assist the party in them; they are marred so far in point of acceptance with God; Eph. ii. 18. As no prayer can be accepted but through Christ's intercession, so none will be offered to God by the Intercessor farther than it is the product of the influence of his own Spirit. Nadab and Abihu's hearth-fire offered with the incense, was a costly lesson of this; Lev. x. 1, 2, 3. So if, through the whole prayer, the Spirit's assistance is wanting, the whole will be unaccepted; if in any of it, that wherein it is wanting will be so.

II. The next head is to show, wherein believers are ready, through their weakness, to mistake, go wrong, and mismanage in their prayers. They are ready to do so both in the matter and manner of them.

First, In the matter of prayer, "We know not what to pray for." Even the things to be prayed for, they are not so well versed in them, but they are ready to go wrong therein. So that they need the Spirit's teaching, to tell them and make them take up their errand, when they are going and come to God in prayer; they need to be set right, and kept right in the very matter of prayer. Their weakness in this point appears, in that,

1. They are apt to pray against their own mercy. Thus did Job, chap. vi. 8, 9, "O that I might have my request; and that God would grant me the thing that I long for! even that it would please God to destroy me; that he would let loose his hand, and cut me off." When Satan was permitted to take all from him, there was an express reserve of his life as the greatest mercy; but he prays very earnestly against it, though

no doubt at long-run Job blessed God from his heart that he did not hear him in that. We are so weak, that in God's dispensations many times we take our friends for our foes, and call what is for our good, evil, as Jacob did when he said, "All these things are against me," Gen. xlii. 36.

2. They are apt to seek what is not so good as God has a mind to give them; 2 Cor. xii. 8, 9, "For this thing I besought the Lord thrice, that it might depart from me. And he said unto me, My grace is sufficient for thee." To be freed from the messenger of Satan was good, but to have God's grace poured in sufficiently to maintain the combat, was better. And therefore Paul upon reflection takes God's way to have been better than what he himself proposed, ver. 9, "Most gladly therefore will I rather glory in my infirmities, that the power of Christ may rest upon me." Narrow asking ofttimes makes narrow receiving. It fares with believers sometimes as with Joash; 2 Kings xiii. 18, 19, "Elisha said unto him, Take the arrows; and he took them. And he said unto the king of Israel, Smite upon the ground; and he smote thrice, and stayed. And the man of God was wroth with him, and said, Thou shouldst have smitten five or six times, then hadst thou smitten Syria till thou hadst consumed it; whereas now thou shalt smite Syria but thrice." They are straitened in their own bowels in asking, and therefore they come not speed.

3. They are apt to seek what would be for their hurt. So did Jonah, when he wished in himself to die, and said, it is better for me to die than to live; chap iv. 8. It would have been very ill for Jonah to have died in such a bad frame and temper of spirit, as he was then in. And if God had struck him immediately, it is like he would immediately have changed his note. David prayed for the life of the child, 2 Sam. xii. 16, but God took it away, for it would have been a living blot upon him. As a foolish child seeks a knife to play with, which he can do nothing with, but hurt himself; so we are apt to seek from God, what in mercy he keeps from us.

4. They are apt to seek food for their corrupt lusts and affections; Matth. xx. 20, 21, "Then came to him the mother of Zebedee's children, with her sons, worshipping him, and desiring a certain thing of him. And he said unto her, What wilt thou? She saith unto him, Grant that these my two song may sit, the one on thy right hand, and the other on the left in thy kingdom." James and John were tickled with a lust of ambition, and they seek honour to satisfy it. And it is God's goodness to his people in such a case, not to do with them as he

did with the lusting Israelites; Psalm cvi. 15, "He gave them their request, but sent leanness into their soul." Men may go wrong here, and not see their error, till the Lord correct it; for they may take lust for love; Luke ix. 54, 55, and so seek to feed their enemies whom they should starve.

5. They are apt, through ignorance or inadvertency,[7] not to pray for what they really need for their case; as the children of Israel, when they "went up to the house of God, and asked counsel of God, and said, which of us shall go up first to the battle against the children of Benjamin?" Judg. xx. 18. To pray for God's presence with them, was not in their head; but that they really needed it, they afterwards felt to their cost. Many sad experiences praying people may have of this, which may show the need of the Spirit's assistance. Hence general and formal prayers, little suited to the particular cases and exigences of the party; which is but trifling in so solemn and serious a matter as prayer to God.

6. Though they do know and advert to it before they go to prayer, they are ready to forget it in the time. There is a forgetting of particular petitions designed or coming of course, which is an effect of the Spirit's influence; in that case the forgotten petition is from one's own spirit, not from the Spirit of God, as in the instance of the prodigal son, Luke xv, what he designed to say to his father, ver. 19, "Make me as one of thy hired servants," when be came to him, he forgets, ver. 21. There is such a forgetting which is an effect of our own weakness; in that case the petition forgotten is from the Spirit of God, the forgetting it from ourselves, Heb. ii. 1.

Thus going to God sometimes, we forget much of our errand, whether by wandering of heart or being left to ourselves in the matter. In a word,

7. *Lastly*, They are apt to pray for things not agreeable to the will of God, that there is neither precept nor promise for. The many petitions in which they are not heard evince this; because "if we ask anything according to his will he heareth us," 1 John v. 14. There is so much remains of corruption in the best, that it is hard even in our prayers to keep within the compass of what is agreeable to his will.

I shall now endeavour to assign the reasons why God's own children are so apt to mistake and go wrong, even in the matter of prayer.

---

7 Heedlessness, unmindfulness.

The great reason is, the remains of darkness that are on the minds of the best, while here; Job xxxvii. 19, "Teach us what we shall say unto him; for we cannot order our speech by reason of darkness." It is true, God's children are not in midnight darkness, but their light is but a twilight, in which they are apt to mistake their way. And the more sensible they are of this, the more need they will find of the Spirit's help in prayer. More particularly, we know not what we should pray for, but are ready to go wrong in the matter of prayer,

1. Because we have at best but little knowledge of our own case; and no wonder that they who are not thoroughly acquainted with the nature of the disease mistake as to the remedy. The blind man, Mark viii. 22–25, is an emblem of the natural man, the true convert, and the glorified saint. The child of God while here, "sees but in part," 1 Cor. xiii. 12. Every believer is a mystery, Cant. iii. 6, a mystery to the world, a mystery to himself. There are many folds and plies in his case, which he himself cannot unfold; plies of grace, sin, temptation, danger, &c.

2. Little knowledge of what is good and best for us, Gen. xlii. 36. We see the weakness of understanding in children makes them often to desire of parents what really is not for them; even so it is with God's children, and therefore it is fatherly love that denies some of their petitions; as in the case of Job, Jonah, and others. We are apt to think that that is best for us that is most pleasant and most easy, but that is often a very deceitful rule.

3. Little acquaintance with the word, particularly the commands and the promises, the measure of our petitions. There is much need of the Spirit's help in that matter, John xiv. 26. We are ready to measure our petitions rather by our own inclinations than by the word; and many read the Bible often, that have but very little skill of making a practical improvement thereof in their prayers, Mark x. 35, 37.

4. We are apt to take the subtle cravings of lust for the cravings of grace or innocent affection, Luke ix. 54, 55. And thence good people unwittingly are made intercessors for their spiritual enemies; which, if they did discern, they would confess their error, and retract their request. Sin dwells in the believer together with grace, and that so closely that the language of the one is often taken for that of the other.

5. Believers are liable to prejudices and wrong notions of things, which they have drunk in from their education, manner of life in the world, &c. Such was the disciples' notion of

the temporal kingdom of Christ, that was the spring of that rash petition of James and John; Mark x. 37, "Grant unto us that we may sit, one on thy right hand, and the other on thy left hand in thy glory." Such was that of the case of Gentiles among the believing Jews, that was the spring of the offence taken at Peter; Acts xi. 2, 3," They that were of the circumcision contended with him, saying, Thou wentest in to men uncircumcised, and didst eat with them." An erring conscience will mislead men under pretence of divine authority, John xvi. 2; Acts xxvi. 9. No wonder then it form wrong requests in prayer, Luke ix. 54.

6. *Lastly*, They are subject to much confusion in prayer, both through natural and spiritual indisposition, Psalm lxxvii. 4. Hence they are ready as Job did, chap. xxxviii. 2, "to darken counsel by words without knowledge." The exercise of their very gift is not always ready at hand with them, far less the exercise of their grace. An influence of the Spirit is necessary both for the one and the other. And when it is wanting, so that they are in no case for praying, no wonder they know not what to pray for.

Secondly, Believers are ready to go wrong in the manner of prayer; "We know not what we should pray for as we ought." It is not in vain our Lord gave his disciples a direction in that point; Matth. vi. 9, "After this manner pray ye," &c. The prayer may be right as to the matter, that yet may be mismanaged in the manner of performance, 1 Chron. xv. 13. And therefore there is need of the Spirit's help in this point too; not only to teach us what, but how to pray. Their weakness in this point appears, in that,

1. They are apt to slip the best season for managing their address before the throne. Thomas missed an opportunity of communion with Christ, that left him under the feet of unbelief, while the rest were delivered from theirs, John xx. 24, 25. The best season is, when the signal is given from heaven to the petitioner, to come forward; sometimes the door is as it were cast open to him, and there is a sign given by some inward motion of the Spirit, or some providential call moving him to come forward. The spouse missed this; Cant. v. 2, 3, "I sleep, but my heart waketh," &c., and she smarted for it; ver. 6, "I opened to my Beloved, but my Beloved had withdrawn himself, and was gone; my soul failed when he spoke: I sought him but I could not find him; I called him, but he gave me no answer."

Moses was very careful to fall in with it immediately; Exod. xxxiv. 8, 9, "And Moses made haste, and bowed his head toward the earth, and worshipped. And he said, If now I have found grace in thy sight, O Lord, let my Lord, I pray thee, go amongst us (for it is a stiff-necked people) and pardon our iniquity and our sin, and take us for thine inheritance."

2. They are apt to enter on prayer with a temper of spirit very unfit for such a holy exercise; being either entangled with worldly cares, or discompesed[8] with unruly passions, Luke xxi. 34; 1 Tim. ii. 8. They both make the Spirit of a man like troubled water, unfit to receive the image of the sun, unfit for divine communications. Jonah's prayer behoved to be marred when he was in a fret. Therefore the apostle exhorts married persons to take heed to their behaviour one towards another, that their prayers might not be hindered, 1 Pet. iii. 7, nothing being more apt to do it than domestic jars, Mal. ii. 13.

3. They are apt to be formal, lifeless, and coldrife in prayer, Cant. iii. 1; Rev. iii. 2. We are called to be "fervent in spirit, serving the Lord." But even where the fire of grace is in the hearth, unless it be blown up by the influence of the Spirit of God, the prayers will be mismanaged, Psalm lxxx. 18. There will be bands of iniquity on the heart which they will not be able to loose, more than to dissolve the ice with their breath; but "where the Spirit of the Lord is, there is the liberty."

4. Their hearts are apt to wander in duty, and will do so if the Spirit fix them not. Therefore David prays, "Unite my heart to fear thy name," Psalm lxxxvi. 11. When Abraham had divided the carcasses, the fowls came down on them; so when one is conversing with God, evil spirits will be at work, to cast in something that may divert him from the present duty, Rom. vii. 21. Many a prayer is lost this way, while the heart steals away after some other thing than what it should then be on.

5. They are apt to content themselves with exercising their gift, without exercising their grace. Therefore Paul warns the Ephesians, chap. vi. 18, "to pray always with all prayer and supplication in the Spirit, and to watch thereunto with all perseverance." Hence many petitions, confessions, thanksgivings, all of them just; yet lost for want of suitable affections coming along with them. For it is the exercise of praying grac-

---

8 Disturb the order of.

es, reverence, faith, love, humility, &c., and not the exercise of praying gifts without them, that is pleasing to God.

6. They are apt to disproportion their concern to the weight of the matters they pray for. This is carefully guarded against in the Lord's prayer, Matth. vi. 9, &c., where the glory of God has the first place, and there is but one petition for temporals, and two for spirituals. But how ready are we to be more concerned for our own interest, than for the honour of God; more fervent for temporal than for spiritual mercies? This makes the prayers like the legs of the lame that are not equal, the affection being disproportioned to the matter.

7. They are apt to be too peremptory in circumstances, without leaving a due latitude to sovereignty. That is limiting the holy One of Israel. This is often done as to time, the timing of mercies, in which we are too apt to take upon us to prescribe to the sovereign manager, John ii. 3, 4, as to the manner of bringing about a mercy, which, short-sighted as we are, we are very ready to determine. And the same may be said as to the measure of mercies.

8. They are apt to mix their own wild fire with the holy fire in prayer. So did the disciples, Mark iv. 38, when they say, "Master, carest thou not that we perish?" The language of passion is sometimes mixed with the language of grace in the prayers of saints; which when they discern, they will be ready to correct, Psalm lxxvii. 7-10. Hence there are expressions of saints unto God, recorded in scripture, not for our imitation, but for our warning of this corrupt bias of the heart; as Job xxx. 21, "Thou art become cruel to me; with thy strong hand thou opposest thyself against me." Jer. xv. 18, "Why is my pain perpetual? and my wound incurable, which refuseth to be healed? wilt thou be altogether unto me as a liar, and as waters that fail?" These he looks on as the ravings of his sick children.

9. They are apt to lay too much weight of their acceptance in their prayers, on what will bear none of it. It is certain, that there is nothing will bear any weight of that, but the merit and intercession of Jesus Christ; Rev. viii. 4. But the natural bias of the heart lies another way, to lay weight on the very performance of the duty, and the way how it is performed, as with such affection, pointedness, length, nay the very voice, as insignificant a thing as it is before the Lord. Hence our Lord cautions against "using vain repetitions" in prayer, "as the Heathen do; for they think (says he) that they shall be heard for their much speaking"; Matth. vi. 7. And that the Heathen

laid much stress on a loud voice in prayer, appears from what Pharaoh says to Moses; Exod. ix. 28, (Heb.) Make ye supplication to the Lord, and much, *i. e.* Make much supplication. Compare 1 Kings xviii. 28, where it is said of Baal's prophets, that "they cried aloud." There are remains of that legal bias in the hearts of God's own children; Matth. xix. 27. And it is only by the Spirit that saints are brought to lay their whole weight on Jesus Christ; Eph. ii. 18; Phil. iii. 3. Otherwise their deceitful hearts will be found disposed to slip aside that way, they being very ready to believe the acceptance of some fluent prayer of theirs, and hard to believe the acceptance of one that goes not so fluently though seriously; yet the blood of Jesus is still the same security.

10. *Lastly,* They are apt to faint and give over, upon the Lord's delaying to answer; whereas it is a chief piece of right management of business at the court of heaven, resolutely to insist and hang on, Luke xviii. 1, 8. We are naturally hasty, and long trials are apt to run us out of breath. There is need of much faith, that patience may have her perfect work; and that is not to be reached without the help of the Spirit; Rom. xv. 13.

I shall now give the reasons why believers are so apt to go wrong in the manner of prayer. They are the following:—

1. Because of the sublimity of the work, that is so far above our reach, that we can by no means know how to manage it, but as we are taught by him with whom we have to do in it. To say a prayer in a formal uttering of words, is no such hard work indeed. But rightly to manage an address at the throne of heaven, on which sits the Sovereign Majesty; and that about the weightiest of all concerns, is such sublime work, that it passes the skill of the greatest orator on earth to do it without the Spirit; Eccl. v. 1, 2. Were any of us to go on business to our earthly king, would we not need to be directed by some knowing the way of the court? How much more do we need direction from the Holy Spirit in our addresses to the throne of grace?

2. Because of the remains of corruption that yet hang about them; Rom. vii. 24. This is a clog at their heels at all times, and will not miss to exert itself in holy duties, ver. 21, "When I would do good, evil is present with me." There is much darkness yet in the minds of the best, as to spiritual things; no wonder they know not how to pray as they ought. Much perverseness there is in the will, both with respect to God's precepts and providences. There is much carnality and disorder in the affections, as they all soundly feel, that are

concerned to get the heart fit for praying, kept right in it, and kept right after it.

3. Because there is a subtle adversary busy to mar them in that their work; Zech. iii. 1. He well knows that all the hope in their case is from the divine help; and therefore while they are before the throne of mercy, he will bestir himself effectually to mar their application. He is an enemy to prayer, and therefore he will keep back from it if he can; if he cannot, he will do his utmost to mar it.

4. *Lastly*, Because of the weakness of grace in them. Grace disposes men to pray; Zech. xii. 10. But the weakness of that grace leaves them in hazard of mismanaging in it. Sometimes it is not in exercise; at best it is but weak, and mixed with corruption, in the struggle with which it will be overcome, if the spirit come not in to its help.

I shall now make some practical improvement.

This doctrine may be of use, both unto strangers to God, and to his own children. And,

First, Ye that are strangers to God, yet in your natural state, without the Spirit, and therefore children of Satan, we may take you up in these two sorts to be spoken to, viz. prayerless natural persons, and praying natural persons.

First, Prayerless natural unconverted persons, such as are living in the state they were born in, and withal living without praying to the God that made them. I have two things to say to you from this doctrine.

1. Learn from it, that this prayerless life of yours declares your case a very sad one. It declares you,

(1.) None of God's children; for whatever mismanagements of it they fall into, they all practise the duty of prayer. So of you that is verified: Deut. xxxii. 5, "Their spot is not the spot of his children." And if so, ye are the children of the devil; John viii. 44, of the family of hell. And his possession of you remains undisturbed to this day, since ye have never been so far awakened, as to set you to, and keep you at prayer.

(2.) Without the Spirit of God; Jude 19. And being without the Spirit, ye are spiritually dead in sin; for so are all naturally; Eph. ii. 1, and it is "the Spirit that quickeneth"; John vi. 63. So that whosoever are without the Spirit are dead still. You are then dead souls in living bodies. It is plain you are dead, for your speech is laid, your senses are gone, there is no moving nor breathing towards God in you, and the Spirit of life is departed from you.

2. Be exhorted from it to reform. And,

(1.) Set about prayer, 1 Thess. v. 17. Remember ye are God's creatures, and therefore obliged to worship him. Ye are men, and not beasts, and therefore should distinguish yourselves from them by religion, Isa. xlvi. 8. Ye have souls that will not die, and therefore ye should be concerned to pray for them, that ye live not in eternal misery.

(2.) Be concerned to partake of the Spirit, and come to Christ for that end, who "hath the seven Spirits of God," Rev. iii. 1. Ye say ye cannot pray. If the Spirit of Christ were in you, it would not be so, Zech. xii. 10, Gal. iv. 6. Ye say ye have no time for prayer, or ye have no place to pray in. If the Spirit of Christ were in you, ye would have a heart to pray; and if ye had the heart for it, ye would find both time and place.

Secondly, Praying natural unconverted persons. People may be praying persons, and yet in the gall of bitterness, and none of God's children; praying persons, and yet profane, Isa. i. 15, 16; formal hypocrites, Matth. xxiii. 14, 27, 28. They may have a gift of prayer, that are void of the spirit and grace of prayer. To such I would say from this doctrine, Then,

1. Certainly ye can pray none at all aright; an evidence of which is, All your prayers are rejected of God, Prov. xv. 8, John ix. 31. If God's own children cannot pray aright without the Spirit, how is it possible ye should do so, who neither have the Spirit, nor yet are children of God? If the weak man cannot go without help, sure the man void of life cannot move at all. View your own case in the case of the true saint, and think, if it be so in the green tree, what must it be in the dry? They are God's children, yet cannot pray aright to their Father without the Spirit; how much less can ye who are none of his family, and therefore never have the Spirit? They always have the Spirit dwelling in them as a Spirit of life, yet cannot pray aright without actual influence from him; how, then, can ye ever pray aright, who are so far from his actual influence, that he is not so much as in you, since ye are not in Christ? Hence,

(1.) Your praying, though continued never so many years, without coming to Christ by faith, is but like so many ciphers, which being without a figure at their head, the value is just nought. There is never one right or acceptable prayer among them all, Heb. xi. 6. They are all lost labour. And such a life of duties is but a wandering in the wilderness of duties, like Israel's wandering forty years in the wilderness, where they died at length, and never entered Canaan.

(2.) All your prayers are turned to sin, Psalm cix. 7. If ye have never prayed aright, ye have always prayed wrong, spilled and marred that duty, profaned that holy ordinance. And so what ye reckon so much praying to God, God will reckon so much taking of his name in vain, for which he will not hold you guiltless. Wherefore let praying persons look well to their state.

2. Think not much of your gifts of prayer, for a gift of prayer will go short way before God. If it were never such a ready, full, and taking gift, it cannot make a man pray one petition aright without the Spirit, John iv. 24. Yet how are men puffed up with such a gift, that have it, and have not grace to keep them humble under it? They think themselves something on account of their gift, while God knows they are nothing, as being without the Spirit; for they see wherein they excel others, but see not wherein they come short of true prayer in the sight of God, Gal. vi. 3, 4.

I have four things to say of a gift of prayer without the spirit of prayer.

(1.) It is a "good gift" of God indeed, James i. 17. But it is a left hand gift, which may be lost and taken away from him that has it now; Zech. xi. ult., "Wo to the idol shepherd that leaveth the flock: the sword shall be upon his arm, and upon his right eye: his arm shall be clean dried up, and his right eye shall be utterly darkened"; compared with John x. 12, for the prophecy relates to the Scribes and Pharisees. It is of that sort that is common to Christ's sheep and the devil's goats. The spirit of prayer is a grace-gift, a right hand gift, which can never be quite lost; Rom. xi. 29, "For the gifts and calling of God are without repentance."

(2.) It may be useful to others for the profit of their souls, but in that respect it is useless to yourselves, 1 Cor. xiii. 1, 2, 3. Others may have communion with God in your exercise of your gift, but you yourself can have none, Prov. xv. 8. Gifts are bestowed on hypocrites for the good and behoof[9] of the saints, as the purse bearer to a young prince gets his purse filled for the needs of the prince, 1 Cor. iii. 21–23. The raven, though an unclean creature, was employed to feed Elijah. The gift the carpenters had that built the ark, was of use to the saving of Noah and his family, but they themselves perished in the deluge, for all their skill of ark-building.

(3.) It cannot but be hurtful to your own souls; which hurtfulness is not from the good gift itself, but from the light and foolish heart it is lodged in, Prov. i. 32. The very gospel,

---

9 Benefit, advantage.

2 Cor. ii. 16, is hurtful that way; yea Christ himself is a stumbling-block by that means. A man with a gift of prayer, without the Spirit, is like a ship without ballast; the more sail she has, she is in the greater danger of being overwhelmed.

(4.) You may perish for ever, for all that gift. Judas had a gift of praying doubtless given him with the gift of preaching; yet for all it he fell from his ministry, and is gone to his own place, Acts i. 25. The light of a gift without the warmth of the Spirit of grace, serves to show the way to outer darkness. And such a gift will aggravate the condemnation of the possessor, being like a bag of gold on a drowning man, that makes him only to sink the sooner and the deeper.

3. *Lastly*, Come forward then another step in religion, and be concerned for a higher attainment in it, than ye have yet reached. Ye have come the length of praying, that is good, but it is not all; if ye stick there, ye perish; come forward to Christ, out of all confidence in your prayers, by believing, uniting with the Son of God. Ye have attained to the gift of prayer; come forward till ye reach the Spirit of prayer, which Christ communicates to all his members, John i. 12; with Gal. iv. 6.

Secondly, Ye that are God's own children, to you I would say,

1. Surely many a mismanaged prayer hath gone through your mouths, so that ye may say, "We are all as an unclean thing, and all our righteousnesses are as filthy rags," Isa. lxiv. 6. So much prayer as has been made by you without the Spirit, so much mismanaged unacceptable prayer has there been, for which ye need pardon. Ye may here view,

(1.) The many prayers of yours, that have been the mere lifeless exercise of a gift without the Spirit from the beginning of them to the end. All which have been lost prayers by the lump. Since ye were acquainted with Christ, ye have kept a constant course of praying daily; but at this rate it will be found there have been many days, and perhaps weeks and months, wherein ye have prayed none at all aright and acceptably. So that if ye seek your prayers in heaven, which ye think ye have sent thither, it will be found that many of them never came there; they wanted the wings of the Spirit's influences, and so fell upon the earth, and are lost.

(2.) The many parts of some of your prayers, and some parts of the best of them, that have been the mere product of your own spirits, and not of the Spirit of God. How much of the prayer has been over many times, ere your lips have been touched with the live coal? And perhaps ere ye have done, ye have quenched the coal, provoked the Spirit to depart. And when it has been best with you, the deceitful heart has made a sinful mixture in it. At this rate seeking many a long prayer before the throne, ye would find that but a short part of it came thither; perhaps but a few sentences. For alas! the skin and dung of our sacrifices are often more bulk, than the flesh that comes on the altar.

2. Be humbled under a sense of your mismanagements in the prayers ye have prayed all along to this day; "for in many things we offend all," Jam. iii. 2. See the need ye have of the blood of Christ to purge away the guilt of your prayers, and apply it by faith for that end, Rev. vii. 14. Lament the too little concern ye have had to get the Spirit's help to your praying, and see for the pardon thereof.

3. *Lastly*, Learn that praying is a more solemn serious work than it is generally looked on to be; and that it is not such an easy thing to pray to purpose, as we are apt to imagine. Take these three warnings then.

(1.) Trust not to your gift of prayer, neither be vain of it, Prov. iii. 5; 1 Cor. i. ult. Oh! it is sad to think of that vanity, and airiness, and self-seeking that is to be found in some people's exercise of their praying gift. It is an argument that the person forgets both God and himself. And nothing can be more contrary to the help of the Spirit in prayer. The heart is deceitful in this point, and we have need to watch it.

(2,) Trust not to your frame. One may have a good frame before he go to prayer, and yet when he comes to the work, may not find his hands; hence often least is got when most is expected; because it is expected rather on what we have, than what we look for from the Spirit. A person may have a good frame in prayer, that may quickly leave him; the wheels of the soul in swift motion may suddenly stop, 2 Tim. ii. 1; Prov. xxviii. 26.

(3) When ye go to prayer, be impressed with a sense of your inability to manage it aright, Josh. xxiv. 19; and then, and all along in prayer, lay yourselves open, and look for the help of the Spirit. Lay the sacrifice on the altar, and look to the Lord for fire from heaven to consume it, as Elijah did, 1 Kings xviii. 33, 37, 38. The Spirit is that fire.

I proceed to another doctrine from the text.

DOCTRINE IV. All our praying aright is so far done by the help of the Spirit, that it is justly reckoned his work, his making intercession for us.

In handling this point, I shall shew,

I. What is to be understood by praying aright.

II. That all our praying aright is done by the help of the Spirit.

III. In what respects our praying aright is so far done by the help of the Spirit, that it is justly reckoned his work.

IV. What is the Spirit's work in our praying aright, or what his making intercession for us is.

V. *Lastly*, Apply the whole.

I. I am to show what is to be understood by praying aright.

Negatively, 1. It is not praying aright in a legal sense, without any imperfection in the eye of the law, attending the prayer. There was never a prayer in the world of that sort since Adam's fall, except the prayers of the man Christ. The best prayers of the best saints have always been attended with blemishes visible to the eyes of God, though not to ours, Isa. lxiv. 6. Such praying is our duty indeed, Matth. v. ult., but the attainment of none in this life, by any measure of grace to be expected, Phil. iii. 12.

2. It is not praying aright in a moral sense, wherein the most rigid hearer can discern nothing contrary to the precepts of morality. A prayer may be so far right as no unlawful thing may be prayed for in it, and yet may be naught, Luke xviii. 11. The matter may be very good, where the manner of praying spoils all. If that were enough, the book-prayers of formalists would be sufficient help, in some cases, to pray aright.

3. It is not praying aright in a rhetorical sense, a well-worded prayer, with a suitable delivery. Words, voice, and gesture are of little moment before God, 1 Sam. xvi. 7; 1 Cor. ii. 4. It may be a right prayer, where the expression is far from being polite, where sentences are broken off before they make a complete sense; as in Psalm vi. 3, "My soul is also sore vexed; but thou, O Lord, how long?" The Lord himself knows what is the mind of the Spirit, though the words do not fully express it. And where all these things are accurate and exact, the prayer may be all wrong before God: where there is not a wrong word, there may not be one right affection.

Positively, It is praying aright in an evangelical sense, so that in the eye of the gospel it passes as acceptable prayer before the throne. This implies two things.

1. Sincerity in prayer, 1 Chron. xxix. 17, in opposition to formality and hypocrisy, 2 Tim. iii. 5; Psalm xvii. 1. The righteous God loveth uprightness of heart in duty, Prov. xv. 8;

and though there may be many blemishes in the duty, where the man is sincere in it, the Lord will regard it, notwithstanding of these blemishes. Hereby the heart is really for God as the chief good, and goes along with the tongue in prayer.

2. A perfection of parts in prayer, though not of degrees. That is to say, praying aright is,

(1.) Praying for things agreeable to God's will revealed in his word of command or promise, 1 John v. 14. Nothing can make praying for things without the compass of the command and promise, to be praying aright. For there faith has nothing to bottom itself upon, and "without faith it is impossible to please God." Heb. xi. 6.

(2.) Praying in a right manner in a gospel-sense, Jer. xxxix. 13, "Ye shall seek me, and find me, when ye shall search for me with all your heart." Hereunto are required praying graces and affections in exercise, as faith, fervency, humility, reverence and the like. These are the soul and life of prayer, whereas the expressions of the lips are but the body of it. Where these are wanting, the duty will be reckoned but bodily exercise, 1 Tim. iv. 8.

Such praying is right in so far as it is acceptable in the sight of God, *i. e.* capable of being accepted according to the rule of the gospel. It is a sacrifice fit to be laid on God's altar; a prayer which may be put in the Mediator's hand, that through his intercession it may be actually accepted. For it is not anything in our prayers themselves for which they are accepted, but only the intercession of Christ, for the best things in them are mixed with sin. Only such prayers are fit to be put in the Mediator's hands, and he will take them off the sinner's hand to present them to the Father, and the Father will accept them at his hand; whereas other sorts of prayer, wherein the petitioner is not sincere, or where they are wrong as to the matter of them, or are not made in the right manner, they cannot come into the Mediator's hand, he will never present them for acceptance; and so it is impossible they can be accepted.

Hence it is evident that none who are out of Christ, unregenerate, unconverted, can at all pray aright, or pray as they ought. For what sincerity can be there, where converting grace has never touched? What faith, fervency, or humility can be exercised by unbelievers dead in sin, whose stony heart is not yet removed? Therefore the form of prayer, Matth. vi. begins, "Our Father," &c., shewing that none can pray aright or acceptably but God's own children, or those who have an interest in him as their Father; and it is the Spirit that teaches them so, Gal. iv. 6.

II. I am next to show that all our praying aright is done by the help of the Spirit. This is to be understood as comprehending these two things.

1. It is done by the help of the Spirit dwelling in us, Gal. iv. 6. Ye are not to think that the Spirit as an external agent helps us to pray aright; nay, but the Spirit helping to pray is as a Spirit of life, dwelling in the man as a member of Christ, 1 John ii. 27. So that till we have the Spirit dwelling in us we can never pray aright.

2. It is done by the help of the indwelling Spirit actually influencing us, Gal. iv. 6, "Crying, Abba, Father," *i. e.* so influencing us as to make us cry. Even the indwelling of the Spirit is not enough for that effect; but there is requisite an agency of the Spirit in us, whereby we may be acted in prayer, which is called "the blowing of the wind," John iii. 8, Cant. iv. ult.

Now that all our praying aright is done by the help of the Spirit indwelling and influencing, is clear,

1. From scripture-testimony. The Spirit is the author of our whole sanctification, whereof praying aright is a part, 2 Thess. ii. 13, particularly of all our acceptable worship, Phil. iii. 3. It is by him we have access to God in worship, Eph. ii. 18. And prayer by name, if of the right sort, is owing to his help, Eph. vi. 18, and that as an indwelling Spirit, a Spirit of adoption, Rom. viii. 15, with Gal. iv. 6, and an influencing Spirit, 1 Thess. v. 17, 18, 19.

2. We are spiritually dead without the Spirit indwelling, and spiritually asleep without the Spirit influencing, Eph. ii. 1, Cant. v. 2. Neither a dead man, nor a sleeping man is fit to present a supplication to the king; so neither is a dead sinner, nor a sleeping saint capable to pray aright. The former, praying, is like a ghost walking and talking; the latter, like a man speaking through his sleep. It is the Spirit that quickens the dead soul, John vi. 63, who coming to dwell in the heart makes the first resurrection; and it is he also who awakens the sleeping saint, Cant. v. 4.

3. There is no praying aright without sanctifying grace, nor without that grace in exercise, John ix. 31, Cant. iii. 1. Where sanctifying grace is not, the filth and pollution of sin remains, and defiles all, Tit. i. 15. So that such a man's praying is like the opening of an unripe grave, Rom. iii. 13. Accordingly the praying Pharisees are called "whited sepulchres," Matth. xxiii. 27. Where grace is not in exercise, there is incense

indeed, but no pillar of smoke ascending from it to heaven; spikenard indeed, but no smell thereof. Now it is the indwelling Spirit that works sanctifying grace, 2 Thess. ii. 13, puts that grace in exercise, Cant. iv. 16, and so fits men to pray, Zech. xii. 10.

4. *Lastly*, To praying aright is required light and warmth, a light of the mind, and warmth of affections; the former for the matter, the latter for the manner. And it is a false light and warmth that makes some natural men think that sometimes they pray aright, Isa. lviii. 2. But all genuine light, and vital warmth comes from the Spirit, Eph. i. 17, 18; 2 Tim. i. 7. Hence the emblem of the virtue of the Holy Spirit was "cloven tongues, like as of fire," Acts ii. 3, 4. And the effect thereof is someway compared with that of drunkenness (which excuses it no more than Christ's being compared to a thief excuses stealing, Rev. xvi. 15.); for as the liquor being received to excess, influences the man, so that things come in his head which otherwise would not, and the affections and passions are wrought up by it, Prov. xxiii. 33, so the Spirit indwelling and influencing, presents to the mind matter of prayer, and works up the affections suitable thereto, Eph. v. 18, 19, Cant. vii. 9.

III. I shall show in what respects our praying aright is so far done by the help of the Spirit, that it is justly reckoned his work. That it is so reckoned in scripture, is evident from the text, where his interceding for us with groanings cannot be understood of himself as the subject, but of us according to the analogy of faith. It is plain also from Gal. iv. 6, "Because ye are sons, God hath sent forth the Spirit of his Son into your hearts, crying Abba, Father." Now the Spirit's crying Abba, Father, is meant certainly of our crying so, by the help of the Spirit, not of a crying whereof the Spirit is the subject; for God is not the Father of the Spirit, because it is the second person, and not the third, who is the Son of God; and Father and Son are the relatives. And thus the apostle explains it, Rom. viii. 15, "Ye have received the Spirit of adoption, whereby we cry, Abba, Father." Now the reasons of this are,

1. Because all that is right in our prayers is from the Spirit, and all that is wrong in them from ourselves, either as to matter or manner, 1 Cor. xii. 11; 1 Pet. i. 22; with 2 Cor. iii. 5. In the incense of our prayers there is smoke that goes up towards heaven, ashes that remain behind on the earth; it is the fire from the altar that sends up the smoke, it is the earthly nature of the incense that occasions the ashes. The flesh of any

such spiritual sacrifice is wholly owing to the Spirit, the skin and dung is our own, and ours only. Therefore all our right praying is justly reckoned the Spirit's work.

2. None pray aright but as they are members of Christ, and children of God, Gal. iv. 6, Rom. viii. 15, John xv. 5. Now it is the Holy Spirit of the Head that dwells in and actuates all the members acting as members, 1 Cor. xii. 11, 12. Therefore as the soul sees by the eye, and hears by the ear; so whatsoever the members of Christ do aright as members, is justly ascribed to the Spirit that actuates the mystical body, and is the Spirit of adoption. But there may be a defect in seeing by the eye, and hearing by the ear; these are not to be ascribed to the soul, but to some disease in the eye or ear. So whatever defects may be in the members of Christ, these are not to be ascribed to the Spirit, but to the remains of corruption in them, and their state of imperfection while here.

3. The Spirit is the principal cause of our praying aright, we are but the instrumental causes of it. The act of praying in heart and expression is done by us; but the grace, ability, frame for prayer, and the exciting and bringing forth into exercise that grace and ability, is from the Spirit, Phil. ii. 12, 13. Hence prayer is said to be inwrought in us, Jam. v. 16. If the wind blow not, the spices send not forth their pleasant smell, Cant. iv. 16. As the sound of the horn ceases as soon as one ceases to wind it, so does our praying aright on the withdrawing of the Spirit, 2 Cor. iii. 5.

4. *Lastly*, All our praying graces, as all others, are in their exercise the product of the Spirit, and his work in us, Gal. v. 22, 23. There is a root and stock of grace in the believer, implanted and preserved by the Spirit, 1 John iii. 9. In prayer these are brought forth into exercise, the man acts faith, love, &c., and therein the soul of prayer lies; but look on them as they are so brought forth from the stock, and they are the fruit of the Spirit, though the believer is the tree they hang on. For the Spirit is the vital fructifying sap of the trees of righteousness, Isa. xliv. 3, 4. Thus the holy lustings, longings, and desires of a believer against sin, are called "the Spirit's lusting," Gal. v. 17. (compare ver. 16, 18), in the same sense as the groanings in our text. See 1 John iv. 4.

OBJECT. If our praying aright is the work of the Spirit, what need have we of the intercession of Christ, for the acceptance of our prayers? Surely the Spirit needs no intercessor betwixt him and the Father. ANSW. Though it is the Spirit's work, it is not his work separately by himself without us; but it is his work in us, and so our work too, Gal. iv. 6, with Rom. viii. 15. And so far as it is done by us, we groaning, lusting, crying in prayer, every thing has a sinful mixture from us at best; so there is need of Christ's intercession still. The water comes pure from the fountain, the Spirit; but running through a muddy channel, such as every saint here is, it cannot be accepted in heaven, but as purified and sweetened by the intercession of Christ.

IV. I come now to consider, what is the Spirit's work in our praying aright, or what his making intercession for us is. And here I shall shew,

1. The difference betwixt Christ's intercession and the Spirit's.

2. The help of the Spirit in prayer.

FIRST, I am to show what is the difference betwixt Christ's intercession and the Spirit's.

1. Christ intercedes for us in heaven at the Father's right hand; Rom. viii. 34. The Spirit intercedes in our hearts, upon earth; Gal. iv. 6. We have no intercession made for us in heaven, but by Christ the only intercessor there.

2. Christ's intercession is a mediatory intercession, wherein he mediates or goes between God and us; an office peculiar to him alone; 1 Tim. ii. 5. But the Spirit's intercession is an auxiliary intercession to us, whereby he helps us to go to God in a right manner, prompting us to intercede for ourselves aright.

3. The Spirit's intercession is the fruit of Christ's intercession, and what is done by the sinner through the Spirit's intercession, is accepted of God through the intercession of Christ. Christ by his death purchased the Spirit for his people, and through his intercession the Spirit is sent into their hearts, where he helps them to pray for themselves; and these prayers are accepted of God by means of the Mediator's intercession, John xiv. 16, and xvi. 7, 13; Rev. viii. 4. In a word,

The difference is such as is between one who draws a poor man's petition for him, and another who presents it to the king, and gets it granted. The Spirit does the former, and Christ does the latter, for us.

SECONDLY, I shall consider the help of the Spirit in prayer, which is his making intercession for us, in the style of the scripture. We shall view this work of the Spirit, more generally, and more particularly.

FIRST, More generally, and that in two things. He acts in it,

1. As a teaching Spirit; John xiv. 26. It is our infirmity in point of prayer, "We know not what we should pray for as we ought." He enlightens our minds, and helps our ignorance as to the matter and manner of prayer, 1 John ii. 27. He is the great Teacher of the church, and none teacheth like him. He will teach them who are so weak that no other can teach them; so that hearing some of God's weak children pray, one must needs say, "This is the finger of God."

2. As a quickening Spirit; Psalm lxxx. 18. Therefore the Spirit is compared to fire, which gives both light and heat. He removes spiritual deadness, and stirs up praying graces in the heart; whence his influences are compared to the blowing of the wind, that puts things that were at rest in motion. Thus he is said to "make intercession with groanings which cannot be uttered," setting the gracious heart a labouring and working towards God, with the utmost earnestness, as one groaning.

SECONDLY, More particularly, the work of the Spirit in our prayers lies here.

First, He excites us to pray, Rom. viii. 15, "Ye have received the Spirit of adoption, whereby we cry Abba, Father." He prompteth us to go to the throne of grace, who otherwise would be negligent of it, and backward to it; Cant. v. 2, 3, 4, "I sleep, but my heart waketh, &c. My beloved put in his hand by the hole of the door, and my bowels were moved for him." Thus he leads us to God (Eph. ii. 18, *Gr.*) as an internal moving principle. This lies in two things,

1. He impresses our spirits with a sense of a divine call to it, and so binds it on our consciences as duty to God, Psalm xxvii. 8. *Heb.* "My heart said unto thee, Let my face seek thy face, when thou saidst, Seek ye my face." Thus he applies the general command for praying to particular times, that the man is made in effect to say, now God is calling me to this duty; and so he sees he cannot slight it without disobedience, but must go to it from conscience of duty. This cuts off the low motives to prayer, of custom, credit, regard to the commands of men, &c.

2. He disposes our hearts for it, inclines us to the duty, that we willingly comply with it. "When thou saidst, Seek ye my my face; my heart said unto thee, Thy face, Lord, will I seek," Psalm xxvii. 8. Men may have a sense of the command on them, who for want of a disposition to the duty commanded, either neglect the command, or else are but dragged to obey it. But the Spirit powerfully inclines the will to the duty, so that the man obeys out of choice, Psalm cx. 3; Cant. vi. 12.

This cuts off the low motives of fear of man, and slavish fear of God too, which move many.

Secondly, He gives us a view of God as a gracious and merciful Father in Christ; Gal. iv. 6. Without this there can be no acceptable prayer. Where there is no spiritual view of God at all in prayer, we worship we know not what. Where we view him as an absolute God out of Christ, we may be filled with terror of him, but can have no true confidence in him. But by the Spirit viewing him in Christ, we have at once the sight of majesty and mercy. And hereby he works in us,

1. A holy reverence of God, to whom we pray, which is necessary in acceptable prayer, Heb. xii. 28. By this view he strikes us with a holy dread and awe of the majesty of God, whereby is banished that lightness and vanity of heart, that makes such flaunting in the prayers of some, as if they were set down on their knees to show their gift, and commend themselves.

2. A holy confidence in him, Eph. iii. 12, "Abba, Father," speaks both reverence and confidence, whereof the Spirit is the author, Rom. viii. 15. This confidence respects both his ability and willingness to help us, Matth. vii. 11. Without this there can be no acceptable prayer, Heb. xi. 6; Jam. i. 6. This is it that makes prayer an ease to a troubled heart, the Spirit exciting in us holy confidence in God as a Father. Hence the soul, though not presently eased, draws these conclusions. (1.) He designs my good by all the hardships I am under, Rom. viii. 28. (2.) He pities me under them, Psalm ciii. 13. (3.) He knows the best time for removing them, and will do it, when that comes, 1 Sam. ii. 3.

Hereby is cut off that unbelieving formality, whereby some expect nothing by prayer, and get as little; as also the despondency, wherewith others are struck, from the sense of God's justice, and their own sinfulness.

Thirdly, He gives us a view of ourselves in our own sinfulness and unworthiness, John xvi. 8. This always accompanies the view the Spirit gives of God, Isa. vi. 5, "Wo is me, for I am undone, because I am a man of unclean lips, and I dwell in the midst of a people of unclean lips; for mine eyes have seen the King, the Lord of hosts." We are very ready to become strangers to ourselves, and to lose sight of our sinfulness. But the Spirit of prayer, according to the measure of his influence, opens out the man before his own eyes, casts abroad the many foul plies of his heart and life, Luke xviii. 13; Isa. lxiv. 6. Hereby he works in us,

1. Humiliation of heart before the Lord, fills us with low thoughts of ourselves before him, Gen. xviii. 27; makes us see ourselves unworthy of the mercies, that either we have got, or desire to have, Gen. xxxii. 10; fills us with holy shame, and self-loathing, Luke xviii. 13; Ezek. xxxvi. 31. This fits us for the receipt of mercies of free grace; and the want of it makes sinners to be in their prayers, as if they came to buy of God, and not to beg, and so to be sent empty away.

2. Cordial confession, that comes away natively from seen and felt sinfulness, Psalm lxii. 8. Thus the influence of the Spirit in prayer causes full and free confession of sin with the mouth, to the honour of God, and our own shame. And the things thus being impressed on the heart, there follow natively words to express them by; and where they fail, groans do well compensate them before the throne. This cuts off the formal, hale-hearted confessions of sin, wherewith prayers are often vitiated.

3. Hearty thanksgiving for mercies received, Psalm cxvi. 11, 12. Hereby the smallest mercies appear very big; and the sinner, that wondered at other times how he came not to get more mercies, begins to wonder he has any at all left him, Lam. iii. 22. But without a discovery of our sinfulness by the Spirit, all our thanksgivings for mercies are but empty compliment, like the Pharisee's, Luke xviii. 11.

4. A high value for the Mediator, and his righteousness, which lies out of the view of the unhumbled heart, Phil. iii. 9. As the stars are best seen from the bottom of a deep and narrow pit, so Christ crucified is best discovered in his excellency and suitableness, by the humbled soul. The lower the soul is in its own eyes, the higher will the Mediator be in its eyes; and the higher the Mediator is, the more fit one is to pray.

Fourthly, He gives us a view of our wants, and the need we have of the supply of them, Luke xv. 17. This may be seen, comparing the Pharisee's and Publican's prayers, Luke xviii. 11, 12, 13. The Spirit taught the one, and not the other. The want of this mars prayer, Luke i. 53, "He hath filled the hungry with good things, and the rich he hath sent empty away." Here he acts,

1. As an enlightener, opening the eyes of the mind, to discern the wants and needs we are compassed with, Eph. i. 17, 18. The Spirit's shining in on the soul, as the sun on a moth-eaten garment holden up betwixt us and it, the soul gets a broad sight of its wants; whence it is made to say, as Isa. lxiv. 6, "We are all as an unclean thing, and all our righ-

teousnesses are as filthy rags." Luke xviii. 13, "God be merciful to me a sinner." Psalm xix. 12, "Who can understand his errors?" This the Spirit doth by opening up the law in its spirituality, and giving us a view of our own circumstances in a present evil ensnaring world.

2. As a remembrancer, bringing seasonably to mind the wants we have, or might have adverted to, John xvi. 26. To everything there is a season; but ofttimes in the season of getting supply at the throne of grace, our wants and needs escape us, they come not in mind, till the market is over. The Spirit is a remembrancer in this case, seasonably suggesting to us our needs for ourselves or others. So he sets things before us in time of prayer.

3. As a forewarner of what we may need, John xvi. 13. So we find Job not only offering sacrifice, with a view to what he could not know, chap. i. 5; but also possessed with a fear of a trial before it came, chap. iii. 25. Thus men are led to lay up for what they may meet with, and in prayer to have a view to the grace that may be needful in such and such emergents. Hereby he helps us,

(1.) To matter of prayer, sets before us things to be prayed for. Where the Spirit is thus at work in the soul, persons will be taught to pray, and it will supply the want of a form; and therefore they that soothe themselves with that, they cannot pray, do but bewray[10] themselves to be void of the Spirit of God.

(2.) To the right manner of praying; for hereby he,

[1.] Impresses us with a sense of need, that we are made to pray feelingly, that the tongue does but express what the heart feels, Luke xv. 17, 18, 19. Insensibleness of our needs makes us formal in prayer, and therefore to be sent empty away. A mere rational sight of our wants will not cure it; but the light of the Spirit is the light of life, John viii. 12; that will not miss to affect the heart.

[2.] Hereby we are rendered sincere in our addresses to God, Psalm xvii. 1. Feigned lips in prayer proceed from a dark and insensible heart. He that really sees his disease, and is persuaded of the need of the Physician, there is no doubt of his being in earnest for his help.

[3.] Hereby we are made importunate in prayer. Necessity has no law, and hunger breaks through stone walls, as we see in the woman of Canaan, who did hang on, over the belly

---

10 Divulge, betray.

of discouragement, and would take no refusal. Importunate praying is prevailing, Luke xi. 8; and felt need that one cannot bear without relief, makes importunity.

[4.] Hereby we are made particular in prayer, laying our hand on our sores, and laying out our particular wants before the Lord, Luke xviii. 41. General prayers, like general preaching, have little of the Spirit in them. They that go where help is to be found, being indeed pinched, will readily tell where they are pinched.

Fifthly, He gives us a view of the grace and promises of the covenant, Psalm xxv. 14; John xiv. 26. Without this, the sinner, pressed with a sense of need, has nothing to support him, and therefore cannot pray in faith. Our Lord Jesus Christ has purchased all the grace and promises of the covenant for his people, and there is enough there for all they can need. It is the office of the Spirit to open them out before their eyes, and apply them. And here the Spirit,

1. Brings to their remembrance the grace and promises suited to their case, Gen. xxxii. 11, 12. The promises are the rule and encouragement of prayer; but while they lie out of our sight, we can neither have suitable direction nor encouragement from them; but when the Spirit draws near with the promise to us, there is help at hand in prayer.

2. He unfolds that grace and these promises, causing to understand them in a spiritual and saving manner, 1 Cor. ii. 12. The letter of the promise can only help to words in prayer; but the Spirit shining on the promise, will help to pray in a gracious manner, for the demonstration of the Spirit is always with power. Hereby,

(1.) The Spirit teaches what to pray for, according to the will of God. While the promises rightly understood regulate our prayers, and they are agreeable to the grace of the covenant, we may be sure we do not err in the matter, 2 Sam. vii. 28, 29. These are God's bills and bonds to his people, and by them he shows what he allows us to ask of him. What he is debtor to his faithfulness for, we may crave.

(2.) In what terms to pray for it, the terms of the promise, terms agreeable to the grace of the covenant. And this is the rise of some expressions of God's children in prayer, which may seem strange and uncouth to others, that have not their view of the grace of the covenant, which want makes them appear unseemly to them; yea, they may seem strange to themselves. And hence also is the agreement to a nicety, that is sometimes to be found betwixt the answer of prayer, and their expression in prayer.

(3.) Hereby he fills our mouths with arguments, helping us to plead and pray, Job xxiii. 3, 4. The grace and promises of the covenant, held before the eyes by the Spirit shining on them to the soul in prayer, is such a fountain of heavenly oratory that will make a weak and unlearned Christian plead and pray at the rate that others are strangers to, and which themselves at another time are quite unable to reach.

(4.) Hereby he stirs up in us a faith of particular confidence as to the thing prayed for, so that we are helped to pray believingly, and not doubtingly and distrustfully. The necessity of this faith in prayer is evident from the scriptures, Matth. xxi. 22; Mark xi. 24; 1 Tim. ii. 8; James i. 6; and the Spirit is the author of it, 2 Cor. iv. 13. He gives a view of the promise and grace of the covenant with relation to that thing, and helps to regulate the prayer thereby, strengthens to believe the accomplishment of the promise in that particular for the Mediator's sake, and consequently the hearing of prayer in that particular. Hereby it appears what this faith is, namely, a confidence agreeable to the promise as demonstrated by the Spirit; absolute as to the particular thing, where the promise is demonstrated absolute, or by the Spirit particularly applied to the thing, Psalm cxix. 49, which may be in things not absolutely necessary, as Mark v. 27, 28, 34. Or indefinite, where the promise is left so by the Spirit, that is to say, a confidence of the thing itself, or of what is as good. And hereby also this faith is distinguished from presumption, in that it is founded on a word of God, and the merit of Christ.

(5.) *Lastly*, Hereby he works in us a holy boldness in prayer, Eph. iii. 12. Faith coming before the throne, and spreading out the word of promise with the grace of the covenant, makes bold there for a gracious answer. How bold was Jacob in that case, "I will not let thee go, except thou bless me?" Gen. xxxii. 26. Foolish men have ignorantly censured this boldness in the prayers of God's children, but God is well pleased with it, when he says, "Ask me of things to come concerning my sons, and concerning the work of my hands command ye me," Isa. xlv. 11; though the counterfeiting of this holy oil must needs be dangerous. It is distinguished by its attending humility, as in Jacob, Gen. xxxii. 10, "I am not worthy of the least of all the mercies, and of all the truth which thou hast shewed unto thy servant."

Sixthly, He raiseth in us holy desires for the supply of our wants; "groanings which cannot be uttered." The Spirit working as fire, fires the heart in prayer, sets it in motion, Cant. v. 4, a lusting, longing, panting for what may tend to the perfection of the new creature, either removing the impediments of its growth, or supplying it with fresh incomes of grace for its growth. Of this more afterwards. But thus we are made to pray fervently, Jam. v. 16; Rom. xii. 11.

Seventhly, He gives us a view of the merit and intercession of the Mediator, Eph. i. 17. This is the work of the Holy Spirit, without whose illumination Christ will be a hidden beauty to us. He shewed Zechariah the intercessor, at his work, Zech. i. 12, and Stephen, Acts vii. 56, and he shews believers the same sight for substance by the eye of faith, 1 Cor. ii. 12. Hereby,

1. He points us to the only way of acceptance of our prayers, John xiv. 6; while hypocrites overlooking Christ lose all their requests. He teaches us to pray as we ought, and so to pray in the name of Jesus Christ, depending on his merit and intercession allenarly.[11]

2. He lays before us a firm foundation of confidence before the Lord; 1 John ii. 1, "If any man sin, we have an advocate with the Father, Jesus Christ the righteous"; an Advocate who never loses the plea he takes in hand, John xi. 42, having an undisputable ground to go upon, namely, the purchase of his own blood. A fresh view of this makes faith in prayer renew its strength, and fills with confidence; Eph. iii. 12, "In whom we have boldness and access with confidence by the faith of him."

3. *Lastly,* He furnishes us with an answer to all objections, that an unbelieving heart and a subtile devil can muster up against us, in prayer; Rom. viii. 33, 34, "Who shall lay anything to the charge of God's elect? It is God that justifieth: who is he that condemneth? It is Christ that died, yea, rather that is risen again, who is even at the right hand of God, who also maketh intercession for us." Are we sinful and vile? The merit of Christ is of infinite value. Are we unworthy for whom God should do such a thing? Yet the Mediator is worthy. Can our prayers, smelling so rank of sinful imperfections, not be accepted at our polluted hands? Yet being perfumed with his merit, they can be accepted at his hand, Rev. viii. 4.

Eighthly, He manages the heart and spirit in prayer, which every serious soul will own to be a hard task; Jer. x. 23,

---

11 Alone, exclusively.

"O Lord, I know that the way of man is not in himself; it is not in man that walketh to direct his steps." Gal. v. 16. Therefore the psalmist says, Psalm xxxi. 5, "Into thine hand I commit my spirit." And,

1. He composes it for prayer; Psalm lxxxvi. 11. "Unite my heart to fear thy name." He frames the heart, that is out of frame for it; commands a heavenly calm in the soul, whereby it may be fitted for divine communications; saying to the heart tossed with temptations, troubles, and risings of corruption, "Peace and be still"; and he blows up the fire of grace into a flame, 2 Tim. i. 7. So the preparation of the heart is owing to him; Psalm x. 17, "Lord, thou hast heard the desire of the humble; thou wilt prepare their heart, thou wilt cause thine ear to hear."

2. He fixes it in prayer, that it wander not away in the duty; Ezek. xxxvi. 27, "I will put my Spirit within you, and cause you to walk in my statutes, and ye shall keep my judgments, and do them." There is need not only of quickening grace in duty, but of establishing grace; for the heart itself is apt to wander off from the serious purpose, and the powers of hell exert themselves to divert from it. But the supply of the Spirit in prayer keeps the heart fixed. And, in the case of wandering,

3. He reduces it from its wanderings in prayer; Psalm xxiii. 3, "He restoreth my soul; he leadeth me in the paths of righteousness for his name's sake." It will always cost a struggle to hedge in the heart in duty, and the help of the Spirit is necessary to maintain the struggle, Rom. vii. 21; Gal. v. 17. But sometimes the heart is quite carried off by its wandering disposition, that the prayer is quite marred, the heart leaving the tongue. In this case the Spirit convinces and humbles the soul under the sense of that sin, and so makes it more serious than before, from thence shewing the corruption of nature, Rom. viii. 37.

Ninthly, and *Lastly*, The Spirit causes us to continue in prayer from time to time, till we obtain a gracious answer; and so makes us pray perseveringly, Eph. vi. 18. The Lord may keep his people long hanging on for an answer ere they get it. The promise may be big with the mercy prayed for, and yet it be not only many months but years ere it bring forth, as in the case of Abraham and David. This is a sore trial, and there would be no keeping from fainting if the Spirit did not help our infirmity. But he helps to hang on,

1. By accounting for the delay of our answer, in a way consistent with God's honour and our good, and so satisfying us in that point; Psalm xxii. 2, 3, "O my God, I cry in the day-time but thou hearest not; and in the night season and am not silent. But thou art holy O thou that inhabitest the praises of Israel." He helps to discern the unsoundness of the subtile reasonings of unbelief, tending to despondency, and so hinders from making rash conclusions; Psalm lxxvii. 10, "I said, this is my infirmity; but I will remember the years of the right hand of the Most High." And so he keeps up in us kind thoughts of God's dispensations.

2. By strengthening faith and hope, which have the battle to fight in this case, Eph. iii. 16. Hangers on at the throne of grace may get a long stand, but they will get their strength renewed, Psalm xxvii. 13, 14. This the Spirit does, by shining anew on the promise; adding other promises to it tending to the same scope; giving some present experience and off-fallings from the Lord's hand, whereby the soul is refreshed in the time; and helping to observe the signs of the approaching day while yet the night continues.

3. *Lastly*, Continuing and reviving on our spirits the sense of our need, which, pinching us anew, obliges to renew our suit for relief until the time we get it, 2 Cor. xii. 8, "For this thing I besought the Lord thrice, that it might depart from me." If in this case we were left to our own spirits, we would seek our help from another quarter, than hanging on about the Lord's hand, and our sense of need would wear off, and we would drop our petition. But the Spirit perfects what he begins; Psalm cxxxviii. ult., "The Lord will perfect that which concerneth me."

I shall now make some practical improvement of this subject.

USE I. Of information. This may let us see,

1. That men in this world are under the influence of that part of the other world which they are in the road to. If ye are in the road to the happy part of the other world, ye are under the conduct and influence of the Holy Spirit, prompting and helping you to do your duty to God. Whence ye may gather, that they are in the road to destruction, who are under the conduct and influence of the spirit of the world, prompting and helping them to a course of sin. Consider the prevailing course of your lives, and trace it to the spring, and ye will find it is the spirit ye are acted by, 1 John iv. 4. One part of men is led by the Spirit of God, and they are holy, heavenly,

and spiritual; another by the evil spirit, and they are unholy, hellish, and carnal. He is a spirit of covetousness in some, of uncleanness in others, &c.

2. Praying is another thing than men generally take it to be. It is not the exercise of a gift, but of grace; not a piece of task laid on men, but a privilege they are advanced to; not a work to be done in our own strength, but by help from heaven; not a piece of the form of religion, but of experimental religion. Consider prayer in this scripture view of it, and among many that bow their knees in prayer to God, there will be found few really praying persons; many whose hearts must say on what they have heard of it, Ezek. xx. 49, "Doth he not speak parables?"

3. True praying will always make people holy and humble; for the Spirit by which it is done is the Spirit of holiness and light, Matth. iii. 11. Does a man value himself upon, and appear proud and conceited of himself on the account of his good praying? still continue in his profane, untender, unholy course? His prayers are his own, they are not by the help of the Spirit in him. God regards them not.

4. Great is the encouragement that poor sinners have to apply themselves to serious and spiritual praying. The weakest are left inexcusable, if they neglect prayer still; and the formal professor, if he continue with his formal task-work of praying still. We have the Hearer of prayer to go to, the Father of our Lord Jesus, with our petitions; an Intercessor in heaven, to present them; and an Intercessor on earth, to draw them for us, and help us to make our petitions. This is the office of the Holy Spirit. Therefore,

Use II. Of exhortation. Set yourselves for praying in the Spirit, Eph. vi. 18. Prayerless persons, give yourselves to praying, and to this kind of praying. Praying persons, satisfy not yourselves without this kind of praying. Stand not still in the outer court of prayer, with hypocrites and formalists; come in to the inner court, with God's own children. Look for the help of the Spirit, employ the Spirit in all your duties, and particularly your prayers. Remember that all the prayers are lost that are not done in the Spirit.

I shall give you some advices, how to get the help of the Spirit in prayer.

1. Come to Christ in the way of believing the gospel. The fulness of the Spirit is lodged in Christ, Rev. iii. 1. He communicates the Spirit to dead sinners, 1 Cor. xv. 45, with John xx. 22, and this in the word of the gospel, Gal. iii. 2. It is vain

to expect the help of the Spirit in prayer, till once we have received the Spirit to dwell in us, Eph. iii. 17, with 1 John iii. ult. To receive the word of the gospel as an engrafted, quickening word, whereby we close with Christ for all, is the necessary foundation for all this.

2. Beware of maltreating the Spirit. And so,

(1.) Resist not the Spirit, Acts vii. 51. Do not stave off convictions, and awakenings out of a state or course of sin. Beware of sinning over the belly of light, and persisting in sin against calls to repentance. That is to resist the Spirit, and so to provoke him to leave you.

(2.) Quench not the Spirit, 1 Thess. v. 19. If this holy fire begin to burn at any time, so as you see the light and feel the heat of it, do not withdraw fuel from it by neglecting the motions and operations of it, not taking care to cherish them; do not smother them; by not giving them vent in prayer: far less drown it out, by taking your swing in any sinful course; Luke xxi. 34, "Take heed to yourselves, lest at any time your hearts be overcharged with surfeiting, and drunkenness, and cares of this life."

(3.) Grieve not the Spirit, Eph. iv. 30. The Spirit is grieved by undervaluing his graces, comforts, influences, and his means of communicating them; by sins gross in their nature or aggravations, whereby the conscience is wasted and signally defiled, whereby some have quite withered away, the Spirit leaving them.

(4.) Vex not the Spirit; Isa. lxiii. 10. Vex him not by your still relapsing into the same sins; Numb. xiv. 22, especially after convictions of the ill of them, confessions thereof, resolutions against them, and smarting for them. This is the great trial of the divine patience, whereby men are in hazard of being given up of God, Numb. xiv. 27.

(5.) Blaspheme not the Spirit in his operations, particularly praying in the Spirit. Take heed of making a mock of religion, preaching, praying, seriousness, talking slightingly of these things, and of making persons the objects of your derision and spite on these accounts. Sometime these things were only to be found among malignants and persecutors; but now they are to be found among people that pray themselves, and partake of the Lord's table. These Satan is training up for greater service, when such times shall come again. But take heed, it is a dangerous course, as these young blasphemers of the Spirit in his operations felt; 2 Kings ii. 23, 24, "As Elisha was going up by the way, there came forth little children out of the city, and mocked him, and said unto him, Go up, thou bald head; go up, thou bald head. And he turned back, and looked on them, and cursed them in the name of the Lord; and there came forth two she-bears out of the wood, and tare forty and two children of them."

3. Walk tenderly and circumspectly; Eph. v. 15. A loose and untender walk, wherein people let down their watch over the frame of their heart, and the course of their life in words and actions, provokes the Spirit to withdraw; when a tender walk is followed with the tokens of his favour; John xiv. 21, "He that hath my commandments, and keepeth them, he it is that loveth me, and he that loveth me, shall be loved of my Father, and I will love him, and will manifest myself to him."

4. When ye go to prayer, be convinced of your absolute need of the Spirit. Look for him, and wait, and lay yourselves open to his influences; Luke xi. 13. Labour to revive that conviction at every occasion of prayer, and to keep it up throughout it. Look for the Spirit in the promise, believing it with application; Ezek. xxxvi. 27, "I will put my Spirit within you," &c. Lay yourselves down at his feet, to be enlightened, quickened, &c., Jer. xxxi. 18, as one lays open himself to receive the fresh air.

5. Be habitually concerned for answers of prayer. They that are in good earnest to have their petitions granted, will be careful to have them right drawn; but they that are indifferent in the one, will be so in the other too; Psalm v. 3, "In the morning will I direct my prayer unto thee," says David, "and will look up." If ye be concerned for Christ's intercession for you in heaven, so will ye be for that of the Spirit in your own heart.

6. Let the Bible be dear to you, and look on it as God's word to you in particular, Rom. xv. 4, "For whatsoever things were written aforetime, were written for our learning; that we through patience and comfort of the scriptures might have hope." Rev. iii. ult., "He that hath an ear, let him hear what the Spirit saith unto the churches." The word is the vehicle wherein the Spirit is conveyed to us; it is the channel of communicating his influences to us; and the instrument he works by in us, in all the parts of his working in us, exciting, enlightening, &c. Isa. lix. ult, "As for me, this is my covenant with them, saith the Lord, My Spirit that is upon thee, and my words which I have put in thy mouth, shall not depart out of thy mouth, nor out of the mouth of thy seed, nor out of the mouth of thy seed's seed, saith the Lord, from henceforth and for ever."

7. Be careful observers of providence, Psalm cvii. ult., "Whoso is wise, and will observe these things, even they shall understand the loving kindness of the Lord." The spirit is in these wheels; and the more people are set to observe their motions, the more they will readily get to observe. This is a way to carry you off formality in prayer, and give you an errand in good earnest to the throne of grace, whether in the way of petition, confession, or thanksgiving.

8. *Lastly*, Be watchful in prayer, Eph. vi. 18. The evil spirit watches against us at all times, and in a special manner the fowls come down on the carcases of our spiritual sacrifices. When ye sit down on your knees, the heart will be apt to fall a-wandering, and it will be much if before the end it do not give the slip. The Spirit of the Lord only can manage our spirits, and he will be provoked by our wanderings to withdraw. Therefore take that watchword, Prov. iv. 23, "Keep thy heart with all diligence; for out of it are the issues of life."

I shall now proceed to the last doctrine observable from the text.

DOCTRINE V. ult. The Spirit helps believers to pray, particularly, causing in them gracious groanings, which cannot be uttered.

In discoursing this point, I shall,

I. Consider the nature of these groanings caused by the Spirit in believers.

II. Show how the Spirit makes intercession for believers with groanings.

III. In what respects these groaning are groanings that cannot be uttered.

IV. Conclude with two or three reflections.

I. We shall consider the nature of these groanings caused by the Spirit in believers. And here I shall shew,

1. Of what kind they are.

2. The moving causes of them.

FIRST, I am to show of what kind these groanings are. There is a twofold groaning.

First, A natural groaning, the effect of pain, and any heavy pressure that lies on men's spirits, Jer. li. 52, "Through all her land the wounded shall groan." This is common to men with beasts, Joel i. 18, "How do the beasts groan?" And men may groan so, without any gracious movings of heart towards God; therefore they are none of the groanings in the text, Job xxxv. 9, 10, "By reason of the multitude of oppressions, they make the oppressed to cry; they cry out by reason of the arm of the mighty. But none saith, Where is God my maker, who giveth songs in the night?"

Secondly, Spiritual and gracious groanings, whereby the gracious soul natively expresses its movings towards God under some heavy pressure, 2 Cor. v. 4, "We that are in this tabernacle do groan, being burdened." These are they with which the Spirit helps believers, and which he causes in them. When men are in a swoon, they groan none; but when they are recovering, they will discover it by groaning; an argument that their sense and feeling is returned. So by these groanings believers are distinguished from the dead in sin.

These spiritual groanings of believers speak,

1. Their feeling of a weight and pressure upon them, 2 Cor. v. 4, above cited. Such is the imperfection of our state in this life, that if there is life in a soul, it must groan, because there is no escaping of pressures, from an evil world without, and an evil heart within. And the easy jovial life that men lead without these groanings, they owe it to spiritual death, which has taken away their feeling, Eph. iv. 18, 19.

2. Their labouring under these pressures, like one under a burden, Psalm vi. 6, "I am weary with my groaning," (*Heb.*) "Laboured to weariness in my groaning." This imports,

(1.) An earnest endeavour to get them off, or to bear them while they are kept on. The new creature is surrounded with weights of various kinds, which in their own nature tend to hinder its growth, and coming to perfection; and there are mighty labourings and workings of it against them, that it may get forward to its desired perfection; Phil. iii. 14.

(2.) Great difficulty in that labouring, so that the man is as it were out of breath wrestling with his harden which natively issues in a groan, Eph. vi. 12. There is difficulty in the Christian life, that will try what metal men are of, and will put them to the exerting of their utmost vigour; and therefore it is compared to the exercise of wrestlers and runners.

3. The working of their affections under them; especially,

(1.) Grief of heart, Jer. xlv. 3. Groaning is the natural expression of sorrow: and sighs, sobs, and groans, are what a heart pierced and weighed down with grief naturally vents itself in. Christ was "a man of sorrows," and so we find him groaning, John xi. 38; and true Christians, whatever their natural temper is, will be found to resound as an echo to a groaning Saviour.

Particularly, groans are the more heavy, when they arise from a double grief, a grief for such a thing, and a grief that it is beyond our power to help it; and of this sort mostly are the groans of believers, Rom. vii. 24.

(2.) Earnest desire of help and relief, 2 Cor. v. 2. Here the heart of the believer in these groanings moves directly towards God, with eyes lifted up to heaven. And hence these groanings are prayers in effect, and are so reckoned before God, Rom. viii. 27. Whence it appears how the Spirit makes intercession for us with groanings, that helping to groan before the Lord, he helps to pray. These groanings may be considered two ways.

[1.] As they are joined with solemn prayer. When a Christian is seriously praying, and is so weighted, that his prayers are here and there interrupted with groanings; these groanings which the prayers are interspersed with, are in God's account parts of the prayer, and as acceptable parts as are in it all; whether they come in when a sentence is closed, or come in before it be perfected, Psalm vi. 3, "My soul is sore vexed; but thou, O Lord, how long?" Men know not distinctly the meaning of such groans, but the Lord sees it as plain as if expressed by words.

[2.] As they are separate from solemn vocal prayer. And thus we may also consider them two ways.

(1.) As they come in the room and stead of vocal prayer intended.

I believe it is very possible, that a child of God may go to his knees to pray, and may rise again without having been able to speak a word, but only to groan; and though he thinks he could pray none at all, he is mistaken; as far as the Spirit helped him to groan, he helped him to pray, though none could understand that prayer of his but God himself who searcheth the heart, Rom. viii. 27. As a full bottle does not orderly empty itself, so a heart may be too full to empty itself by words, but by groans, Psalm lxxvii. 4, "Thou holdest mine eyes waking; I am so troubled that I cannot speak."

(2.) As they are without any design of solemn prayer. When a man is walking or sitting, musing on the sinfulness of his own heart and life, or on the wickedness that is done in the world, with the dishonour that comes on the holy name of God thereby; till his heart, swelling with grief, natively vents itself in a groan; that groaning is in God's account a prayer, and a prayer that shall be heard at length, as proceeding from the influence of his own Spirit. What was it that set the wheel of providence in motion, to stop the wicked career the Egyptians were in, Exod. ii. 24. ? Why, God heard the groaning of the children of Israel.

SECONDLY, I come now to show the moving causes of these groanings of believers. Believers by the Spirit, have their groanings unto the Lord,

1. Under a pressure of trouble. While they are here, they cannot miss so much of a suffering lot, as will make them groan; Rom. viii. 18, 23; and by the Spirit, these groans are directed towards God, as those of a child, under the difficulties of the way, are directed to his father.

(1.) Sometimes they are groaning to him under outward troubles. So Israel groaned under the Egyptian bondage; Exod. ii. 23, 24; yea Christ himself; John xi. 33, 38. These are weights that press their spirits, make them to groan, and look upward for relief; Rom. viii. 23, longing for the day when they shall be beyond them.

(2.) Sometimes they are groaning under inward troubles; Psalm xxx. 7, "Thou didst hide thy face, and I was troubled." While here they are liable to spiritual desertions, wounds in their spirits under the apprehensions of the Lord's anger against them. And they groan out their case towards the hand that smites them. Both outward and inward troubles often meet together, as in the case of David; Psalm vi. 2, 3, 6, "Have mercy upon me, O Lord, for I am weak; O Lord, heal me, for my bones are vexed. My soul is also sore vexed; but thou, O Lord, how long? I am weary with my groaning, all the night make I my bed to swim; I water my couch with my tears"; and in that of Job: chap. xxiii. 2, "Even to-day is my complaint bitter; my stroke is heavier than my groaning."

2. Under a pressure of temptations. These are a heavy weight to a gracious soul; they made Paul to go groaning to God again and again; 2 Cor. xii. 7, 8. Our Lord Christ had experience of an hour of the power of darkness; Luke xxii. 53, "When I was daily with you in the temple, ye stretched forth no hands against me; but this is your hour, and the power of darkness." And his followers will not want experience of the same, wherein temptations come on thick and vigorous. These cause groanings,

(1.) Because of their disturbing the peace of the soul; they turn the calm into a storm, that the soul is tossed thereby as on a raging sea, which makes them cry, "Lead us not into temptation."

(2.) Because of the difficulty of one's keeping his ground against them; Eph. vi. 12, 16. Every temptation has a friend within us, and men's nature is unto temptation as tinder to sparks of fire, apt to take fire; so that it requires hard wrestling to keep our ground.

(3.) Because of the danger of falling thereby into sin. Temptation is the precipice, and sin is the devouring gulf; and they who have a sense of their danger, no wonder they groan, groan under the pressure, and groan for relief.

3. Under the pressure of sin. This is a light burden to the most part of mankind, but it is the heaviest burden to a child of God, and causes in him, through the Spirit, the heaviest groans. For it is of all things the most contrary and opposite to the new nature in him, whence are these continued strugglings; Gal. v. 17, "The flesh lusteth against the Spirit, and the Spirit against the flesh; and these are contrary the one to the other; so that ye cannot do the things that ye would." Many troubles Paul met with; but did any of them all ever cause in him such an exclamation as that; Rom. vii. 24, "O wretched man that I am! who shall deliver me from the body of this death?" Now the children of God groan,

1*st*, Under the weight and pressure of their own sin, the sin of their nature, and the sin of their life; Psalm li. 3, 5, "I acknowledge my transgressions; and my sin is ever before me. Behold, I was shapen in iniquity; and in sin did my mother conceive me." It lies on them heavy as a body of death, while others being dead in sin, it is no burden to them; no burden to their heart, though sometimes it may be to their conscience. And there are three things in their sin that press them sore.

(1.) The filthiness of it, that deformity that is in it, being the quite contrary of the holiness of God expressed in his law. The soul seeing the glory of the holiness of God, and how its sin is the very reverse of that glory; that fills it with shame; Ezra ix. 6, and self-loathing; Ezek. xxxvi. 31. Beholding itself in the glass of the pure and holy law, as a polluted and defiled creature, it groans under it as one pressed down to the earth with a burden; Jer. iii. ult., "We lie down in our shame, and our confusion covereth us; for we have sinned against the Lord our God."

(2.) The prevailing power of it; Psalm lxv. 3, "Iniquities prevail against me, (*Heb.*) Have been mightier than I." The new nature struggles against sin; Gal. v. 17. The new man of grace and the old man of sin are engaged in combat; and ofttimes the old man prevails, and the new man is cast down.

Now the believer taking part with grace against corruption, groans under this prevailing power of corruption (Rom. vii. 23, 24,) as an insupportable tyranny that he longs to be rid of.

(3.) The guilt of it; Psalm li. 4, "Against thee, thee only have I sinned, and done this evil in thy sight." In the eyes of a believer, life lies in the favour of God, the shinings of his countenance; but their guilt binds them over to his anger, and overclouds his countenance. And that is a weight that makes them groan; that when it is removed, they rejoice as one that has got a harden taken off his back; Psalm xxxviii. 4, "Mine iniquities are gone over mine head; as an heavy burden they are too heavy for me." Compared with Hos. xiv. 2, "take away all iniquity, and receive us graciously; so will we render the calves of our lips."

2*dly*, Under the weight and pressure of the sin of others; Ezek. ix. 4, "Go through the midst of the city, through the midst of Jerusalem, and set a mark upon the foreheads of the men that sigh and that cry for all the abominations that be done in the midst thereof." As one cannot but loath an abominable thing on another as well as on himself; so sin, wherever it appears, on others, as well as on ourselves, will be a burden to a gracious soul, that will make it groan; Isa. vi. 5, "Wo is me, for I am undone, because I am a man of unclean lips, and I dwell in the midst of a people of unclean lips." Thus Lot was under a continued burden in Sodom, while he was among them; 2 Pet. ii. 7, 8. And none groan spiritually under their own sin, that do not groan also under the sins of others amongst whom they live. There are three things in the sins of others that make them groan.

(1.) The dishonour to the holy name of God that is in them; Rom. ii. 23, 24. To see men trampling under foot the holy laws of God, and, by their profane courses, affronting the God that made them, and walking after their own lusts, cannot but be a burden to any who truly love the Lord, and are concerned for the honour of his name; Psalm cxix. 136, "Rivers of waters run down mine eyes," says David, "because they keep not thy law." Zeal for the honour of God, as it is native to his children; so, where it cannot prevail against sin, natively vents itself in groaning under the burden; Psalm lxix. 9.

(2.) The ruin to the sinner's own soul that is wrapt up in it; Jer. xiii. 17. There needs no prophetical eye, but an eye of faith in the Lord's word, to foresee the ruin of those that go on impenitently in their sinful course; Rom. vi. 21. When sinners are fighting against God, by going on in their trespasses; it is easy to see whose head must be wounded in the encounter; Psalm lxviii. 21, and who must fall at length, however long they keep foot; Deut. xxxii. 35. Now the prospect of this is enough to make a gracious soul groan for those that cannot groan for themselves; Psalm cxix. 119, 120, "Thou puttest away all the wicked of the earth like dross; therefore I love thy testimonies. My flesh trembleth for fear of thee, and I am afraid of thy judgments." So Hab. iii. 16.

(3.) The hurt that is in it to others. It is Solomon's observation that "one sinner destroyeth much good," Eccl. ix. ult. And there is a woe pronounced on the world, because of offences, Matth. xviii. 7. Sin is a noxious vapour, spreading its infection over many; wounding some, and killing others; grieving to the godly, and hardening to the wicked. And a serious view of the mischief it does to others, beside the sinner himself, makes the godly groan.

From what is said it appears that sin is the fundamental and chief cause of the believer's groaning. Troubles outward and inward rise from it, temptations lead to it. That is it within them, and that is it without them that makes them groan. That is the burden to the Spirit of God that grieves him, as one groaning under a burden, Amos ii. 13; Isa. i. 24. That is it that makes the whole creation groan, Rom. viii. 22. And it is that which makes the believer groan.

II. The second general head is to show how the Spirit makes intercession for believers with groanings.

1. He works in them a spiritual feeling of their burdens; Rom. viii. 23, "And not only they, but ourselves also, which have the first fruits of the Spirit, even we ourselves groan within ourselves." The time was, when they lay with the rest of the world without sense or feeling of the burden on them, and he gave them life; and sometimes spiritual life in them has been so low, that they could have but little true feeling of their own case; and it was a burden to them to bestir themselves to rid themselves; Cant. v. 3, "I have put off my coat; how shall I put it on? I have washed my feet; how shall I defile them?" But the Spirit excites grace, and gives them a lively feeling of their spiritual case; ver. 4, "My Beloved put in his hand by the hole of the door and my bowels were moved for him."

2. He gives them a view of the free and unburdened state wherein mortality is swallowed up of life, 2 Cor. v. 4. There is such a state, it is represented in the word of truth. The Spirit strengthens the eye of faith, whereby the soul sees it clearly,

though afar off; a state wherein there is an eternal putting off of the burden of trouble, temptation, and sin.

3. He excites in them ardent desires of riddance from their burden, and of arriving at the unburdened state; 2 Cor. v. 2, "For in this we groan, earnestly desiring to be clothed upon with our house which is from heaven." Rom. viii. 23, "Even we ourselves groan within ourselves, waiting for the adoption, to wit, the redemption of our body." What ardent desire of deliverance would a man have who was kept lying among dead corpses, rotting and sending forth their stench into his nostrils? Such ardent desire will a Christian have, when, through the Spirit, grace is put in lively and vigorous exercise, while the dead world without him, and the body of death within him, conspire to annoy him with their savour of death, Rom. vii. 24. Hence,

4. He engages them in earnest wrestling with their burden, in order to get clear of it, that the new creature of grace may get up its back, and run the way of God's commandments, Gal. v. 17. Here grace has a mighty struggle with its enemy, longing and panting for the victory, and pressing towards a state of perfection, Phil. iii. 14.

5. *Lastly*, Finding themselves still entangled with their burden, notwithstanding of all their wrestling, he helps them to groan out their case before the Lord, as a case that is beyond their reach to help; Rom. vii. 23, 24, "I see another law in my members, warring against the law of my mind, and bringing me into captivity to the law of sin which is in my members. O wretched man that I am! who shall deliver me from the body of this death?" But the groaning through the Spirit's aid is not groaning and dying, but,

(1.) Groaning and looking to the Lord for help; Psalm cxxiii. 1, "Unto thee lift I up mine eyes, O thou that dwellest in the heavens." The believer groans and looks upward to God for relief. His burden of trouble, he will lie under it, till the Lord take it off, and will not take any sinistrous[12] course for his deliverance; Isa. xxviii. 16, "He that believeth shall not make haste." The burden of sin, he is never to be reconciled with that, but however long he wrestles with it without the desired success, he will ever be looking and longing for deliverance, Phil. iii. 13, 14.

(2.) Groaning and waiting for relief, Rom. viii. 23. Unbelief makes one to groan and despair of deliverance, either

---

12 Disasterous, unlucky.

in temporals or spirituals, Jer. ii. 25. But the Spirit makes the believer to groan and wait in hope, Gal. v. 5. Though the eyes fail while they wait for their God, yet still they will wait in hope of the promise, Luke xviii. 1.

III. I come now to show in what respects these groanings are groanings that cannot be uttered.

1. The working of their affections, thus set in motion by the Spirit, is sometimes such as stops the coarse of the words. This is often seen in the workings of natural affections, how that either joy or grief filling the heart, mars the ordinary course of words; the heart being too full, to be vented easily in expression. It is not then to be thought strange, that it so falls out in the case of spiritual affections pat in mighty motion by the Spirit. Yea they do,

(1.) Sometimes interrupt the expression, and the groaning fills up what is wanting in the words, Psalm vi. 3. Even as a hurt and pained child tells his case to his mother, in imperfect expressions, filling up the want with tears, sighs, and sobs; so that she may have difficulty to understand what ails him; but our Father in heaven has no difficulty in coming at the meaning of his children so expressed, Rom. viii. 27, "He that searcheth the hearts, knoweth what is the mind of the Spirit." Our elder Brother sometimes spoke by broken sentences from the same cause, Luke xix. 41, 42, "And when he was come near, he beheld the city, and wept over it, saying, If thou hadst known, even thou, at least in this thy day, the things which belong unto thy peace! but now they are hid from thine eyes." So Gen. iii. 22.

(2.) Sometimes stop the expression altogether, like as a multitude of people rushing all together to a door, they all stick, and none can get out, Psalm lxxvii. 4, "I am so troubled that I cannot speak." So a child of God may go to prayer, and not be able to speak a word. But let them go to their knees before the Lord for all that; and if they cannot speak a word, let them groan their case before the Lord. That is a proper way of praying in the Spirit, and God will certainly hear and accept that kind of praying, though there be nothing but groaning in it. Do ye put away dumb people without an alms, because they cannot speak? are ye not more moved with their signs and humming noise, than with the cries of common beggars? Do not the sighs and sobs of your frighted or hurt children move you more than their complaints formed in words? And do ye think that God will disregard the groans and sighs of his people, when they cannot speak a word to him? No, surely; he will hear the groaning of the prisoner, Psalm cii. 20.

2. What they feel and see in this case, by the Spirit, is always beyond what they can express in words. I own that what a child of God sometimes feels and sees in prayer, is so small, that their words may sufficiently express it; but when the Spirit helpeth them to these groanings, it is quite otherwise, their words cannot come up to their affections. When the Spirit gives a Christian an experimental feeling of the burden of sin, realizes to him the glory of the unburdened state, and makes him groan between the two, there is something there that is truly unspeakable. As the gift of Christ is unspeakable to those who truly see it, 2 Cor. ix. 15, and the joy in the Holy Ghost to those that feel it, 1 Pet. i. 8, so are the groanings by the Spirit unutterable to the groaners.

I conclude with two or three reflections.

1. God's people are a groaning people. For they have the Spirit of Christ, and he makes intercession for them with groanings; they have put on Christ, and he was a groaner. And those that are strangers to these groanings, their groaning time is coming; walking now in the vanity of your minds, will make eternal groaning.

QUEST. How are God's people regarded when they get leave to groan on? ANSW. They must abide the trial of their graces, and be conformed to the image of a groaning Saviour. In due time their burden will be taken off, and they will groan no more.

2. Prayer is a business of great weight and seriousness. It is one thing to say a prayer, another thing to pray indeed acceptably. Wherefore from this, and all that has been said,

3. *Lastly*, Learn to pray by the help of the Spirit, for no other praying is acceptable to God; look to him in all your addresses to the throne, and depend upon his guiding and influence; that through Christ Jesus ye may have access by one Spirit unto the Father, Eph. ii. 18.

III. Of Praying in the Name of Jesus Christ[13]

Whatsoever ye shall ask the Father in my name, he will give it you.
John xvi. 23

Our Lord Jesus is here comforting his disciples under the want of his bodily presence which they had so long enjoyed, showing them that it should be well made up to them. They should see him again after his resurrection, though not to return to that familiarity with them as before; they should see him by the Spirit, in his exalted state; and should find God so reconciled to them by his sacrifice of himself, that they should have a boldness of access to the throne in heaven, which they had not before; that in that day they should ask him nothing in that manner they used while he was with them in the days of his flesh; but in a manner more to his honour and their comfort. Here he declares,

1. What that manner is, and that in two things. (1.) They should apply themselves, in asking or petitioning, directly to the Father as their God and Father allowing them access to him, for the supply of all their needs. (2.) They should apply to him in the name of the Son, the exalted Redeemer, expressly, seeing more clearly the way of sinners treating with God through the Mediator, than either the Jewish church had done, or they themselves while they had his bodily presence with them.

2. The success of that manner of applying to God. It should be successful in all points. Whatsoever, in spiritual or temporal things, they should petition the Father in the name of Christ, he should give it them for his sake.

---

13 The substance of some Sermons preached at Etterick in the year 1728.

The following doctrine arises from the words.

DOCTRINE.—Whosoever would pray to God acceptably, must pray to him in the name of Jesus Christ.

In treating this point, I shall,
I. Show what it is to pray in the name of Jesus Christ.
II. Give the reasons why acceptable prayer must be in the name of Christ.
III. *Lastly*, Apply.

I. I am to show what it is to pray in the name of Jesus Christ. That this takes in whatever is necessary in prayer, both as to matter and manner, is evident from the text, "Whatsoever ye shall ask in my name," &c. And no man can thus pray but by the Spirit, 1 Cor. xii. 13.

Negatively, It is not a bare mentioning his name, in prayer, and concluding our prayers therewith, Matth. vii. 21, "Not every one that saith unto me Lord, Lord, shall enter into the kingdom of heaven." We must begin, carry on, and conclude our prayers in the name of Christ, Col. iii. 17, "Whatsoever ye do in word or deed, do all in the name of the Lord Jesus, giving thanks to God and the Father by him." The saints use the words, "through Jesus Christ our Lord," 1 Cor. xv. 57; but the virtue is not in the words, but in the faith wherewith they are used. But alas! these are often produced as an empty scabbard, while the sword is away.

Positively, we may take it up in these four things.

FIRST, We must go to God at Christ's command, and by order from him. This is the import of the phrase "in his name," Matth. xviii. 20, "Where two or three are gathered together in my name, there am I in the midst of them." If a poor body can get a recommendation from a friend to one that is able to help him, he comes with confidence and tells, such a one has sent me to you. Our Lord Christ is the friend of poor sinners, and he sends them to his Father to ask supply of their wants; and allows them to tell that he sent them; John xvi. 24. And coming that way, in faith, they will not be refused. This implies,

1. The soul's being come to Christ in the first place; John xv. 7, "If ye abide in me, and my words abide in you, ye shall ask what ye will, and it shall be done unto you." Sense of need brings the soul to Christ, as the poor man's friend, who has the favour of the court of heaven, that through his means the soul may get its wants supplied there. See Acts xii. 20.

We must first come to Christ by faith, ere we can make one acceptable prayer to God.

2. That however believers in Christ are relieved of the burden of total indigence; John iv. 14, yet while they are in the world, they are still compassed with wants. God will have them to live from hand to mouth, and so to honour him by hanging on daily about his hand for their supply from time to time. In heaven they shall be set down at the fountain; but now the law of the house is, "Ask, and ye shall receive"; Matth. vii. 7.

3. That Christ sends his people to God by prayer, for the supply of their wants. This he does by his word, commanding them to go, and by his Spirit inclining them to go. For thus the whole Trinity is glorified by the praying believers, the Father as the Hearer of prayer, the Son as the Advocate and Intercessor presenting their prayers to the Father, and the Spirit as the Author of their prayers; Eph. ii. 18, "For through him we both have an access by one Spirit unto the Father."

4. That acceptable prayer is performed under the sense of the command of a God in Christ; Isa. xxxiii. 22, "For the Lord is our judge, the Lord is our lawgiver, the Lord is our king, he will save us." Men may pray, though not acceptably, with little or no sense of the command of God on their consciences; that is, not serving God, but themselves. They may pray under the sense of the command of an absolute God out of Christ; that is but slavish service to God. But the believer has the sense of the command, as from Jesus Christ, where majesty and mercy are mixed in it; and that is son-like service.

5. *Lastly*. That the acceptable petitioner's encouragement to pray is from Jesus Christ; Heb. iv. 14–16, "Seeing then that we have a great High Priest, that is passed into the heavens, Jesus the Son of God, let us hold fast our profession. For we have not an High Priest which cannot be touched with the feeling of our infirmities; but was in all points tempted like as we are, yet without sin. Let us therefore come boldly unto the throne of grace, that we may obtain mercy, and find grace to help in time of need." It is Christ's token that he has given them to carry with them, that affords them all their confidence with God; that is the promises of the covenant sealed with his own blood. Faith laying hold on these, carries them as Christ's token to the Father, upon which a poor criminal may expect to find acceptance and supply.

SECONDLY. We must pray for Christ's sake, as our motive to the duty. This also is imported in the phrase, "in his name";

Mark ix. 41, "Whosoever shall give you a cup of water to drink, in my name, because ye belong to Christ,—he shall not lose his reward." As we must be influenced by his command, as the reason of our praying, so with regard to him as our motive. As there is no coming to God but by him; so there is no kindly drawing of us to God, but by the allurement of the glory of God in the face of Jesus; 2 Cor. iv. 6. Any other sight of the glory of God would fright the sinner away from him, as from a consuming fire. So we must behold God in Christ, and go to him as the object of our love and adoration. This implies,

1. An high esteem of Christ in the acceptable petitioner; 1 Pet. ii. 7, "Unto you which believe, he is precious." No man's prayer will be acceptable to God, who wants a transcendent esteem of the Lord Christ; for God is honoured in his Son; John v. 23. And the more the esteem of Christ has place in one's heart, the more it will be found, he will give himself to prayer.

2. Complying with the duty out of love to Christ; Heb. vi. 10, "God is not unrighteous, to forget your work and labour of love." The soul must discern Christ's stamp on every duty, and so embrace it for his sake. The duty of prayer some embrace and use, because of the usefulness of it to themselves; but God's children embrace it for the sake of Christ; 2 Cor. v. 14, "For the love of Christ constraineth us." Love natively leads to desire communion with the party beloved; and love to Christ recommends prayer to a holy heart, as a means of communion with God in Christ.

3. Complying with the duty out of respect to his honour and glory; Phil. i. 21, "For to me to live is Christ." Christ humbled himself, and therefore the Father has glorified him; chap. ii. 9-11. And every act of praying in his name glorifies him, being an acknowledgment before God of the unspeakable dignity of his merit and intercession, as procuring that access for sinners unto God, that no other way could have been obtained.

4. *Lastly*, Doing it with heart and good-will; for what is done for Christ's sake by a gracious soul, must needs be so done; Isa. lxiv. 5, "Thou meetest him that rejoiceth, and worketh righteousness, those that remember thee in thy ways." One praying indeed in the name of Christ, is acted by a principle of lore to him, which, oiling the wheels of the soul, sets all in motion, so that the heart is poured out like water before the Lord. And where that principle is wanting, there is acting by constraint.

Thirdly. We must in praying to God act in the strength of Christ. This also is imported in the phrase; Luke x. 17, "And the seventy returned again with joy, saying, Lord, even the devils are subject unto us through thy name." So Zech. x. ult., "I will strengthen them in the Lord, and they shall walk up and down in his name." We must go to prayer, as David went against Goliath; 1 Sam. xvii. 45, "I come to thee in the name of the Lord of hosts." And here consider,

1. What this pre-supposes.
2. Wherein it lies.

First, Let us consider what this acting in prayer in the strength of Christ pre-supposes. It pre-supposes,

1. That praying acceptably is a work quite beyond any power in us; 2 Cor. iii. 5, "Not that we are sufficient of ourselves to think any thing as of ourselves." The want of this persuasion mars many a prayer, and makes many a rash and inconsiderate approach unto God. To manage aright an address to God on his throne of glory, cannot miss to appear such a work in the eyes of all, who have due thoughts of God's majesty, or of their own ignorance and weakness.

2. That there is a stock of grace and strength in Jesus Christ, for our help, as to other duties, so for this duty of prayer; 2 Cor. xii. 9, "My grace is sufficient for thee." Man at first had his stock of grace in his own hand, and he made a sad account of it. Now the Lord has lodged it in the Mediator, as the head of believers; Col. i. 19, "For it pleased the Father, that in him should all fulness dwell." In him there is not only a fulness of sufficiency for himself, but of abundance for his people, as of water in a fountain, or of sap in the stock of a tree; John iii. 34, "God giveth not the Spirit by measure unto him."

3. Sinners are welcome to partake of this stock of grace and strength in Christ; 2 Tim. ii. 1. For it is lodged in him as a storehouse, to be communicated. The fountain stands open, and whosoever will may come and take; Zech. xiii. 1. They are very welcome; as it is an ease and pleasure for the mother to have the full breast sucked by her babe, so it is a pleasure to Christ to communicate of his fulness; Isa. lxvi. 12, 13, "For thus saith the Lord, Behold, I will extend peace to her like a river, and the glory of the Gentiles like a flowing stream; then shall ye suck, ye shall be borne upon her sides, and be dandled upon her knees. As one whom his mother comforteth, so will I comfort you; and ye shall be comforted in Jerusalem."

4. We must be united to Christ, as members to the head, and branches to the vine, if we would act in prayer or any oth-

er duty in the strength of Christ; John xv. 5, "I am the vine ye are the branches; he that abideth in me, and I in him, the same bringeth forth much fruit; for without me ye can do nothing." We cannot partake of the stock of grace and strength for duty in Christ, without partaking of himself; Rom. viii. 32. As the soul in a separate state doth not quicken the body, so the soul not united to Christ cannot be fitted for duty by strength derived from him. The graft must knit with the stock, ere it can partake of the sap.

SECONDLY. I am to show wherein acting in prayer in the strength of Christ lies. It lies in two things:—

1. The soul's going out of itself for strength to the duty; that is, renouncing all confidence in itself for the right management of it; 2 Cor. iii. 5, forecited. Every duty is to be undertaken, begun, and I carried on, under a sense of utter weakness and insufficiency for it in ourselves.

(1.) Gifts are not to be trusted to; Prov. iii. 5. That is the way to get gifts blasted, for they are but an arm of flesh; Jer. xvii. 5, 6. And though ye should have the free exercise of your gift; yet a bare gift can never make a man do a duty graciously. The work will still be but a dead work, without the life of grace derived from Christ the Lord of life.

(2.) Nay grace received and implanted in us is not to be trusted to for this end. Learn ye, that even of our gracious selves we can do nothing; 2 Cor. iii. 4, 5. There must be continued supplies of grace from Christ unto us, else we will bring forth no fruit; John xv. 5. It is true, grace is a seed that in its nature tends to fruit; but what will come of the seed, if the showers, and dew, and heat of the sun be withheld?

2. The soul's going to Christ for strength to duty, by trusting on him for it; Isa. xxvi. 4, "Trust ye in the Lord for ever; for in the Lord Jehovah is everlasting strength." This is the exercising of faith, by which the saints live; Gal. ii. 20, and derive grace and strength from Christ their head; John i. 16. Faith is that grace by which the weak soul fetches in strength and grace from the fountain of it in Christ. So he prays in the name of Christ, in this respect, who goes about the duty in confidence of, and trusting in Christ for, strength and ability to manage it acceptably; Psalm lxxi. 16, "I will go in the strength of the Lord God; I will make mention of thy righteousness, even of thine only." To make this more plain, consider,

(1.) By faith a Christian sees, in the glass of the word, an utter inability for duty in himself, believing, on the testimony of the word, that of himself he is unable to work any good work, Isa. xxvi. 12; nay, not to begin it well; Phil. i. 6, to will it; chap. ii. 13, nor so much as to think it; 2 Cor. iii. 5. In all which the Christian's faith is strengthened by experience.

(2.) By faith he sees also a fulness of grace and strength treasured up in Christ the head, to be communicated to the members of his body; 2 Cor. xii. 9, "And he said unto me, My grace is sufficient for thee; for my strength is made perfect in weakness." Col. i. 19, "It pleased the Father, that in him should all fulness dwell." And he beholds the promises he has made of it, as the conduit pipes by which it is conveyed unto them; 2 Pet. i. 4, "Whereby are given unto us exceeding great and precious promises; that by these you might be partakers of the divine nature." These things the Christian believes on the testimony of the same word of God; and thus he sees a sufficiency to oppose to his own emptiness, and a fulness of strength to remedy his own weakness.

(3.) By faith he trusts that this fulness in Christ shall be made forthcoming to him, in a measure of it, for the duty, according to the promise; Psalm xviii. 2, "The Lord is—my God, my strength, in whom I will trust." Hab. iii. 19, "The Lord God is my strength, and he will make my feet like hinds' feet, and he will make me to walk upon mine high places." Thus there is a particular application in faith, that the Christian trusts in the word of promise, that grace and strength shall be given to him. So the word holds it out for particular application by faith; 2 Cor. xii. 9, "My grace is sufficient for thee"; and this is the way to bring in strength, as the Psalmist's experience testifies; Psalm xxviii. 7, "The Lord is my strength and my shield, my heart trusted in him, and I am helped"; and so the promise secures it; Jer. xvii. 7, 8, "Blessed is the man that trusteth in the Lord, and whose hope the Lord is. For he shall be as a tree planted by the waters, and that spreadeth out her roots by the river, and shall not see when heat cometh, but her leaf shall be green, and shall not be careful in the year of drought, neither shall cease from yielding fruit." Take away that trust, that particular application, the soul is left helpless, having nothing to gripe to, and the communication of strength is blocked up; according to what the apostle James says, chap. i. 6, 7, "Let him ask in faith, nothing wavering; for he that wavereth is like a wave of the sea, driven with the wind, and tossed. For let not that man think that he shall receive any thing of the Lord."

FOURTHLY. We must in praying to God pray for Christ's sake, as the only procuring cause of the success of our prayers; Dan. ix. 17, "Now therefore, O our God, hear the prayer of thy servant, and his supplications, and cause thy face to shine upon thy sanctuary that is desolate, for the Lord's sake." Going to God in prayer, we must as it were put off our own persons, as not worth noticing in the sight of God, and put on the Lord Jesus Christ; come and receive the blessing in the elder Brother's clothes, having all our hope from the Lord's looking on the face of his Anointed. This is the main thing in the text, a relying on the Lord Jesus for the success of our prayers in heaven. Here I shall shew,

1. What is pre-supposed in this.
2. Wherein it consists.

FIRST. I am to show what is pre-supposed in praying to God for Christ's sake. It pre-supposes,

1. That sinners in themselves are quite unacceptable in heaven, even in their religious duties. Not only are the wicked so; Prov. xv. 8, but even the saints considered in themselves; Isa. lxiv. 6. The reason is plain, God is holy, we are impure and defiled. There is such a rank smell of sinful pollution about us, that the opening of a sinner's mouth in prayer is like the opening of an unripe grave; Rom. iii. 13. It is too strong, that we cannot sweeten ourselves. The loathsome savour of the sins about the best, cannot be mastered by any sweet savour of their duties, but only by the sweet savour of the sacrifice of Christ; 2 Cor. ii. 15, with Eph. v. 2.

2. Christ is most acceptable there; he is the darling of heaven, the prime favourite there; Matth. iii. ult., "This is my beloved Son, in whom I am well pleased." He is acceptable there as God, the only begotten of the Father from eternity; but that is not it. He is acceptable as God-man, Mediator, who has in our flesh fulfilled his Father's will, by his obedience and death; Eph. v. 2, "Christ—hath given himself for us, an offering and a sacrifice to God for a sweet-smelling savour." And he is acceptable to the Father,

(1.) In himself; Matth. iii. ult., above cited. The Father is well pleased with his person, and delights in him, as the brightness of his own glory, and his own express image. He is well pleased with his undertaking the work of our redemption, and his management of that work; he is pleased with his holy birth, righteous life, and complete satisfaction; so pleased with his humbling himself, that he has "highly exalted him"; Phil. ii. 9.

(2.) He is so well pleased with him, that he accepts sinners for his sake; Eph. i. 6, "He hath made us accepted in the Beloved." For his sake rebel sinners are accepted to peace and favour, criminals, to eternal life, their performances, mixed with much sinful imperfections, are accepted as pleasing in his sight. The sweet smell of his sacrifice so masters the rank savour of sin about them, that they are for his sake brought into his presence and made near. The Father knows not to refuse him any request; John xi. 42, "I knew that thou hearest me always."

3. Sinners are warranted to come to the throne of grace in his name; Heb. iv. 15, 16, "We have not an High Priest which cannot be touched with the feeling of our infirmities; but was in all points tempted like as we are, yet without sin. Let us therefore come boldly unto the throne of grace, that we may obtain mercy, and find grace to help in time of need." It is sinners of mankind, not of the angel tribe; chap. ii. 16, "For verily he took not on him the nature of angels: but he took on him the seed of Abraham." Whatever be our case, he will do for us to the uttermost; Heb. vii. 25. He is an Advocate that will take our most desperate causes in hand, carry them through, and that in a way agreeable to justice; 1 John ii. 1, "If any man sin, we have an Advocate with the Father, Jesus Christ the righteous." The petitions put into his hand cannot miscarry.

SECONDLY, I am now to show wherein this praying to God for Christ's sake consists. And,

First, In general, it consists in our relying on the Lord Jesus only, for the success of our prayers in heaven. And,

I. Consider what we are in this matter to rely on him only for.

(1.) We are to rely on him only, for access to God in our prayers; Eph. iii. 12, "In whom we have boldness and access with confidence by the faith of him." In vain do we pray, if we get no access to the prayer-hearing God; and there is no access to him, but through Christ; John xiv. 6. Whoever attempt to draw near to God otherwise, will get the door of heaven cast in their face; but we must take hold of the Mediator, and come in at his back, who is Heaven's favourite and the sinner's friend.

(2.) For acceptance of our prayers; Eph. i. 6, forecited. Our Lord Christ is the only altar that can sanctify our gift; Heb. xiii. 10, 15. If we lay the stress of our acceptance on any person or thing, but Jesus Christ, the crucified Saviour, we cannot be accepted. For our best duties being mixed with sinful imperfections, cannot be accepted of a holy God but through a Mediator; and there is no Mediator but he; 1 Tim. ii. 5.

(3.) For the gracious answer of prayer in granting our petitions. So the text, "Whatsoever ye shall ask the Father in my name, he will give it you." We have forfeited all other pleas for Heaven's favours, by Adam's fall. And now no prayers can be heard and answered in heaven; but for Christ the second Adam's sake. A sinner cannot have the least favourable glance from the throne of God, but what is given for Christ's sake. What men get otherwise, they get with a vengeance, an impression of wrath on it; Hos. xiii. 11; Psalm lxxviii. 29.

2. Consider how we are to eye Christ as the object of this reliance. We are to eye him in it as our great High Priest; Heb. iv. 15, 16, forecited. A believer is to eye Christ in his prayers, in all his offices. We are to eye him as our Prophet, teaching us by his Spirit how and what to pray for; as our King, having the office of distributing Heaven's favours to poor sinners; but in point of our access, acceptance, and hearing, we are to eye him as a Priest; for it is in that office only we can find what to rely on before God, for these ends. And here we find,

(1.) The infinite merit of his sacrifice to rely on; Rom. iii. 25, "Whom God hath set forth to be a propitiation, through faith in his blood." Man by sin lost himself, and all Heaven's favours from the greatest to the least, from heaven's happiness to the least drop of water to refresh him. Accordingly Christ redeeming sinners by his blood, paid the ransom not only for their persons, but for all Heaven's favours to them, from the greatest to the least. Therefore he says, "Incline your ear, and come unto me; hear, and your soul shall live, and I will make an everlasting covenant with you, even the sure mercies of David"; Isa. lv. 3. He bought their seat in heaven, their peace, and pardon, yea and their seat on earth, their bread, and their water; Isa. xxxiii. 16, "He shall dwell on high; his place of defence shall be the munitions of rocks, bread shall be given him, his waters shall be sure." Now, would we pray in his name?

Then in prayer eye Christ on the cross, bleeding, dying, and by his bloody death and sufferings paying for the mercy thou art seeking. Is it a spiritual mercy, or a temporal mercy? It is a purchased mercy, the purchase of the blood of Christ; seek it of God as such, as the purchase of the blood of Jesus.

(2.) His never-failing intercession to rely on; Heb. vii. 25, "Wherefore he is able also to save them to the uttermost, that come unto God by him, seeing he ever liveth to make intercession for them." Our great High Priest having offered his sacrifice on earth, is now gone into the heavens, presenting there the blood of his sacrifice in the infinite merit thereof before his Father; that he may obtain the purchased mercies for his people. So that the supply of the needs of his people, is his business in heaven, as well as it is theirs on earth. And he offers their prayers to his Father; Rev. viii. 4. Therefore if ye would pray in his name,

In prayer eye Christ as your Intercessor at the right hand of God, Rom. viii. 34. If the price of his blood was extended to the purchasing of all the mercies we need; surely his intercession extends from the greatest to the least of them also. And therefore we need not stick to put our petitions for any mercy we need, in his hand. Hence it may appear,

Secondly, More particularly, wherein praying in the name of Christ, and for his sake consists,

1. Renouncing all merit and worth in ourselves, in point of access, acceptance, and gracious answer, saying with Jacob, Gen. xxxii. 10, "I am not worthy of the least of all the mercies, and of all the truth, which thou hast shewed unto thy servant." If we stand on personal worth, from the consideration of our doings or sufferings, or any thing in or about ourselves, we pray in our own name, and will speed accordingly. Self-denial is absolutely necessary to this kind of praying, that stopping our eyes to all excellencies in ourselves or duties, we may betake ourselves to free grace only.

2. Believing that however great the mercies are, and however unworthy we are, yet we may obtain them from God through Jesus Christ; Heb. iv. 15, 16. There can be no praying in faith without this. If we do not believe this, we dishonour his name, whether our unbelief of it arise from the greatness of the mercy needed, or from our own unworthiness, or both. For nothing can be beyond the reach of his infinite merit and never-failing intercession.

3. Seeking in prayer the mercies we need of God, for Christ's sake accordingly. So we present our petitions "in his name"; John xvi. 24. We are to be ashamed before God in prayer, ashamed of ourselves, but not ashamed to beg in the name of his Son. Our holy shame respects our unworthiness; but Christ's merit and intercession are set before us, as a ground of confidence.

4. Pleading on his merit and intercession; Psalm lxxxiv. 9, "Behold, O God our shield, and look upon the face of thine Anointed." We are not only to seek, but to plead in prayer, as needy petitioners whose pinching necessity makes them fill their mouths with arguments; Job xxiii. 3, 4. Christ's merit

and intercession is the fountain of these arguments; and to plead on mere mercy, mercy for mere mercy's sake, is too weak a plea. But faith founding its plea on Christ's merit, urges God's covenant and promise made thereupon; Psalm lxxiv. 20, his glorious perfections shining in the face of Jesus, the honour of his name manifested in Christ.

5. *Lastly*, Trusting that we shall obtain a gracious answer for his sake; Mark xi. 24, "What things soever ye desire when ye pray, believe that ye receive them, and ye shall have them." The soul praying according to the will of God, is to exercise a faith of particular confidence in God through Christ, which is not only warrantable, but necessary; Jam. i. 6, 7. This glorifies the Mediator, and glorifies the faithfulness of God in the promise; and the want of it casts dishonour on both.

II. The second general head is, to give reasons why acceptable prayer must be in the name of Christ. I offer the following:—

1. Because sinners can have no access to God without a Mediator, and there is no other Mediator but he; Isa. lix. 2; 1 Tim. ii. 5. Innocent Adam might have come to God immediately in prayer, and been accepted; for while there was no sin, there was no need of a Mediator. But now the justice of God bars the access of sinners to him; and there is none to mediate a peace betwixt God and the sinner but Christ; John xiv. 6.

2. Because the promises of the covenant were all made to Jesus Christ, as the party who fulfilled the condition of the covenant; Gal. iii. 16. The promises are the measure of acceptable prayer; what God has not promised, we cannot warrantably pray for. In prayer we come to God to claim the promises; and we cannot claim them, but in the right of Christ the head of the covenant, to whom they were made; that is to say, we cannot pray acceptably but in his name.

3. Because our praying in the name of Christ is a part of the reward of Christ's voluntary humiliation for God's glory and the salvation of sinners; Phil. ii. 9, 10. He gave his life a ransom for sinners, and a price of redemption of their forfeited mercies; therefore God has statuted and ordained, that sinners shall crave and receive all their mercies in his name, that they shall kneel in him to receive the blessing, as his members.

4. Because it is not consistent with the honour of God, to give sinners a favourable hearing otherwise; John ix. 31, with 2 Cor. v. 19, 21. Where is the honour of God's justice, if Heaven's favours be bestowed on sinners otherwise than on the account of a satisfaction?—the honour of his holiness, if they

may have communion with him as they are in themselves? — of his law, if they may get their petitions of mercy answered, but in the name of one who has answered its demands? They dishonour God, his Son, and his mercies, that ask any thing but in the name of Christ.

5. Nothing can savour with God, that comes from a sinner, but what is perfumed with the merit and intercession of Christ; 2 Cor. ii. 15; Eph. i. 6. It is not the inward excellency of the prayers of the saints, that makes them acceptable in God's sight; but the righteousness of Christ, which is by faith on the praying saint praying in faith; Heb. xi. 4. The merit of his righteousness, presented in his intercession, with the prayer, makes it acceptable; Rev. viii. 4. It savours in heaven out of his mouth.

6. *Lastly*, The stated way of all gracious communication between heaven and earth, is through Jesus Christ, who opened a communication between them by his blood, when it was blocked up by the breach of the first covenant; John xiv. 6. Whatever favour is conveyed to us from heaven in a way of grace and love, whatever we offer to God in a way of duty or desire, must go through him. This was represented in Jacob's ladder; Gen. xxviii. If we would come to God, or present a petition to him, it must be through Christ; Heb. x. 19, 20. If the Lord comes to us, or sends us a gracious answer, it is through him; 2 Cor. v. 19.

I shall now make some practical improvement of this subject.

USE I. Of information. From this doctrine we learn,

1. What a holy God we have to do with in prayer, who hath said, "I will be sanctified in them that come nigh me, and before all the people I will be glorified"; Lev. x. 3. He sits on his throne of majesty, and we can have no access to him, being sinners, but through Christ. His very throne of grace, from which he breathes love and good-will to sinners, is founded on justice and judgment; Psalm lxxxix. 14. We must come to him under the covert of the Mediator's broad righteousness and efficacious blood; otherwise we cannot stand before his spotless holiness.

2. Let us prize the love of Christ, in making an entrance for us into the holy place, through the vail of his flesh; Heb. x. 20. The flaming sword of justice, which guarded the way to the tree of life, was bathed in his blood, to procure us access to God. He bought again the estate that Adam forfeited for us,

and he bought it with his precious blood; that since we could not have it again in our own name, we might have it in his.

3. There can be no acceptable praying to God but by believers united to Christ, having on the garment of his righteousness; John ix. 31, "God heareth not sinners." An unregenerate man, living in his natural state, may pray; but can never pray acceptably, while in that state; for he cannot pray in the name of Christ, which is not the work of the tongue using these words, but the work of the heart by faith relying on Christ, his merit and intercession.

4. Even believers cannot pray in the name of Christ, and so not acceptably, without faith in exercise. It is not enough for this end, that one have faith in the root and principle; but faith must be exercised in every duty; Gal. ii. 20, "The life which I now live in the flesh," says Paul, "I live by the faith of the Son of God." It is as necessary to every acceptable performance, as breathing to the common actions of life; John xv. 5.

5. *Lastly*, We have great need not to be rash in our approaches to God in prayer, but that we prepare our hearts and compose them aforehand for such a solemn duty; Eccl. v. 1. We should beware lest custom in these things, and particularly in the more frequent and less solemn approaches to God in prayer, at our meals, turn us to formality; but should labour to impress our hearts with the holiness of God, the necessity of a Mediator, and stir up grace in our hearts.

USE II. Of reproof to all those who approach unto God in prayer, otherwise than by and in the name of Jesus Christ. The idolatrous Papists allow other mediators of intercession, besides the one only Mediator; and pray to, employ, and rely on saints and angels, to intercede in heaven for them, though religious worshipping of the creature is directly forbidden; Matth. iv. 10, and angel-worship; Rev. xix. 10, and the saints departed are not acquainted with our particular cases; Isa. lxiii. 16. But those also among us are to be reproved, as approaching to God in prayer otherwise than in Christ's name,

1. Who make approach unto God in prayer, as an absolute God, without consideration of the Mediator. This is the effect of the natural blindness and ignorance of men's minds; not knowing God, nor discerning the flaming sword of justice guarding the tree of life, they rush forward on the point thereof to pull the fruits. Let such consider their dangerous rashness, and reform; Heb. xii. ult., "For our God is a consuming fire"; knowing they can never worship God acceptably in that way; John v. 23, "He that honoureth not the Son, honoureth

not the Father which hath sent him." Hence the knowledge and belief of the doctrine of the Trinity is the foundation of all acceptable worship, without which it cannot subsist; Eph. ii. 18, "For through him we both have an access by one Spirit unto the Father"; and the Christian, church is thereby distinguished from the rejected Jews; 1 Thess. i. 1, and it must be practically improved in every piece of true worship.

2. Those who, in their approaches to God, put other things in the room of the Mediator, or join other things with him. For as there is no access to God without a Mediator, so there is none but by the one Mediator only; John xiv. 6, "No man cometh unto the Father, but by me." But who do that? Even all those who in their approaches by prayer, lay the stress of their access and acceptance with God, in whole or in part, on any thing but Christ. Whatever then reliest on for these ends, besides Christ, has his room, and so mars the duty; Phil. iii. 3, and provokes God; Jer. xvii. 5, 6. There is a bias in the hearts of the best this way.

There are four things which men are apt to put thus in the room of Christ in whole or in part,

(1.) Their own worth, in respect of their qualifications and good things done by them; Judg. xvii. ult. This the proud Pharisee relied on in his approach; Luke xviii. 11, 12, "God, I thank thee," says he, "that I am not as other men are, extortioners, unjust, adulterers, or even as this publican. I fast twice in the week, I give tithes of all that I possess." So proud and conceited professors go to their prayers, and with their money in their hand miss the opened market of free grace. They say they beg for Christ's sake, but yet in reality they have more expectation from their own personal worth, than from the merit of Christ's blood. Their want of a humbling work of the Spirit raises the value they have for themselves; and the want of saving illumination sinks the value of Christ's merit with them.

(2.) The mercy of an unatoned God, that is, mercy considered in God without a view to the satisfaction of his justice by the Mediator. This the ignorant and profane are apt to stumble on, whose eyes are open to the mercy of God, but blind to his justice, which therefore they are in no concern about the satisfaction of. It never enters into their hearts, to question, how it is consistent with the honour and justice of God to accept them; but the notion they have framed of the mercy of God answers all their difficulties. Howbeit, no such mercy is proposed to sinners in the gospel; Isa. xxvii. 11; Psalm lxxxv.

10. It is true, it was a good prayer of the publican, Luke xviii. 13, "God be merciful to me a sinner"; but his words bear an eye to mercy through a propitiation; and so was the mercy of God held forth to the Old Testament church in the mercy-seat, as well as to the New.

(3.) The manner of their performing the duty itself. Great weight is laid here, as if a well-said prayer were sufficient to recommend itself and the petitioner too. Cain laid such weight on his sacrifice; Gen. iv. 4, 5. A flash of affections and seeming tenderness in prayer, is in the eyes of many a prayer that cannot be rejected; Isa. lviii. 3, "Wherefore have we fasted, say they, and thou seest not? wherefore have we afflicted our soul, and thou takest no knowledge?" Enlargement in duty raises the value of it so in their own eyes, that they cannot think but it must be valuable in the eyes of God too. So in the earnestness of the prayer, and many words used; Matth. vi. 7. Let men examine their expectations, and they will be fair to find more weight laid there than on the merit of Christ, though this only can bear weight.

(4.) Their own necessity; Hos. vii. 14, "They have not cried unto me with their heart, when they howled upon their beds; they assemble themselves for corn and wine, and they rebel against me." Sense of need is a necessary qualification in acceptable prayer; but pinching necessity, where the heart is unhumbled, is apt to be set in a room higher than becomes it, as if of itself it were a sufficient plea. When it is thus abused, may be known by this, That on the not hearing of the prayer, the heart riseth against God; a sign that the petitioner is not as a needy beggar craving an alms, but a needy creditor craving his own. Our necessity should quicken us to seek, but it is the merit and intercession of Christ alone that is to be relied on for our access.

Use III. Wherefore rely on Christ, and on him only, for access to God in, and acceptance of, your prayers; that is, pray in the name of Christ.

Mot. 1. In this way of praying ye may obtain any thing ye really need. So says the text, "Whatsoever ye shall ask the Father in my name, he will give it you." There is no mercy so great, nor any sinner so unworthy, but he may have it, coming to God this way; Heb. vii. 25, with John xi. 42. God can bestow it in that way with the safety of his honour, the sinner may confidently expect it on good grounds. For Christ's merit is infinite, his intercession always prevalent.

2. There is no access to God, nor acceptance of prayer another way; John xiv. 6. It is through him our persons can be accepted, Eph. i. 6; and through him our duties can be so; Heb. xi. 4. Every sacrifice not offered on this altar, however valuable it seems, will be rejected. There is no return of prayer in a gracious manner otherwise.

I conclude with giving you a few directions for praying in the name of Christ.

1. Labour to impress your hearts with a sense of the spotless holiness and exact justice of God, Psalm lxxxix. 7. This will show the necessity of a Mediator to interpose, as in Israel's case.

2. Be sensible of your need of, and look for, the help of the Spirit in every approach, Rom. viii. 26. As the sending of the Spirit is the fruit of Christ's merit and intercession; so the Spirit being come leads back to the Mediator, Eph. ii. 18.

3. Shake off all confidence in yourselves, and see your utter unworthiness of the least mercies, how great soever your need of them be, Gen. xxxii. 10. As Jacob put off his own raiment to put on his elder brother's for the blessing, so do ye cast off your own filthy rags, and put on the Lord Jesus Christ.

4. Satisfy not yourselves with bare seeking for Christ's sake; that is not enough: but be confident that ye shall get access, acceptance, and a gracious return for his sake, Mark xi. 24. Raise a believing expectation in him.

QUESTION, How may one reach that? ANSWER, (1.) By a believing view of Christ on the cross purchasing, and at the Father's right hand, interceding for, our mercies; and particularly eying his sufferings, agreeable to your wants, as in the case of your want of light, the darkness came on him; in the case of your want of bread, his hunger, &c. (2.) By a believing application of the promises suitable to your needs. (3.) Considering this as God's ordinance for communication between heaven and earth, Gal. iii. 8.

5. *Lastly*, Watch against your hearts going off to any confidence in the duty itself; for that is to dishonour the name of Christ, and will provoke the Spirit of the Lord to depart from you.

IV. Of God's Hearing of Prayer[14]

O thou that hearest prayer, unto thee shall all flesh come.
Psalm lxv. 2

What avails prayer, if it be not heard? But God's people need not lay it aside on that score. Our text bears two things with respect to that matter.

1. A comfortable title ascribed to God, with the unanimous consent of all the sons of Zion, who are all praying persons, "O thou that hearest prayer." He speaks to God in Zion, or Zion's God, that is, in New Testament language, to God in Christ. An absolute God thundereth on sinners from Sinai, there can be no comfortable intercourse betwixt God and them, by the law; but in Zion from the mercy-seat in Christ, he is the hearer of prayer; they give in their supplications, and he graciously hears them. Such faith of it they have, that praise waits there for the prayer-hearing God.

2. The effect of the savour of this title of God, spread abroad in the world, "Unto thee shall all flesh come"; not only Jews, but Gentiles. The poor Gentiles, who have long in vain implored the aid of their idols, hearing and believing that God is the hearer of prayer, will flock to him, and present their petitions. They will throng in about his door; where by the gospel they understand beggars are so well served. They will "come in even unto thee," (Heb.) They will come in even to thy seat, thy throne of grace, even unto thee thyself, through the Mediator.

The doctrine I chiefly propose speaking to, is,

---

14 The substance of some Sermons preached at Etterick in the year 1728.

DOCTRINE, God in Christ is the hearer of prayer.

In handling this doctrine, I shall shew,
I. Wherein God's hearing of prayer lies.
II. The import of his being the hearer of prayer.
III. What prayers they are that God hears.
IV. More particularly consider the hearing and answering of prayer.
V. *Lastly*, Apply.

1. I am to show wherein God's hearing of prayer lies. God being omniscient and every where present, there can nothing be said or done in the world, but he hears or discerns it. But the hearing of prayer in the sense of the scripture is a peculiar privilege of the Lord's people, and lies in the following things.

1. God's accepting of one's prayer, Psalm cxli. 2, "Let my prayer be set forth before thee as incense; and the lifting up of my hands as the evening-sacrifice." Many prayers are said in the world, that are so far from being accepted of God, that they are an abomination to him, Prov. xxviii. 9. God turns them away from him, as one flings a petition over the bar, that he is displeased with, Psalm lxvi. ult. But the prayers that he hears, he is well pleased with them, he approves of them. Hence he is said to attend, hearken to the voice, and consider prayer, as one listens to a sound that pleases him, and dwells on a pleasing thought, Psalm lxvi. 19, "Verily God hath heard me; he hath attended to the voice of my prayer." He delights in the petition, Prov. xv. 8, "The prayer of the upright is his delight." He loves to hear the petitioner's voice, Cant. ii. 14, "Let me hear thy voice; for sweet is thy voice." He accepts the petitioner's person, and his petition too, as the angel said unto Lot, Gen. xix. 21, "See I have accepted thee concerning this thing also, that I will not overthrow this city, for the which thou hast spoken." For where prayer is heard, the person is accepted too, as Gen. iv. 4, "The Lord had respect unto Abel, and to his offering"; Job xlii. 9, "The Lord also accepted Job."

2. His granting the request, Psalm xx. 1, 4, "The Lord hear thee in the day of trouble;—grant thee according to thine own heart, and fulfil all thy counsel." The sinner coming to God with a petition, lays it before him, and his desire is granted. God wills it to be unto him accordingly, Matth. xv. 28, "O woman," said Christ to the woman of Canaan, "great is thy faith; be it unto thee even as thou wilt." The mercy prayed for

is ordered for the sinner, in kind or equivalent. Thus prayer is heard in heaven, heard and granted.

3. His answering of prayer, Psalm cii. 2, "In the day when I call answer me speedily." This is more than granting the request, being a giving unto the petitioner's hand what is desired. It is an answer not in word to the believer's faith only, but in deed to the believer's sense and feeling. Thus Hannah prayed for a child, and she got one; Paul prayed for the removal of a temptation, and he got grace sufficient to bear him out against it. Thus prayer heard in heaven comes back like the dove with the olive-branch of peace in her mouth.

II. I shall show the import of God's being the hearer of prayer. These comfortable truths are imported in it.

1. God in Christ is accessible to poor sinners, 2 Cor. v. 19, "God was in Christ, reconciling the world unto himself, not imputing their trespasses unto them." Though he sits on the throne of glory, and we are guilty before him; yet he is on a throne of grace, so as we may have access to him with our supplications. The flaming sword of justice guards the tree of life, on the side of the law; so that on that part our God is a consuming fire, which sinners are not able to dwell with; yet behold him in Christ, and through the vail of his flesh he is accessible to the worst of sinners.

2. He is a sin-pardoning God, Exod. xxxiv. 6, 7, "And the Lord passed by before him, and proclaimed, The Lord, The Lord God, merciful and gracious, long suffering, and abundant in goodness and truth, keeping mercy for thousands, forgiving iniquity, and transgression, and sin." Prayer is made particularly for the pardon of sin; the daily cry at the throne is, "Forgive us our debts." If then he is the hearer of prayer, he is a sin-pardoning God. We cannot pay our debt, but God can forgive it, and will forgive it to all that come to him in Christ for forgiveness. All kinds of sin he forgives freely, Micah vii. 18; Isa. i. 18. There is no exception, but of the sin against the Holy Ghost, which in its own nature makes the guilty refuse pardon, Matth. xii. 31. The pardon is proclaimed in the gospel, Acts xiii. 38; not to encourage presumption in any, but to prevent despondency in all, Psalm cxxx. 4, "There is forgiveness with thee; that thou mayest be feared."

3. He is an all-sufficient God, Gen. xvii. 1, "I am the Almighty God," (*Heb.*) "All sufficient." He is self-sufficient for himself, and all-sufficient for his creatures. If he were not so, he could not be the hearer of prayer; the needs of praying persons would soon exhaust his treasure. But though all flesh

come to him for supply of their various wants, he is the hearer of prayer; he has enough for them all, to answer all their needs, come as oft as they will. He is a fountain of goodness, that never runs dry, but is ever full.

4. He is a bountiful and compassionate God, Psalm lxxxvi. 5, "Thou, Lord, art good, and ready to forgive; and plenteous in mercy unto all them that call upon thee." He is willing and ready to communicate of his goodness and mercy to poor sinners for the supply of all their needs. He is more ready to give, than we to ask; we are not straitened in him, for he is the hearer of prayer; but in our own bowels. He has laid down a method, how we are to ask; and in that method, it is ask and have, James i. 5, 6, 7, "If any of you lack wisdom, let him ask of God, that giveth to all men liberally, and upbraideth not; and it shall be given him. But let him ask in faith, nothing wavering; for he that wavereth is like a wave of the sea, driven with the wind, and tossed. For let not that man think that he shall receive anything of the Lord." The faith of this is necessary to acceptable prayer, Heb. xi. 6. "For he that cometh to God, must believe that he is, and that he is a rewarder of them that diligently seek him."

5. He is an omnipresent and omniscient God, Psalm cxxxix. 7, "Whither shall I go from thy Spirit; or whither shall I flee from thy presence?" Heb. iv. 13, "Neither is there any creature that is not manifest in his sight; but all things are naked, and opened unto the eyes of him with whom we have to do." How else could he be the hearer of prayer? What part of the world soever the petitioner is in, whether he prays with the voice or with the heart only, God is the hearer of prayer. Idolaters might choose high places to worship their idols in; but it is all one to the hearer of prayer, whether the petitioner be on the top of the highest mountain, or as low as the centre of the earth. Jonah was heard out of the whale's belly. Though thousands of voices be going in prayer to the throne at the same time, the infinite mind comprehends them all, and every one, as easily as if there were but one at once.

6, *Lastly*, He is a God of infinite power, Rev. iv. 8, "They rest not day and night, saying, Holy, holy, holy, Lord God Almighty."—While there is such a variety of cases, that the creatures have to lay before him in prayer, he could not be the hearer of prayer, if there were anything too hard for him to do. But nothing is impossible with him; he calleth things that are not to be as if they were, at the voice of prayer.

III. I proceed to show what prayers they are that God hears. It is not every prayer, nor every one's prayer that God hears. But it is the prayers of his children, for things agreeable to his will, made by the assistance of his Spirit, and offered through Christ.

1. They are the prayers of his own children, who are justified by faith, and reconciled to him, James v. 16, "The effectual fervent prayer of a righteous man availeth much." Our Lord teaching how to pray, teaches as to call God "our Father"; which can be only through faith. Our persons must be accepted in justification, ere any work of ours can be so. Where there is no peace betwixt God and the sinner, what communion can be there? Amos iii. 3, "Can two walk together, except they be agreed?" The scripture is plain, "God heareth not sinners," John ix. 31. God's way of giving graciously, is to give other things with Christ, Rom. viii. 32, "He that spared not his own Son, but delivered him up for us all, how shall he not with him also freely give us all things?" It is in the covenant only that one can have a bottom for acceptance of his prayers.

OBJECTION. Then it is in vain for any to pray, but true believers. ANSW. There is less evil in praying by an unbeliever, than in his omitting it; and consequently less punishment will be. But going to pray, go to Christ by faith, and so your prayer shall be accepted; and no otherwise.

2. They are such prayers of theirs as are for things agreeable to God's will, 1 John v. 14, "This is the confidence that we have in him, that if we ask anything according to his will, he heareth us." Even in saints there are remains of a corrupt will, and so it is not left to them to pray for what they please; not what is the choice of their corruption, but what is the choice of their grace. When James and John would have prayed for fire from heaven to consume the Samaritans, Christ rebuked them, and said, "Ye know not what manner of spirit ye are of," Luke ix. 54, 55. Elias did it, but they might not, not having his spirit.

3. They are prayers made by the assistance of the Holy Spirit, hence called "inwrought," (*Gr.*) Jam. v. 16. No language is acceptable in heaven, but what is learned from thence. It is not the art of payer, but the Spirit of prayer, that is pleasing in the sight of God. The former may be reached by God's enemies, whose false heart may vent itself by a flattering tongue, as Israel did, Psalm lxxviii. 36, 37, "Nevertheless, they did flatter him with their mouth, and they lied unto him with their tongues. For their heart was not right with him,

neither were they stedfast in his covenant." The latter is the peculiar privilege of God's children, yet common to them all; Gal. iv. 6, "Because ye are sons, God hath sent forth the Spirit of his Son into your hearts, crying, Abba, Father."

4. *Lastly*, They are prayers offered to God through Christ the Mediator, the soul trusting on his merit and intercession alone for the hearing of them, Dan. ix. 17, "Now therefore, our God, hear the prayer of thy servant, and his supplications, and cause thy face to shine upon thy sanctuary that is desolate, for the Lord's sake." John xiv. 14, "If ye shall ask anything in my name, I will do it." Christ is the altar on which our spiritual sacrifices can be accepted; and it is not consistent with the honour of God, to hear the prayers of sinners otherwise.

The doctrine being thus explained in the general, I come in the next place more particularly,

1. To confirm it, and show that there is such a thing as hearing of prayer, the privilege of the Lord's people in this lower world.

2. To show in what manner the Lord hears prayer.

FIRST, I am to confirm it, and show that there is such a thing as hearing of prayer, the privilege of the Lord's people in this lower world, God is in heaven, they are on the earth; voices from heaven, or angel-messengers to report the acceptance of prayers there, are not to be expected. Nevertheless we are sure there is such a thing still in being, and it is necessary to prove it.

1. For the sake of a profane generation, who, as they are strangers to, so they are despisers of, communion with God.

2. For the sake of formalists, who go about the duty of prayer as a task, but are in no concern for the fruit of it; send away the messenger, but look for no report.

3. For the sake of discouraged Christians who go bowed down, because they cannot perceive it as they desire.

That God is the hearer of prayer, and will hear the prayers of his people, is evident from these considerations.

First, The supernatural instinct of praying that is found in all that are born of God, Gal. iv. 6, forecited. It is as natural for them to pray to fall a praying when the grace of God has touched their hearts, as for children when they are born into the world to cry, or to desire the breasts; Zech. xii. 10, "I will pour upon the house of David, and upon the inhabitants of Jerusalem the spirit of grace and of supplications." Compared with Acts ix. 11, where, in the account that is given of Paul, at his conversion, it is particularly noticed, "Behold he prayeth."

Hence the whole saving change on a soul comes under the character of this instinct; Jer. iii. 4, 19, "Wilt thou not from this time cry unto me, My Father, thou art the guide of my youth? I said, Thou shalt call me, My Father, and shalt not turn away from me." This supernatural instinct being the work of God in the new nature, cannot be in vain. Accordingly it is determined; Isa. xlv. 19, "I said not unto the seed of Jacob, Seek ye me in vain." But it would be a vain appetite, if it were not to be satisfied by hearing.

Secondly, The intercession of Christ; Rom. viii. 34, "It is Christ that died, yea rather, that is risen again, who is even at the right hand of God, who also maketh intercession for us." It is a great part of the work of Christ's intercession, to present the prayers of his people before his Father, Rev. viii. 4, to take their causes in hand contained in their supplications, 1 John ii. 1. So we find him interceding for his church of old in her low condition, Zech. i, and in the New Testament, John xvii. He is ever at the work, and cannot neglect it, Heb. vii. 25, and it cannot be without effect; John xi. 42, "I knew that thou hearest me always," said Jesus to his Father.

Thirdly, The promises of the covenant, whereby God's faithfulness is impawned[15] for the hearing of prayer; as Matth. vii. 7, "Ask, and it shall be given you; seek, and ye shall find; knock, and it shall be opened unto you." Isa. lxv. 24, "And it shall come to pass, that before they call, I will answer, and whiles they are yet speaking, I will hear." Psalm cxlv. 19, "He will fulfil the desire of them that fear him; he also will hear their cry, and will save them." The promise of hearing of prayer, is one of the great lines of the covenant; Hos. ii. 20, 21, "I will even betroth thee unto me in faithfulness, and thou shalt know the Lord. And it shall come to pass in that day, I will hear, saith the Lord, I will hear the heavens," &c.; and it is so proposed with his being his people's God; Zech. x. 6, "I am the Lord their God, and will hear them."

Fourthly, The many encouragements given in the word to the people of God, to come with their cases unto the Lord by prayer. He invites them to his throne of grace with their petitions for supply of their needs; Cant. ii. 14, "O my dove that art in the clefts of the rock, in the secret places of the stairs, let me see thy countenance, let me hear thy voice; for sweet is thy voice, and thy countenance is comely." He sends afflictions for to press them to come; Hos. v. ult, "I will go and

---

15 Pledged.

return to my place, till they acknowledge their offence, and seek my face; in their affliction they will seek me early." He gives them ground of hope of success, Psalm l. 15, whatever extremity their case is brought to; Isa. xli. 17, "When the poor and needy seek water and there is none, and their tongue faileth for thirst, I the Lord will hear them, I the God of Israel will not forsake them." He shews them, that however long he may delay for their trial, yet praying and not fainting shall be successful at length; Luke xviii. 8, "I tell you that he will avenge them speedily."

Fifthly, The gracious nature of God, with the endearing relations he stands in to his people; Exod. xxii. 27, "And it shall come to pass, when he crieth unto me, that I will hear; for I am gracious." Matth. vii. 9-11, "What man is there of you, whom if his son ask bread, will he give him a stone? or if he ask a fish, will he give him a serpent? If ye then being evil, know how to give good gifts unto your children, how much more shall your Father which is in heaven give good things to them that ask him?" He wants not power and ability to fulfil the holy desires of his people; he is gracious, and will withhold no good from them that they really need. He has the bowels of a Father to pity them, the bowels of a mother to her sucking child. He has a most tender sympathy with them in all their afflictions, the touches on them are as on the apple of his eye; and he never refuses them a request, but for their good; Rom. viii. 28.

Sixthly, The experiences which the saints of all ages have had of the answer of prayer. The faith of it brings them to God at first in conversion, as the text intimates; and they that believe cannot be disappointed. Abraham, Moses, David's and Job's experiences of this kind are in record, with many others, Paul's, &c. The Psalmist sets up his case as a way-mark to all the travellers to Zion; Psalm xxxiv. 6, "This poor man cried, and the Lord heard him; and saved him out of all his troubles." And to this day the saints' experience seals the truth thereof.

Lastly, The present ease and relief that prayer sometimes gives to the saints, while yet the full answer of prayer is not come; Psalm cxxxviii. 3, "In the day when I cried, thou answeredst me; and strengthenedst me with strength in my soul." The unbosoming of themselves to the Lord in prayer, comforts and strengthens the heart; 1 Sam. i. 18. This is on the faith of the Lord's hearing of prayer; Micah vii. 7, "I will look unto the Lord; I will wait for the God of my salvation; my God will hear me."

SECONDLY, I come to show in what manner the Lord hears prayer. For clearing of this, I lay down the following observations thereon,

FIRST, A thing desired of God may be obtained, and yet the prayer not heard and accepted, as in Israel's case; Psalm lxxviii. 29, "So they did eat, and were well filled; for he gave them their own desire." For as it is plain on the one hand, that sinners out of Christ may sometimes obtain a thing they pray for, as in the case of the Ninevites, it is as plain on the other, that no prayer of theirs can be accepted of God, according to John ix. 31, "God heareth not sinners." It is one thing to get a thing prayed for, another to get it as an answer of accepted prayer; Psalm lxxviii. 34–38. Now this falls out in two cases,

1. When the thing prayed for is given downright in wrath, as it was in the case of the Israelites seeking a king; Hos. xiii. 11, "I gave thee a king in mine anger." Men often need no more to ruin them, but to get their will; and God may give it them with a vengeance. They get their desire, but it is far from being accepted; for it is in anger it comes to them.

2. When it is given in the way of uncovenanted condescendence. Thus sinners out of Christ may get particular requests of theirs answered, as Ahab; 1 Kings xxi. 29. For though God does not accept their persons, nor any performance of theirs; yet he may show regard to his own ordinance of prayer, and therefore make it not fruitless even to them. And thus the Lord does to train sinners to the yielding themselves to him, and to depending on him by faith and prayer; Hos. xi. 3, "I taught Ephraim also to go, taking them by their arms."

Answers of accepted prayer come in the way of the covenant of grace, but these in the way of common providence. And they may be discerned by these attending signs.

(1.) Wilfulness and unhumbledness of spirit in asking; 1 Sam. viii. 19, "Nevertheless the people refused to obey the voice of Samuel; and they said, Nay, but we will have a king over us." When one's will is peremptory, and is not brought to a holy submission to God in the matter, but they will wring the mercy out of God's hand, and have it at any rate, whether with or without his good will; be sure that is what comes in the way of common providence only.

(2.) Strengthening and feeding of lusts by them when received, Psalm lxxviii. 29, 30. Hence on such receipts men commonly grow worse, and their mercies are short-lived; being greedily snatched off the tree of providence, ere they are ripe, their teeth are set on edge with them, vers. 30, 31.

(3) A frame of spirit, in asking and receiving, not of the mould of the gospel, but of the law; whereby more stress is laid upon our own necessity than on the intercession of Christ; there is much desire of the mercy, but no believing dependence on the Lord for it in the promise as a free promise through Christ; and ordinarily it leaves the heart fixed on the gift, and does not carry it back to the Giver.

Secondly, A prayer may be heard and accepted, and yet the desire of it not granted. That is to say, God may be pleased with, and accept of the prayer as service to him; and yet may see meet not to grant the thing prayed for. Even as a father going to correct one of his children, may be very well pleased with another child of his interposing for sparing, though he may not see it meet to for-bear for all that.

The truth of this is put out of doubt, in the case of Jesus Christ himself, Matth. xxvi. 39, who prayed, saying, "O my Father, if it be possible, let this cup pass from me; nevertheless, not as I will, but as thou wilt." Compare, Heb. v. 7, "Who in the days of his flesh, when he had offered up prayers and supplications, with strong crying and tears, unto him that was able to save him from death, and was heard, in that he feared." If it was so done with the Head, no wonder it be so with the members too, as David, 2 Chron. vi. 8, 9, "But the Lord said to David my father, Forasmuch as it was in thine heart to build an house for my name, thou didst well in that it was in thine heart; notwithstanding, thou shalt not build the house, but thy son which shall come forth out of thy loins, he shall build the house for my name." A thing may be very agreeable to the command of God, to be prayed for, which yet may be otherwise ordered in the holy wise providence of God. It is one thing what he requires of us by his revealed will, another what in his secret will he minds to do, Deut. xxix. ult., "The secret things belong unto the Lord our God: but those things which are revealed, belong unto us, and to our children for ever, that we may do all the words of this law."

Now of prayers accepted and not granted, it is to be observed,

1. They are not absolute and peremptory, but with holy submission to the divine pleasure, as of our Lord's, Matth. xxvi. 39. If we pray absolutely, for what God has not so promised, and such a prayer is not granted, it is not accepted nei-

ther. So all that this amounts to is, that God sees meet to refuse what the petitioner did seek, but with submission to his will either to grant or refuse it.

2. Where a prayer is accepted and not granted, there is in the bosom of the denial an unseen greater mercy. Had that cup passed from Christ, where had been the glory of God the Father, Son, and Holy Ghost, in the salvation of an elect world, that was wrapt up in the denial of that sinless desire of Christ's holy human nature? Had David's child lived for whom he prayed, he had been a lasting stain on his father's reputation; but God refused David's petition in that, where the refusal was a greater mercy than the granting would have been.

3. Hence that treatment of such prayers is agreeable to the chief scope and aim of the petitioner, which is God's glory and his own good. This is the design of believers in all their accepted prayers, which, being agreeable to the promise, there is no jarring there betwixt God and them. Only, they in this case look on such a thing as they pray for to be the most proper mean for that end; God sees it is not, and therefore refuses it. So all that this amounts to is, as if one should desire one to lead him such a way to such a place; he refuses not to lead him to the place, but he will not lead him that way, but a nearer and better way.

QUESTION. How may I know such prayers of mine to be accepted, when they are not granted?

ANSWER 1. When the heart is brought to submit to the denial as a holy and righteous dispensation; Psalm xxii. 2, 3, "O my God, I cry in the day time, but thou hearest not; and in the night season, and am not silent. But thou art holy, O thou that inhabitest the praises of Israel." When the sinner from his heart clears the Hearer of prayer, leaving his complaint on his unworthy self, such an effect is an argument of prayer accepted, though not granted.

2. When though the thing be denied, yet divine support under the denial is granted, and made forthcoming, Luke xxii. 42, 43. Christ having prayed, saying, "Father, if thou be willing, remove this cup from me; nevertheless, not my will, but thine be done; there appeared an angel unto him from heaven, strengthening him." And he was carried through all his sufferings by his Father, so that he was victorious over death itself. Thus often God, denying the petitions of his children, with respect to temptations, troubles, &c., yet testifies his acceptance of their prayers by the supports given under

the same; Psalm cxxxviii. 3, "In the day when I cried," says David, "thou answeredst me; and strengthenedst me with strength in my soul."

3. *Lastly*, When such a soul is helped to go back to the same God with new petitions in faith and hope of hearing; 2 Sam. xii. 20, "Then David arose from the earth, and washed, and anointed himself, and changed his apparel, and came into the house of the Lord and worshipped." This argues a faith of the promise of all things working together for good, Rom. viii. 28, a leaving a latitude of dispensation to sovereignty, well becoming a submissive and resigned petitioner.

Thirdly, The desire of a prayer may be heard and granted, and yet it may be long ere it be answered. That is to say, all prayers not answered to our sense and feeling, are not lost; they may stand granted in heaven, and yet it may be many a day ere the answer of them come to us. A prayer may be granted, and yet the mercy prayed for be still withheld, so that the petitioner may be obliged to send new petitions day by day for it still.

I shall first confirm this, and then show why it may be so ordered.

First, To confirm the truth of this, consider,

1. Scripture instances. Abraham prayed for an heir, it was granted, Gen. xv. 3, 4, yet it was more than thirteen years before that prayer was answered, in the birth of Isaac., Gen. xvii. 25. So the Israelites in Egypt, Exod. ii. 23, 24; and Daniel, chap. ix. 23. Such instances are recorded for our learning.

2. There is a difference betwixt the granting of a petition, and the intimation of that grant to us; betwixt Heaven's order for our getting of the mercy, and the execution of it. The one is the hearing and grant of prayer, the other is the answer; and though these sometimes may come both in one instant, as Matth. xv. 28, "Jesus answered and said unto her, O woman, great is thy faith; be it unto thee even as thou wilt; and her daughter was made whole from that very hour"; yet often they are at a great distance of time, as in Abraham's case.

3. The hearing and granting of prayer is an object of faith, the answer of prayer an object of sense and feeling, 1 John v. 14, 15; Matth. xv. 28. A prayer made through the assistance of the Spirit, according to the will of God, and offered to God through Christ, is heard and granted in that instant wherein it is made; and this is what we are to believe, on the ground of the faithfulness of God in the promise, before we get the answer to our sense and feeling; for "faith is the substance

of things not seen, and we walk by faith not by sight"; and therefore this is the ordinary way to put the grant and answer at some distance of time, though not always, Isa. lxv. 24.

Secondly, I shall show why the answers of prayers heard and granted, are kept up for a time, and may be for a long time.

1. To keep the petitioners hanging on about the throne of grace; Prov. xv. 8, "The prayer of the upright is his delight." The Lord by this means gives them many errands to the throne, so that they must always be going back again, and renewing their suits. So fathers make their little children follow them, and hang about them, and speak to them as they can; and no father has such delight in the company and converse of his children, as God has in his, Cant. ii. 14.

2. For the trial of their graces; Jam. i. 12, "Blessed is the man that endureth temptation; for when he is tried, he shall receive the crown of life, which the Lord hath promised to them that love him." This life is the time of trial, and God's withholding for a time the answers of granted prayers, is a piece of trial that will go in through and out through the child of God. It tries their sincerity and earnestness for an answer, Job xxvii. 10; with Luke xviii. 7; their patience and disposition to wait on God, Hab. ii. 3; their hope in God, Psalm cxlvii. 11; and xlii. 5; especially it tries their faith in the word of promise, and that is a trial of great estimation in the sight of God; 1 Pet. i. 6, 7, "Wherein ye greatly rejoice, though now for a season (if need be) ye are in heaviness through manifold temptations. That the trial of your faith being much more precious than of gold that perisheth, though it be tried with fire, might be found unto praise, and houour and glory at the appearing of Jesus Christ." Every new act of faith in the word, is more valuable than all the famed exploits of carnal, selfish men; especially when faith keeps hold of the promise like a rope in the water, while providence is bringing one wave after another over the man's head, Psalm lvi. 10. So Matth. xv. 21–28.

3. Till they be prepared and fitted for receiving the answer; Psalm x. 17, "Lord, thou hast heard the desire of the humble; thou wilt prepare their heart, thou wilt cause thine ear to hear." Mercies we need, but we are not at all times meet to receive them. God gives his left-hand gifts to strangers, in the way of common providence, whether they be prepared for them or not; and hence many are ruined getting much laid to their hand before they have the grace or wisdom to manage it, for God's honour and their own good. But his right-hand gifts

to his children, in the way of the covenant, though they be ready for them, yet he will keep them back till they be made ready and prepared for them too. So he is at pains to humble them, and work them for that thing. Saul was brought to the kingdom easily, but David not so.

4. *Lastly,* Till the best time come, for their getting it, when it may come to them with the greatest advantage; Eccl. iii. 14, "I know that whatsoever God doth, it shall be for ever; nothing can be put to it, nor any thing taken from it; and God doth it, that men should fear before him." There is much in the timing of a favour; the same thing may be worth double to a man at one time, beyond what it will be at another. And be sure, if God is keeping back the answer of a granted prayer, he is only reserving till the best time of bestowing it; John xi. 14, 15, and ii. 4.

QUEST. How may a Christian know his prayer is heard and granted, while yet it is not answered?

ANSW. 1. If ye have prayed in faith, no doubt your petition is heard and granted, though it should not be answered for ever so long after; Matth. xxi. 22, "All things whatsoever ye shall ask in prayer, believing, ye shall receive." God refuses not, nor rejects any prayer for things agreeable to his will, made in faith of the promise, through the assistance of the Spirit, and offered to him through his Son. And ye ought to believe, that such prayers are granted, but that God for holy wise ends delays the answer.

2. If ye are strengthened to hang on about the Lord's hand for the answer, hoping and waiting for the Lord; Psalm cxxxviii. 3. It is a certain truth, which ye may build upon; Gal. vi. 9, "In due season we shall reap, if we faint not." This is the very character of an elect believer, on his trials for glory; Luke xviii. 7, "Shall not God avenge his own elect, which cry day and night unto him, though he bean long with them?" Granted prayer brings something in hand, namely, grace to wait on; Psalm xxvii. ult., "Wait on the Lord; be of good courage, and he shall strengthen thine heart; wait I say on the Lord." Compare ver. 13, "I had fainted, unless I had believed to see the goodness of the Lord in the land of the living."

3. *Lastly,* It is a good sign when ye are encouraged to wait for the desired answer, by the Lord's answering you in other things that fall out in the meantime of the delay. For the Lord lays these to your hand to support your faith and hope in point of the delayed answer. How was David's faith of the promise of the kingdom kept up, so many years during Saul's

reign? Why, David in that time had many experiences of answers of prayer, and fulfilling of promises in other things, as Psalm xxxiv. 6, "This poor man cried, and the Lord heard him; and saved him out of all his troubles."

FOURTHLY, Prayers accepted and granted, shall certainly be answered to the believer's sense and feeling at length. The answer may be delayed, but it cannot be forgotten nor miscarried. Such prayers will surely be turned into praise at long-run; and faith will bring in sense and feeling, when it is tried a while.

I shall first confirm the truth of this, and then show when they shall be so answered to their sense and feeling.

First, To confirm this, consider,

1. The interest the Mediator has in the matter, which secures and puts it beyond doubt. It is upon his merit that the prayer is accepted, on his intercession that it is granted; so that he is nearly concerned in the obtaining of the answer; and then he is the great Steward in heaven, into whose hands the whole fulness of covenant-benefits for sinners' supply is put. How then can it fail, when the mercy petitioned for is lodged in the hand of our Intercessor?

2. The faithfulness of God in his word; Psalm lxxxix. 8, "O Lord God of hosts, who is a strong Lord like unto thee? or to thy faithfulness round about thee?" This stands as a rock immoveable in all the changes that befall his people. His word must be accomplished, and his promise fulfilled, whatever stand in the way of it. Heaven and earth shall rather be removed than it fail, or fall a minute behind the set time of its bringing forth; Hab. ii. 3, "For the vision is yet for an appointed time, but at the end it shall speak, and not lie; though it tarry, wait for it, because it will surely come, it will not tarry."

3. The love and pity God has to his children that cry to him "His ears are open to their cry"; Psalm xxxiv. 15. He forgets it not; Psalm ix. 12. As he is their God, so he will be "a God to them," as the expression is; 1 Chron. xvii. 24, namely, to do the part of a God to them; that is, to hear and answer their prayers.

4. *Lastly*, Such prayers are the product of his own Spirit in them; Rom. viii. 26. And be sure, the mouths that he opens, he will fill; the holy appetite and desires that he creates in them, he will satisfy.

Secondly, I shall show when they shall be answered to their sense and feeling. There are two periods in general, wherein God gives answers of prayers accepted and granted. Answers of prayer are given,

1. In time, during the petitioner's life in this world; Psalm lviii. ult., "Verily there is a reward for the righteous; verily he is a God that judgeth in the earth." Believers in this life have communion with God, and do get answers of prayer, as provision allowed them of their Father, for their journey through the wilderness. But one may wait a long time of his life for an answer of some prayers, and ere he go off be made to say, "Lord, now lettest then thy servant depart in peace, according to thy word; for mine eyes have seen thy salvation"; Luke ii. 29, 30.

Of the seasons of life for answers of prayer, we may say in the general, there are four seasons thereof.

(1.) A time of the Lord's return to a church and people from whom he had hid his face; Psalm cii. 16, 17, "When the Lord shall build up Zion, he shall appear in his glory. He will regard the prayer of the destitute, and not despise their prayer." The children may cry long to their Father, ere he let on he notices them, when he is angry with their mother; but when he is pleased with her, they get speedy answers from him; Dan. ix. 1, 2, 23. Times of reformation, and outpouring of the Spirit on a land, are times of answers of prayer to particular persons; which should move us to carry along the public case, with our private cases, as David did; Psalm li. 18, 19, "Do good in thy good pleasure unto Zion; build thou the walls of Jerusalem"; &c.

(2.) A time of greatest extremity, when matters are carried to the utmost point of hopelessness; Deut. xxxii. 36, "For the Lord shall judge his people, and repent himself for his servants; when he seeth that their power is gone, and there is none shut up, or left." When God's people are brought to that, they can do no more, then is the special season of God's doing for them; Isa. xli. 17, "When the poor and needy seek water, and there is none, and their tongue faileth for thirst, I the Lord will hear them, I the God of Israel will not forsake them." When the child was laid by for dead, the well was discovered. When the knife was at Isaac's throat, the answer comes from heaven, "Stay thine hand." A sentence of death is often passed on all probable means, the thing is put as it were in the grave, and the stone sealed; and then comes the resurrection of it; 2 Cor. i. 8-10. Psalm cxxvi. 1, "When the Lord turned again the captivity of Zion, we were like them that dream."

(3.) A time of the petitioner's deepest humiliation, when he is beat down from all his heights, and brought as low as the dust of the Lord's feet, as in Job's case; chap. xlii. 6, 7, &c., and the woman of Canaan's; Matth. xv. 27, 28. It is the Lord's way with his children to lay them very low, before he raise them up; to empty them soundly of themselves, before he fill them. They must be made to see their own utter unworthiness, that God is no debtor to them, be wholly resigned to the divine pleasure, and become as a weaned child. And that may cost much hewing; but it is the way they are prepared for mercy; Psalm x. 17.

(4.) *Lastly*, A time wherein the mercy may come most seasonably for God's honour and their comfort, Gal. vi. 9, "In due season we shall reap, if we faint not," The husbandman expects to reap his crop in the harvest, for that is the most proper season. Our God is the best judge of time for this or that purpose, and he does all in judgment, Deut. xxxii. 4. So that the petitioner shall be fully satisfied as to the delay of the answer, and the whole steps of providence in the matter, and be made to sing as Rev. xv. 3, saying "Great and marvellous are thy works, Lord God Almighty; just and true are thy ways, thou King of saints."

2. In eternity, when the believing petitioner is got into another world, then will be a season of answers of prayer, Mal. iii. 17, 18, "They shall be mine, saith the Lord of hosts, in that day when I make up my jewels, and I will spare them as a man spareth his own son that serveth him. Then shall ye return and discern between the righteous and the wicked; between him that serveth God, and him that serveth him not." I do not say, they will pray in another world, but prayers poured out in this world will be answered in another world, partly after death, and fully and completely at the resurrection. For consider,

(1.) There are accepted and granted prayers that are never answered on this side of time; yet they cannot miss to be answered, Psalm ix. 18, "For the needy shall not alway be forgotten; the expectation of the poor shall not perish for ever." Therefore they are answered in eternity. Such is that prayer of all the children of God, Rom. vii. 24, "O wretched man that I am, who shall deliver me from the body of this death?" The complete victory over all their enemies, and being set beyond their reach, which is delayed till the resurrection, 1 Cor. xv. 26, "The last enemy that shall be destroyed, is death."

(2.) There are prayers that are answered here in part, but are not fully answered till the petitioner comes into another world. The prayers for the coming of Christ's kingdom are begun to be answered now, but they will not be fully answered till the last day. Petitions for deliverance from temptation, the power of lusts and corruptions, are answered so as an earnest is given, but the full answer is till then in reserve, Rom. xvi. 20, "The God of peace shall bruise Satan under your feet shortly."

(3.) *Lastly*, All the accepted prayers of those that wait for the Lord, whether for their souls or their bodies, will be at once answered in heaven fully; there the promises will be told out to them for ever in full tale. There are many prayers for deliverance from temptations, trials, and troubles, which God sees not meet to answer now; but they will be all answered at once then, Rev. xxi. 4, "God shall wipe away all tears from their eyes; and there shall so no more death, neither sorrow, nor crying, neither shall there be any more pain; for the former things are passed away."

Therefore, let none think that all the prayers are lost that are not answered during this life; for prayers here made in faith, may be delayed as to their answer, till the petitioner come home to his Father's house; and there will be a second crop there of prayers here answered.

QUEST. When an answer of prayer comes, how shall it be known to be an answer of accepted and granted prayer, and not come in the way of common providence?

ANSW. 1. Mercies that come so make the soul more holy, tender, and watchful, whereas others prove snares and fuel to men's lusts, Psalm vi. 8, "Depart from me, all ye workers of iniquity; for the Lord hath heard the voice of my weeping." Common providence filled the rich man's barns, then said he, "Soul take thine ease."

2. They enlarge the soul in thankfulness to God, Psalm cxvi. 1, 12, "I love the Lord, because he hath heard my voice, and my supplications. What shall I render unto the Lord, for all his benefits towards me?" And they make it to rejoice more in the Giver, than in the gifts, 1 Sam. ii. 1, "My heart rejoiceth in the Lord." The signature of God's good will that is upon the mercy, makes it of a great bulk, though it may be a small thing in itself, Gen. xxxiii. 10, "I have seen thy face, said Jacob to Esau, as though I had seen the face of God, and thou wast pleased with me." Thus coming from God in the way of the covenant, it leads back to God; but others not so.

3. *Lastly*, They come seasonably, the heart being in some measure prepared for the receipt. Psalm x. 17, when the soul is moulded in a submissive disposition. Exercised souls will be afraid of a mercy coming too soon.

Fifthly, God answers prayer, either by giving the very thing itself asked, or the equivalent of it. As a man may pay his bond, either in money, or money worth. So there are two ways of God's fulfilling his promises, and answering his people's prayers.

1. Sometimes God answers prayer by giving the very thing desired. So he answered Hannah's prayer for a child, and Solomon's prayer for wisdom. And what comes that way will bear much bulk in the eyes of a gracious soul, because of the good will of God that is stamped on it, whereby it is distinguished from what comes in the common road.

And what comes that way, readily comes with a good incast[16] to it, especially if the petitioner has been kept long hanging on for it. Such an incast got Solomon, 2 Chron. i. 12, "Wisdom and knowledge is granted unto thee, and I will give thee riches, and wealth, and honour, such as none of the kings have had, that have been before thee, neither shall there any after thee have the like." They that wait long for their answer, ordinarily get as it were both the stock and interest together. So Abraham and Sarah waited long for the promised seed, even till they were come to extreme old age; and then they got it with a renewing of their age.

2. Sometimes by giving, though not the thing itself, yet the equivalent of it, that which is as good; as one may pay his bond, by giving, though not money, yet what is as good as money. Thus though God did not give David the child's life, yet he gave him a Solomon, a mercy as good and better. Paul, though he got not free of the temptation at his asking, yet he got grace sufficient to bear him up under it, 2 Cor. xii. 9.

And God's as-good that he gives his people, will readily be found better, all things considered. That is best which is best for God's honour and our good, and God knows better than we what is most suitable to these purposes. It would have been more easy for Paul, to have been freed from the messenger of Satan; but it was more for God's honour and his spiritual good, to be helped to fight that messenger and overcome.

---

16 An amount given by a seller above the exact measure.

Learn then, that your prayers may be answered, though ye get not the very thing ye ask. Though God answer you not in kind, if he answer you in kindness, you have no reason to say your prayer is not heard. If he take not off your burden, yet if he gives you support, he hears you, Psalm cxxxviii. 3. There are two ways how God gives his people as good.

(1.) Sometimes he gives them as good in the same kind: though he gives them not the same temporal mercy they would have had, he gives them another of the same kind as good as it. Though he gave not David the life of the child he asked, he gave him a Solomon. So God reserves to himself the choosing.

(2.) Sometimes he gives them as good in another kind; as not giving them such a temporal mercy, he gives them a spiritual mercy and enjoyment in the room of it; and surely there is no loss there.

QUESTION, How may one know that God answers his prayer, by giving him the as-good.

ANSWER 1. When that which is given answers or serves the purpose as well as the thing desired would have done. David desired the child's life as a token of God's reconciliation with him; but Solomon's birth answered the same purpose, 2 Sam. xii. 24, 25. So there was no loss as to the main thing in view.

2. When the heart is brought to rest contented with what is given in the room of what was desired. So Moses was sufficed with a sight of the land from Pisgah, instead of entering into it. When the thing given takes the heart off what is withheld, it is a sign it comes as an answer of prayer by the way of an as-good.

3. When a person is to his own conviction a gainer by the choice God makes for him. Thus the Lord sometimes answers his people's prayers in trouble for deliverance, by giving them manifestations of his love and mercy, which they would not have gotten if the trouble had been removed, Lam. iii. 57, "Thou drewest near in the day that I called upon thee; thou saidst, Fear not."

Sixthly, God's answer of prayer sometimes agrees with the expression used in prayer, though not with the preconceived design and desire of the petitioner. There is a special help of the Spirit allowed God's people in prayer, beyond what they have otherwise, Rom. viii. 26. Hence going to God on such a particular errand, they are sometimes carried so to express their desire, that the answer agrees exactly to the expression used in the petition, though the petition as expressed doth swerve somewhat from what they intended.

It will therefore be profitable on the receiving an answer of prayer, to compare it with the expression in which the petition was made; and the harmony betwixt them being observed, will set the matter of the answer in a clear light.

Lastly, One mercy may be the answer of the prayers of many. Whether it be a public mercy to a society, or a private mercy to a particular person, it may be given in answer to the prayers of many, and many may take the comfort of that answer. As when the prayers of a congregation are heard, or a mercy is given which many have privately prayed for, though the answer is one, it may belong to many.

QUESTION, How may one know that in such a case there has been any regard had to his prayer for the mercy?

ANSWER 1. If thy heart did join in prayer for the mercy, with others, thy affections being touched with earnest desire of the mercy, thy soul lifted up to depend on the merit and intercession of Christ for the granting it, thou needest not doubt but it is an answer to thy prayer as well as to others, Matth. xviii. 19, "I say unto you, that if two of you shall agree on earth, as touching any thing that they shall ask, it shall be done for them of my Father which is in heaven."

2. If thou findest thy heart enlarged in thankfulness to God for the mercy when it is obtained, that is another evidence that it is an answer to thy prayer as well as others, 2 Cor. iv. 15, "For all things are for your sakes, that the abundant grace might, through the thanksgiving of many, redound to the glory of God." Many a prayer had been put up for the coming of the Messiah; Simeon when he saw him is transported with thankfulness of heart, as having obtained his desire, Luke ii. 29.

I shall now shut up this subject with some practical improvement.

USE I. of information. Hence see,

1. How much we poor sinners stand indebted to free grace providing a Saviour for us. We could have had no access with our prayers to an absolute God; justice would have barred our acceptance. So fallen angels have no access to God allowed them; for Christ took not on their nature. But great is our privilege in this point; 1 John ii. 1, "For if any man sin, we have an Advocate with the Father, Jesus Christ the righteous."

2. The heinousness of the sin of neglecting prayer. A price is put in men's hands to get wisdom, but they have no heart

to it. The door of mercy and grace stands open, but they will not come to it; God sits on a throne of grace, ready to answer petitions; but they have none to put in his hand.

3. The impiety and profaneness that is in abusing of prayer, making a scorn of it in ordinary conversation, as "God pity you, help you, bless us, save us," &c. How lamentable is it, that the name of God, and the ordinance of prayer, should be thus prostituted to the lusts of men at every trifle! The day will come, when God's pity, help, &c., which ye make so light of now, will appear more valuable than ten thousand worlds, and ye shall not have them, if ye repent not of that contempt which ye now treat them with.

4. The folly of those who are in no concern for the hearing of their prayers. Surely, they forsake their own mercy. Ye would have little satisfaction in your meat, if it did not feed you; in your clothes, if they did not keep you warm. What satisfaction then can ye have in your praying, if ye cannot find it is heard?

5. *Lastly*, This shews why serious souls do so much value prayer, and betake themselves thereto in all their straits. Slight it who will, it will not be slighted by those who have experience of the Lord's hearing their prayers, Micah vii. 7, "I will look unto the Lord; I will wait for the God of my salvation; my God will hear me." Daniel was such a man; and he would rather venture on the den of lions, than forego his praying to God. The neglect of it, is a sign of unacquaintedness with that.

USE II. Of direction and comfort to the people of God, in all the trials and troubles they meet with in the world. Here is your course ye should take, go to God with your case, whatever it be, and make your prayer to him about it, Phil. iv. 6, "Be careful for nothing; but in everything by prayer and supplication with thanksgiving, let your requests be made known unto God." Here is your comfort, God is the hearer of prayer, Isa. xlv. 19, "I said not unto the seed of Jacob, Seek ye my face in vain." There are four things I would suggest to you here for your direction and comfort.

1. God has made the way to heaven lie through many tribulations, that his children might have the more errands to his throne of grace. That this is the path-road to the kingdom of God, is clear from scripture testimony, Acts xiv. 22, "we must through much tribulation enter into the kingdom of God"; John xvi. ult, "In the world ye shall have tribulation"; and the experience of Christ the Head, and the saints

in all ages. That this is the design of it, appears also from the word, Hos. v. ult. "I will go and return to my place, till they acknowledge their offence, and seek my face; in their affliction they will seek me early." Prosperity seldom fails to issue in forgetting of God, Deut. xxxii. 15. Adversity causes to feel a need of his help, Zeph. iii. 12. So God keeps the thorn of affliction at the breast of his people, to keep them waking, and sends the cross to invite them to the throne of grace.

2. The way to heaven in that respect never alters, though the external circumstances of the church in the world do alter. Sometimes there is persecution in the church, sometimes peace; but in the most peaceable time of the church, God's people shall go through the world to the kingdom through much tribulation. The seed of the serpent will vent their enmity one way or other against the people of God, though they have not law on their side to bear them out in persecuting them. God will have his people tried, and caused to suffer in their bodies, goods, liberty, and life, if not by the hands of persecutors, yet by his own hand one way or other. For that is a perpetual rule, Matth. xvi. 24, "If any man will come after me, let him deny himself, and take up his cross, and follow me." Luke xiv. 26, "If any man come to me, and hate not his father, and mother, and wife, and children, and brethren, and sisters, yea, and his own life also, he cannot be my disciple." So there is no change, but only as to the means and instruments of trial.

3. Whatever be your trial, whether it be in temporal or spiritual things, ye are welcome to the throne of grace with it, Phil. iv. 6, forecited. Whether it come on you immediately from the hand of God, or men, ye may carry it to God by prayer, and pour out your heart before him as a prayer-hearing God, in confidence that he can help you, and will do it in due time.

4. The more trials and afflictions God's people meet with, the more experience readily they will be found to have of God's hearing prayer; Rom. v. 3, 4, "And not only so, but we glory in tribulations also, knowing that tribulation worketh patience, and patience experience; and experience, hope." Of all the patriarchs Jacob had the most trials, and accordingly was richest in experiences. The more battles the Christian soldier is engaged in, the more is he enriched with spoil. The Israelites had not sung that triumphant song recorded Exod. xv, had they not been in that great strait at the Red Sea.

USE last, of exhortation. Then,

1. Improve your privilege of access to God through Christ in prayer. Since God has cast open the gates of mercy, come enter in by them; since he is saying to you, "What is thy petition and it shall be granted thee?" slight not the golden season of petitioning. Consider,

(1.) Your need is great. Whatever ye have or want in temporals, surely ye need a resting place for your conscience and for your heart; you need something to make you happy in time and eternity.

(2.) The whole creation cannot answer your needs. There is an emptiness in every creature, that it cannot be a resting place to you, Isa. lv. 2. The soul is of such a make, that no less than an infinite good can satisfy it. Only God in Christ can make you happy.

(3.) He offers to supply all your needs; Psalm lxxxi. 10, "I am the Lord thy God; open thy mouth wide, and I will fill it." Ask in faith, and ye shall receive.

(4.) *Lastly*, This door of access will not always stand open; Matth. xxv. 10, 11, 12, "And while they went to buy, the bridegroom came, and they that were ready went in with him to the marriage, and the door was shut. Afterward came also the other virgins, saying, Lord, Lord, open to us. But he answered and said, Verily I say unto you, I know you not." Now is the accepted time.

2. Be concerned for God's hearing of your prayers; look after them and see what speed they come. There are two things wherein this concern should appear.

(1.) In making your addresses to the throne of grace, being careful so to manage that, as ye may be accepted. They who are rash in their approaches to God, and careless how their petitions are formed and presented, cannot be duly concerned for a hearing of them. Labour, therefore, so to pray, as your prayers may be heard and accepted.

(2.) In depending and waiting on after prayer for an answer; Psalm v. 3, "My voice shalt thou hear in the morning, O Lord; in the morning will I direct my prayer unto thee, and will look up." Do not drop your suits, but insist for an answer, depending for it on the promise of God in his word.

Thus far of God's hearing of prayer. I shall shut up this with a word to another doctrine for the use of the whole.

DOCTRINE. Such is the glory of God as the hearer of prayer in Christ, that it will make all flesh that discerns it come unto him.

Here I shall shew,

I. What is that glory of God as the hearer of prayer in Christ, that is so attractive.

II. How this glory of God in Christ is discerned by a sinner.

III. What that coming unto God is, that is the effect of discerning that glory.

IV. *Lastly*, Deduce an inference or two.

I. I am to show what is that glory of God as the hearer of prayer in Christ, that is so attractive. It is twofold.

1. The glory of his all-sufficiency; Gen. xvii. 1, "I am God all-sufficient." He is not only all-sufficient for himself, but for his creatures; if he were not so, he could not be the hearer of prayer. But sinners in the darkness of their natural state discern it not; they cannot comprehend what way he can be so, and therefore they traverse the round of the creation, seeking in the creature that sufficiency; till the light of the glory of God's all-sufficiency shine into their hearts in Christ. Then it shines unto them with a threefold ray of glory.

(1.) An absolute suitableness to their case, which must needs be very glorious in their eyes, since that is what they were always seeking, but could never find before, according to that; Isa. lv. 2, "Wherefore do ye spend money for that which is not bread? and your labour for that which satisfieth not? hearken diligently unto me, and eat ye that which is good, and let your soul delight itself in fatness." Therefore with the wise merchant they "sell all to buy the one pearl," Matth. xiii. 45, 46. The heart of man is an empty, hungry thing, going among the creatures seeking a match for itself, in which it may rest; but there they cannot find it; but discovering it in a God in Christ, they are attracted with the glory of that sight.

(2.) A complete fulness for them; Col. i. 19, "For it pleased the Father, that in him should all fulness dwell." In his all-sufficiency the soul sees the fulness of a Godhead, an infinite boundless fulness, to answer and satisfy the boundless desires of an immortal soul. That is a fountain for the thirsty soul to drink at to the full; a treasure to enrich the soul oppressed with poverty; a salve for all its sores, and a remedy for all its wounds. So it cannot miss to attract.

(3.) An ability to help in all possible incidents, Heb. vii. 25, "Wherefore he is able also to save them to the uttermost, that come unto God by him, seeing he ever liveth to make intercession for them." The arm of the creature is weak in all cases, and quite too short in many cases; but so is not the arm of an all-sufficient God; Isa. lix. 1, "Behold, the Lord's hand is not shortened, that it cannot save; neither his ear heavy, that it cannot hear." There is nothing too hard for him, there is nothing that Omnipotency can stick at. Who can but draw towards such a one for a Friend?

2. The glory of his free grace and good-will to poor sinners; hence the heavenly host sang; Luke ii. 14, "Glory to God in the highest, and on earth peace, good-will towards men." When the Lord would show Moses his glory, he proclaimed the name of the Lord before him; Exod. xxxiv. 6, 7, "The Lord, the Lord God, merciful and gracious, long-suffering, and abundant in goodness and truth, keeping mercy for thousands, forgiving iniquity, and transgression, and sin." The glory of all-sufficiency may attract the desire of sinners; but the sinner cannot come to him, while that treasure appears to be locked up from him, a gulf fixed betwixt him and it. But when once an all-sufficient God appears in the glory of his free grace in Christ, the treasure appears open to the sinner, there is a bridge for him laid over the gulf; and so he comes freely away to God in Christ. This shines to the coming sinner with a threefold ray of glory.

(1.) Readiness to forgive sin; Psalm cxxx. 4, 7, 8, "But there is forgiveness with thee; that thou mayest be feared. Let Israel hope in the Lord; for with the Lord there is mercy, and with him is plenteous redemption. And he shall redeem Israel from all his iniquities." He is gracious to pardon the sins for which he might justly condemn the sinner; he is willing to be reconciled to offenders, and receive them into peace, 2 Cor. v. 19. This is an attractive glory where the conscience is awakened.

(2.) Willingness to give and communicate all that is needful to make the sinner happy; Rev. xxi. 7, "He that overcometh shall inherit all things, and I will be his God, and he shall be my son." He is gracious to give, as well as to forgive; Hos. xiv. 2; not only to lay by his wrath against the sinner, but to load him with benefits.

(3.) And all this freely, without any view to any worth in the creature, as Isa. lv. 1, "He, every one that thirsteth, come ye to the waters, and he that hath no money; come ye, buy and eat, yea, come, buy wine and milk without money, and without price." No condition, no qualification is required; only the sinner is welcome to take and have, whatever he has been.

II. The next thing is to shew, how this glory of God in Christ is discerned by a sinner.

1. The mean of discerning it is the gospel; 2 Cor. iii. ult., "Beholding as in a glass the glory of the Lord." As by means of light in the air we discern bodily objects, so by the means of the gospel we discern this glory of God, 2 Cor. iv. 4. By the law we discern the glory of an absolute God terrifying and confounding to a sinner, but by the gospel the glory of God as in Christ, attracting and refreshing to a sinner. It is as a looking-glass wherein we see the image of things; 2 Cor. iii. ult. It brings before us the lovely image of a God in Christ reconciling the world to himself.

2. The organ or instrument of discerning it is faith, Hab. ii. 4. Though there be full light in the air, and the looking-glass presenting the beautiful image of a person, be set before one's face, if the man's eyes be out, he cannot discern it. So the glory of God in Christ is held forth unto men in the gospel; but they are spiritually blind who are unbelievers, they perceive it not; 1 Cor. ii. 14, "The natural man receiveth not the things of the Spirit of God; for they are foolishness unto him; neither can he know them, because they are spiritually discerned." But faith sees the glory; John i. 14, "The Word was made flesh, and dwelt among us, (and we beheld his glory, the glory as of the only-begotten of the Father) full of grace and truth."

3. The author of sinners discerning it is the Spirit, 2 Cor. iii. ult. It is he that illuminates the dark mind, that cures sinners of their natural blindness. He works faith in the soul, brings home the gospel-report to the sinner in particular, demonstrating it to be the word of God, and God's word to him in particular, and so makes the soul embrace it by believing it, Isa. liii. 1.

III. The third head is to show what that coming unto God is, that is the effect of discerning that glory. The sinner discerning the glory of God in Christ as the hearer of prayer,

1. He comes away from all other doors, which before he used to hang about for supply. He despairs at length of coming speed there, Jer. iii. 22, 23, "Return ye backsliding children, and I will heal your backslidings; behold, we come unto thee, for thou art the Lord our God. Truly in vain is salvation hoped for from the hills, and from the multitude of mountains; truly in the Lord our God is the salvation of Israel." The light of the glory of God shining into his heart, discovers the emptiness of all the poor shifts the sinner makes to get supply in his natural state of blindness.

(1.) He comes away from the door of the empty creation, where he had long laboured to find a rest; and despairs of finding it there any more. The profits, pleasures, comforts, and conveniences of this world, appear lying vanities that can never give rest to the heart; and they must have another portion; Jer. xvi. 19, "O Lord, my strength and my fortress, and my refuge in the day of affliction, the Gentiles shall come unto thee from the ends of the earth, and shall say, Surely our fathers have inherited lies, vanity, and things wherein there is no profit."

(2.) From the door of sin, where he expected a satisfaction in the fulfilling of his lusts; and he despairs of ever finding it there, Job xxxiii. 27. He finds that puddle-water will not quench his thirst, that the pleasure of it is but short, but the pain and sting of it lasting.

(3.) From out of the world lying in wickedness, 2 Cor. vi. 17, as he would escape away from lions' dens and mountains of leopards, Cant. iv. 8. He despairs of ever finding his account in the way of the world.

2. He comes away unto God in Christ, for all, and instead of all; Jer. iii. 22, "Behold, we come unto thee, for thou art the Lord our God." And he comes unto him,

(1.) As a Saviour, that will save his submissive supplicants, Jer. iii. 22, 23. Faith apprehends him as God our Saviour, and so comes to him and trusts on him for salvation from sin and from wrath, Matth. i. 21, "Thou shalt call his name Jesus; for he shall save his people from their sins."

(2.) As a portion, that will eternally make up impoverished and ruined creatures, Psalm cxlii. 5, and in which the poor petitioner may find what he has so long sought for in vain, in the world and the way of sin.

(3.) As his resort for ever in all his needs, whatever they shall be, Psalm lxxi. 3. The soul coming unto God, comes to him as one that will never go back to another, but will hang on about his door, though he should die at it.

I conclude with an inference or two.

1. Whoso come not unto God in Christ, as a Saviour, &c., are certainly ignorant of him, and see him not in his glory; "For they that know thy name," says the psalmist, "will put their trust in thee," Psalm ix. 10.

2. Great and powerful must that glory be, which draws sinners from all other doors unto God. By nature we are backward to come unto God; it must be a very ravishing glory that has such an effect on perverse sinners.

3. *Lastly,* Be concerned to discern that glory; to discern it by faith, and by experience, in order to your coming to him as your Saviour, portion, and continual resort.

V. On Acceptance with God: The Doctrine of the Acceptance of Men's Works Explained, and a Practical Regard thereto in all the Duties of Life Inculcated[17]

For if there be first a willing mind, it is accepted according to that a man hath, and not according to that he hath not.
2 Corinthians viii. 12

The Christians in Judea being in much distress and poverty, there was a contribution through the churches of the Gentiles for them. The communion of saints extends not only to spiritual, but temporal things too; that they be ready to help one another out of their substance. And this communication of worldly things to the supply of the saints, is not confined to those of our own church; but is to be extended to strangers on occasion, at the greatest distance. The gospel came from Judea to the Gentiles; and now money must go from the Gentiles for the relief of those of Judea. Hereby God took a trial of the Gentile churches, their love to, and esteem of, the gospel. Many will pretend to great esteem of the gospel, but they must have it for nothing. Any of their money that is desired for any public use, for the furtherance of the gospel, it is all accounted lost.

This contribution is here recommended to the Corinthians. They readily fell in with the proposal, ver. 11. Now they are desired to perform, each according to his ability.

---

17 The substance of several sermons preached at Etterick in the year 1726.

In the text, an objection of the poorer sort is answered, who might fear that any thing they had to give was so little, that it would not be accepted. In answer thereto, they are told that God regards men's works rather by the quality than the quantity; by the mind it is given with, rather than by the thing given.

1. The case of acceptance is put, "If there be first a willing mind, it is accepted." The acceptance here is of a man's work, not of his person; though the former always presupposeth the latter, in the gospel way. And it refers to God, for he only can judge with what mind a thing is done. Now God accepts a man's service, if there be first a willing mind; that is, a readiness and good will to the work of his service. If the heart go before and lead the hand, it is accepted; otherwise it is not.

2. What regard is had in this acceptance of one's work to the quantity of it. (1.) That it be according to one's ability, that it be done to his power. Some are able to do more, and be more useful than others; but if men have a willingness to the work, and do what they are able accordingly, it is accepted through Christ; his that can do but little, as well as his that can do much. But this cuts off the pretences of those who content themselves with lazy wishes, and lay not out themselves to do what they may do. (2.) That want of power to do more, shall not mar the acceptance of what is done according to power with a willing mind, Mark xii. 43. The Lord will take the little piece of service off his people's hand, when the heart is right; as well as the great service of those of his that have great abilities. Not but that where the inability is brought on by people's own fault, it is their sin that they do not do more; but that sin shall be forgiven them, and what they do be accepted, "if there be first a willing mind."

The scope and substance of the text may be taken up in the following doctrines.

DOCTRINE I. Works may be done in service to God, that are not accepted of him.

DOCTRINE II. It should be our main concern in our works, that they may be accepted of God.

DOCTRINE III. Where there is a willing mind carrying out a man to do and serve the Lord to his ability, what is so done is accepted of God.

DOCTRINE IV. Want of power to do more, shall not mar the acceptance of what is done from a willing mind according to one's power. In that case, God will accept of his people's will for the deed.

I shall speak to each of these doctrines in order.

DOCTRINE I. Works may be done in service to God, that are not accepted of him.

In treating this point, I shall,
I. Confirm the doctrine.
II. Assign the reasons thereof.
III. Make some improvement.

1. In order to confirm the doctrine, consider,

1. Oft-times God hides his face from the man and his work too, and people have no communion with God in their services to him; Hos. v. 6, "They shall go with their flocks and with their herds to seek the Lord; but they shall not find him, he hath withdrawn himself from them." When a master will not look on his servant's work, it is an evidence he is not pleased with him, nor it, Isa. i. 15. This may be the case of the godly sometimes, and it is the case of the wicked always. O how many lost services are there this way.

2. Such services may be so far from being accepted, that they are really loathsome to a holy God; Prov. xv. 8, "The sacrifice of the wicked is an abomination to the Lord." He reckons them to be to no purpose, he is full of them, they are vain in his esteem, he cannot endure them, they are a trouble, a burden, and a weariness to him, Isa. i. 11–14. So it is often fulfilled in this case, "That which is highly esteemed amongst men, is abomination in the sight of God," Luke xvi. 15. The man thinks highly of his own work, and others do so too; but in the mean time God abhors it.

3. God may put such services out of the roll of services to him, and set them down in the roll of sins against him. That is a terrible word, Jer. vii. 21, "Thus saith the Lord of hosts, the God of Israel, put your burnt-offerings unto your sacrifices, and eat flesh"; *i.e.*, Put your sacrifices that should be all burnt on the altar, to your other sacrifices, and eat all together as common flesh to fill your bellies; *q.d.*, Let your prayers, and your common discourse, your hearing of sermons and your idle tales go together; I esteem the one no more than the other. And that is another dreadful word; Amos iv. 4, "Come to Bethel and transgress, at Gilgal multiply transgression; and bring your sacrifices every morning, and your tithes after three years"; *q.d.*, Go to your knees now, and take the name of God in vain; go to the church, and put off a little time of a Sabbath day.

4. They may bring a curse and a stroke on men, instead of a blessing and token of God's favour; Hos. viii. 13, "They sacrifice flesh for the sacrifices of mine offerings, and eat it; but the Lord accepteth them not; now will he remember their iniquity and visit their sins." Nadab and Abihu were consumed by a fire that came out from the altar they were serving at; Ananias and Sapphira were struck dead on occasion of selling their land for the service of the church; and men may be smothered with the dung of their sacrifices spread on their faces, Mal. ii. 3.

5. *Lastly*, This may take place while the service stands the man both cost and pains. The Israelites were at cost for spices for the altar, but all was rejected, Jer. vi. 20; they were at pains in attending ordinances, and endured a stress in fasting, but all to no purpose, Isa. lviii. 2, 3. Bodily exercise profiteth little before God, who is a Spirit, and must be worshipped in spirit and in truth.

II. I am next to render the reasons of the point, That works may be done in service to God, that are not accepted of him. God is no austere master, but very indulgent to his servants, and will take a very small service kindly off their hands; but men often serve him in a way that is provoking to him, and to his dishonour; and thence are the reasons why their services are not accepted.

1. Sometimes that is offered for service to God, that is forbidden by him, John xvi. 2, "They shall put you out of the synagogues: yea, the time cometh, that whosoever killeth you will think that he doth God service." A blinded conscience gets the leading of a man, and leads him out of the way of God; it dictates what is sin to be duty, and what is duty to be sin; so that the man thinks he is serving God, while he is really serving his own corruptions; and so instead of a "Well done, good and faithful servant," he meets with a "Wo unto them that call evil good, and good evil; that put darkness for light, and light for darkness," Isa. v. 20; and "lies down" at length "in sorrow," Isa. l. ult.

2. Sometimes that is offered that is not commanded or required; Matth. xv. 9, "In vain they do worship me, teaching for doctrines the commandments of men." Nothing can be acceptable to God, but what is required by some one or other command of his; "for whatsoever is not of faith, is sin," Rom. xiv. ult. See Isa. i. 12. Horrid idolatry is condemned on that very ground, that it was uncommanded service, Jer. vii. 31. It is an affront to the sovereignty of God, and his mastership,

for men to order his service according to the devices of their own hearts, and not to keep precisely to his orders. Hence are the superstitions of Popery, and the uninstituted ceremonies of the Church of England, which are the product of human device, without any countenance from the word of God.

3. Ofttimes, though the work be commanded of God, yet it is marred in the making. There is something about the person, or the work, that ruins all.

1st, About the person, that mars the acceptance. As,

(1.) He may be in a state of separation from Christ, not united to him by faith, and so not accepted of God, John xv. 5. No acceptable work can be done by any man while he is out of Christ; Eph. ii. 10. For a man's person must be accepted, before his work can be accepted, since his work being imperfect, cannot procure the acceptance of his person. Now no sinner's person is accepted but in Christ, Eph. i. 6, and we come to be in Christ by faith; therefore faith in Christ must go before acceptable obedience, Heb. xi. 6. Faith makes the tree good, ere it can bring forth good fruit, Matth. vii. 17. And no fruit of obedience is accepted of God, but what grows on a branch of Christ the true vine. The blasting curse lies on all other. See Gen. vi. 9.

(2.) He may be in a state of enmity with God; and as no man will like the services of his enemies, so God will not accept the services of one not reconciled to him; Amos iii. 3, "Can two walk together, except they be agreed?" Every unbeliever is an enemy to God, Rom. viii. 7, for his sin remains unpardoned, and his nature unchanged; and therefore his best works are but splendid sins, himself but a whited sepulchre; and when he speaks and acts fairest, there are seven abominations in his heart. How then can an all-seeing God accept such services?

(3.) He may be an unregenerate man, and so like Simon "in the gall of bitterness, and in the bond of iniquity," Acts viii. 23. Whosoever are out of Christ, are unregenerate; for it is by being in him, and so partaking of his Spirit and fulness, that we become new creatures, 2 Cor. v. 17; Eph. i. 13. Now how can the corrupt tree bring forth good fruit? or the old nature acceptable obedience? If the fountain be poisoned, can the streams be wholesome? Could one like the best liquor in a vessel wherein there is no pleasure?

(4.) He may be habitually unholy or profane in his life, or as to the body of his conversation; Prov. xxviii. 9, "He that turneth away his ear from hearing the law, even his prayer shall be abomination." So the Lord rejects the sacrifices of the Israelites, Isa. i. 15, 16 The Psalmist tells us, that "the man who shall ascend into the hill of the Lord, and stand in his holy place," must "have clean hands, and a pure heart," Psalm xxiv. 3, 4. The apostle wills to "lift up holy hands, without wrath and doubting"; 1 Tim. ii. 8, if we would be accepted. Their conversation must be of a piece, whose works will be accepted; for God will never accept the services of men, that for the most part serve the devil, the world, and their lusts. Many are like the harlot; Prov. vii. 13, 14, as if they thought their duties would purge away their sins. Nay but their sinful courses otherwise will pollute and render abominable their duties, Hag. ii. 11–14.

2*dly*, About the work, that may mar its acceptance.

(1.) It may be none of the work of the Spirit of Christ in the man, but proceeding from a man's self allenarly. All good works accepted of God are the product of the Holy Spirit in believers, as the sap which the vine-stock communicates to the branches. Therefore to "the works of the flesh"; Gal. v. 19, are opposed "the fruits of the Spirit"; ver. 22. And "all goodness is the fruit of the Spirit"; Eph. v. 9, and a Christian's life is "a walking after the Spirit"; Rom. viii. 1, as a borrowed life. And as no common hearth-fire could be accepted at the altar, but only the holy fire that came from heaven; so no work will be offered to the Father for acceptance by the Son, but what is the work of his own Spirit; and no work will be accepted by the Father, but what is offered by the Son as intercessor. See Eph. ii. 18. See what prayer is accepted, Jam. v. 16. Not the prayer of every one, but of a "righteous man"; not every prayer of a righteous man neither, but "the inwrought" (*Gr.*) "prayer" of his, viz. that which is inwrought by the Spirit.

(2) It may be no work of love to God, or of a willing mind; but done awkwardly and against the grain; 1 Tim. i. 5; some bye-considerations moving the man to serve the Lord; and no liking of him or his service. Forced service can never be accepted, that which people are constrained to. It is the obedience of slaves, not of sons, that natural men do perform; and flows from a spirit of fear, more than a spirit of love; 2 Tim. i. 7. See Isa. lxiv. 5.

(3.) It may be not done in faith, and so cannot be accepted; Heb. xi. 6. Acceptable service is done in the faith of the command, having authority on the man's conscience; and in the faith of the promise, the promise of strength to perform, and the faith of the reward of grace, believing the labour shall not be in vain in the Lord, 1 Cor. xv. ult. But instead of that, most of our good works are done without any regard to God's authority, without any dependence on him for strength, and without the true hope of the gratuitous reward of grace won by Christ to be communicated to us.

(4.) It may be done selfishly; men seeking their own profit in them, more than God's honour; seeking to please their own conscience that otherwise will not let them rest, rather than to please God; seeking a name to themselves, rather than to glorify his name; and to save their own souls from hell by them, rather than to testify their thankfulness to the Saviour, who has purchased salvation by his blood. This is to pervert the end of duties, to use them for unhallowed ends; in a word, to serve ourselves, and not God; and therefore no more to be accepted than a servant's working his own instead of his master's work, Hos. ix. 4; Zech. vii. 6. Yea good things may be done downright to serve a lust, or to satisfy a passion, Matth. xxiii. 14; 2 Sam. iii. 9.

(5.) It may be done by chance rather than design; Lev. xxvi. 21; (*Heb.*) There are who are chance-customers to religion, who fall in with a good work, rather because it falls in their way, than because God lays it in their way; as the Danites, Judg. xviii. 5. God looks to the heart, and undesigned service to him will be reckoned no serving of him, but serving one's own fancy. This is another thing than one's embracing an opportunity which the Lord puts in his hand; Gal. vi. 10, wherein one is glad of an occasion of serving God.

(6.) It may be done by the power of custom, rather than of conscience. Custom, fallen into by education, or otherwise, is the spring of many duties done by men; wherein men move, by that, as a clock by the weights; rather than from an inward principle; which can never be acceptable to the heart-searching God, who requires reasonable service.

(7.) It may be done in a slighting manner, dealing scrimply and grudgingly with God. As when there is no proportion between the work and one's ability, as in the rich men casting in their little piece of brass-money, Mark xii. 41; when men offer to God, not the best, but the most worthless they have; so did Cain, Gen. iv. 3, 4. Thus men by thinking any thing may serve in the service of God, pour contempt on the holy One, and bring on themselves a curse instead of a blessing; Mal. i. 14.

(8) *Lastly*, When it is not offered to God for acceptance through Christ. It is God's appointment; Col. iii. 17, "What-

soever ye do in word or deed, do all in the name of the Lord Jesus." A young pigeon would have been accepted on the altar of Jerusalem, when a bullock would not have been accepted on the altar of Bethel. If the service of men be never so great and costly, if it is offered to God otherwise, and the acceptance of it looked for because of its own worth, it will be rejected, Rev. vii. 14. No works savour with God, but as they savour of Christ, 2 Cor. ii. 15.

I now proceed to make some short improvement of what has been said,

1. People may do much in the service of God, and yet do nothing to purpose, Eccl. x. 15. A man may go many a weary foot, and yet never come to the place he designed, while he wanders from the right way, 2 John 8. Such wanderers in religion are all unregenerate men, who set about duties; they are busy doing nothing. They do many good things like Herod, and yet they never do one thing acceptably. For their persons are not accepted; and so their works cannot be so.

2. Even among the duties of a godly man, there may be much refuse; many unaccepted duties. A believer's person is always accepted of God, Eph. i. 6, for the state of justification is perpetual. But such may be the prevalence of faithlessness, selfishness, &c., in some particular works of his, that they may never come to be accepted of God; for sanctification has its ups and downs, being liable to many changes.

3. How little reason is there to boast of our works! There is nothing we can do, can be accepted for its own worth. If it be accepted, the meanness of it is seen, the soul is humbled, and no acceptance of is looked for, but for the sake of Christ. If we be so conceited of our work, as to boast of it; it is an evidence that God accepts it not; hence said our Lord unto the Pharisees, Luke xvi. 15, "Ye are they which justify yourselves before men; but God knoweth your hearts; for that which is highly esteemed amongst men, is abomination in the sight of God."

4. What will come of them that do nothing in the service of God at all; but live in the habitual neglect of known duties, are prayerless, slighters of the means of grace, &c.? 1 Pet. iv. 18. If they that set off to the heavenly city may miss the way, and never reach it; sure those that sit still, and never move that way, will never see it. Many soothe themselves in the neglect of duties, because some that do them walk so unlike them; but the case of such is very dangerous; for no habitual

neglecters of duties can be saved; and it is in vain for men to make the practice of others an excuse for evil doing.

5. *Lastly*, Take heed how ye perform duties, and satisfy not yourselves with the bare performance, without being solicitous as to the manner, Luke viii. 18. Better is one duty so managed as to be accepted than a hundred otherwise; as one piece of gold is more worth than a hundred counters. But this brings me to

DOCTRINE II. It should be our main concern in our works that they may be accepted of God.

In handling this point, I shall
I. Show what is the acceptance of our works with God.
II. Give the reasons of the doctrine.
III. Make improvement.

I. I shall show what is the acceptance of our works with God. It lies in these two things.

1. His being pleased with them; Col. i. 10, "That ye might walk worthy of the Lord unto all pleasing." The accepted work God approves of, and is well pleased with. Though the saints do no works that they are every way pleased with themselves; yet there are some works of theirs that are very pleasing to God. He delights in them, Prov. xv. 8. They are sweet to him, as honey to the mouth, Cant. v. 1. They are sweet as music to the ear, and as beauty to the eye, Cant. ii. 14.

This pre-supposeth them to be good, and agreeable to his will. For evil cannot be pleasing to him, Psalm v. 4. He who is goodness itself, can never be pleased but with what is good, Heb. xiii. 16. The unregenerate do nothing good, Psalm xiv. 2, 3, and so nothing they do is accepted, Heb. xi. 6. The saints do some things good, some things evil; the good is accepted, and the refuse is cast away.

2. His taking them off their hand, as service done to him. God testified his acceptance of the sacrifice by fire, Lev. ix. ult. for the fire made them go up in flames towards heaven, Judg. xiii. 20. See Psalm xx. 3, Gen. iv. 4, 5. So he received them off their hand. He reckons such a work a piece of service done to him, sets it down as it were in his book, in due time to give it a reward of grace, Lev. vii. 18, Mal. iii. 16.

Hence is the after-notice God takes of the good works of his people;—in time, as it fared with Moses, who, refusing to be called the son of Pharaoh's daughter, was afterwards advanced to be king in Jeshurun;—in eternity, as Matth. xxv. He will not forget any of them, Heb. vi. 10, but a plentiful sowing of them will have a plentiful reaping. So they are the surest riches, 1 Tim. vi. 18. Not that the reward is given for their sake, but for Christ's sake; and such is the covenant connection.

QUESTION. How can any of our works be accepted of a holy God, or he be well pleased with them, &c., since there is so much sinfulness attending the best of them?

ANSWER 1. In point of justification they are not, nor cannot be accepted; *i. e.* our persons cannot be accepted as righteous for our works, since they are not legally perfect, perfect in every point. In the way of the covenant of works, the work was first to be accepted for its own sake, as absolutely perfect; and then the person for the works' sake. So that whosoever seek by their works to be accepted of God, they go back to the covenant of works; and must either bring works every way perfect, or be rejected; and because they cannot do such works, "therefore by the works of the law shall no flesh be justified," Gal. ii. 16.

2. In point of sanctification the good works of the justified may be accepted; *i. e.* one's person being accepted, his works may be accepted, being evangelically perfect, though not legally; being perfect in parts, though not in degrees. For in the way of the covenant of grace, the person is first accepted in Christ, and then his work though imperfect. Hence it appears,

(1.) That to a person's being accepted of God in Christ, there is no working, but believing required; Mark v. 36. For till the person be accepted of God in Christ, he can do no acceptable work. He can yield no savoury fruit till he be ingrafted by faith in Christ.

(2.) That the way to bring sinners to good works, is to bring them to Christ in the first place by faith, that they may be justified and accepted in him. Men may be made proud legalists otherwise, but not evangelical Christians; whited sepulchres, but still full of rottenness.

(3.) That there is very good reason why the good works of unbelievers are rejected, because they are imperfect; and yet the good works of believers are accepted, though they be imperfect. For besides that the principle, motives, and ends of their works are vastly different, there is a great odds between,

[1.] Their states. The one is the King's friend, the other an enemy; the one the King's son, the other but his hired servant. If a man is pleased with a little piece of service that his own child does him, can the hired servant expect that as little will be taken off his hand? Can our enemy expect the same acceptance of his service, as our friend?

[2.] The desired acceptance. The unbeliever desires his work may be accepted for his salvation; but the believer desires his work may be accepted as only a token of his gratitude to his Saviour, who has saved him already. Can any man rationally think, that as little can be accepted at his hand, for the price of salvation, as may be accepted for an acknowledgment of salvation received?

But further to clear this question, consider,

1. Even the acceptance in point of sanctification, is not for the sake of the work itself, nor for the worker's sake neither; but for Christ's sake, and by the means of his intercession. This is clear from the necessity of Christ's intercession to the acceptance of our works; and that intercession being a pleading of the merit of his own obedience and death; Col. iii. 17; Rev. vii. 14, and viii. 3. It is for the same merit of Christ, that first the believer himself, and then his imperfect works are accepted of God.

2. The sinfulness and imperfections that attend the works of the believer, are not, nor cannot be ever accepted. God is displeased and angry with the dross of sin that cleaves to the believer's best performances; and he never is so well pleased with the good in them, as to accept the ill too. Yea, he may write his indignation against these, when he is pleased with the substance of the work.

3. The main of the accepted work is good, however sinfulness attends it. For the matter of it, it is commanded; for the form of it, it proceeds from a right principle, the love of God; it is done in faith, and to the glory of God. And this is the work of God's own Spirit in the believer; the weaknesses that attend it, proceed from the believer himself. And such works as are good in the main, God will not reject, for the infirmities that attend them. As for those works even of believers that are not thus good in the main, they are not at all accepted.

4. Christ separates the precious from the vile part, and offers the former perfumed with his merit, unto the Father for acceptance, Heb. x. 21, 22; Rev. viii. 3. In every sacrifice there were two very different things, the flesh and the skin and dung. The former came to the altar, the latter never. So Christ separates in a believer's duties that which is from his own Spirit, and that which is from the believer himself puts away this, and presents that to his Father. This was lively represented in the burning of the incense, where the fire being

set to it, the finer part went up in flame and smoke, towards heaven; and the gross part, the ashes, remained, and a priest came and carried them away in a golden dish. So is the case here,—the finer part in the saints' services, that which is done by the assistance of the Spirit and in faith, ascends to heaven for acceptance; and the ashes that remain are carried away, in virtue of the free promise, Ezek. xxxvi. 25.

5. *Lastly*, The Father then accepts the precious part for the Son's sake, and for the same sake pardons the guilt of the vile part, the infirmities attending it, Rev. viii. 4; Psalm cxli. 2. The accepted duties go through two hands, first the believer's, then Christ's; their prayers are first said on earth by themselves, then they are repeated in heaven by the Mediator. It is from the second hand only, and on the repetition only, that they are accepted, 1 Kings viii. 32; and in the second hand, and on the repetition, they are not so bulky, but better.

II. I shall next give the reasons of the point, That it should be our main concern in our works that they may be accepted of God. Because,

1. As God is the first cause, so he is the chief end of all things; Rom. xi. ult., "For of him, and through him, and to him are all things." So as we are his creatures, our chief end in all our duties should be to please him; as all the waters coming from the sea do return to it again. This was the duty of Adam in the covenant of works, as sure as he was not to have another God, as in the first command; though he was to gain life by his works, which we are not, and therefore it is surely ours much more.

2. Our duties are a matter of gratitude; we owe them to God, not only in point of justice, but thankfulness, for benefits received, creation, preservation, and redemption; Exod. xx. 2, "I am the Lord thy God, which have brought thee out of the land of Egypt, out of the house bondage." We are in debt to him, and we cannot pay, but only acknowledge by small tokens, Hos. xiv. 2. If we are to offer to a fellow creature a token of our obligation to him, the first question is, What is it that I can give that will be most acceptable to him? How much more should the first question be, What is it that I can give that will be most acceptable to God?

3. God looks mainly to the heart with which a duty is done, and knows whether he gets it or not, 1 Chron. xxviii. 9. Though a servant do well, yet if he hath no regard to his master's pleasure in what he does, it is disobliging; and whatever men do, if it is not their main aim to please God, it is provok-

ing. Our aims may be hid from men; but they are as open to God as our overt actions.

4. *Lastly*, It is a necessary ingredient in a good work, so that a work cannot be good without it, 1 Cor. x. 31. For such a work is pointed wrong as to the end of it, Zech. vii. 5. It is a sacrifice wanting the heart, the thing that God mainly requires and delights in, Prov. xxiii. 26. So whatever we may account it, God will not account it a good work.

I come now to the practical improvement of this doctrine, which I shall discuss in a twofold use, viz., of conviction, and of exhortation.

USE I. This doctrine may serve for conviction, humiliation, and reproof to men, who generally are strangers to it, and at best very defective in it. It may convict men,

1. In point of ill works. These are fruitful in the world, things that are altogether evil, and cannot be good, Gal. v. 19. In the midst of gospel-light they overflow, and there is no true repentance for them, because there is no reformation. To such workers I would say,

(1.) How far are ye from regarding at all God's acceptance of your works, who take the liberty to do against the letter of his law, what ye know his soul abhors? The drunkard, swearer, sabbath-breaker, or unclean person, is not so abandoned as to think that these his actions can please God. But the truth is, the pleasing of God is what he is not anxious about, but he is resolved to please himself in his lust, let his Maker take it as he will. What must be the end of these things? Rom. i. 18, "For the wrath of God is revealed from heaven against all ungodliness, and unrighteousness of men, who hold the truth in unrighteousness."

(2.) Ye thereby evidence, that it is not the pleasing of God, but yourselves, that ye seek in your good works; and that therefore your ill works and your good works will all go one way, being rejected of God; your swearing and your praying, &c. will be reckoned all one. If it were your main design in one thing to please God, it would be so in all, Jam. ii. 10, 11; and therefore since ye do not endeavour to please him in all, know that ye can please him in nothing; Psalm cxxv. ult., "As for such as turn aside unto their crooked ways, the Lord shall lead them forth with the workers of iniquity."

2. In point of good works, namely, those that for the matter of them are good, wherein men may be accepted of God, if they rightly manage them. These are of three sorts:—

1st, Natural good works, such as eating and drinking, sleeping, &c. I call them good works, because they are commanded of God, are necessary to be done, and it would be sin to omit them. They are duties of the sixth command, the neglect whereof is sinful, Col. ii. ult., and one may be accepted of God in them, Rom. xiv. 3, or rejected of him, Zech. vii. 6. Bring these works of ours to this rule, That it should be our main concern in our works, that they may be accepted of God; and how may we stand convicted of,

(1.) Regardlessness of God's approbation and acceptance in these things; having no eye to God in them, but going about them as men without God in the world, or as beasts, Matth. xxiv. 38, without any regard to God's command requiring our use of them, dependence on God for the benefit of them, or design to be strengthened by them for serving God in the duties of religion and our particular calling.

(2.) Dishonouring of God in them. In the way of purchasing them, many an ill shift is made for the belly; and if men can get it, to satisfy the appetite, they are not anxious about their right to it before God, whether it be with a good conscience their own bread, got with honest labour and industry, 2 Thess. iii. 12; or whether doing their utmost with their industry, they have a right to it as charitable supply. In the way of using them, without conscientious moderation, by gluttony or drunkenness; a sinful eagerness to satisfy a lust for them; and unfitting themselves for the service of God by them.

It is but a little the time of eating and drinking will last; there is an eternity to be spent without them. If we endeavour to be accepted of God in them while they last, it will be our comfort when we shall for ever lay them aside; if not, the regardlessness and dishonouring of God in them, will be an eternal sting in the conscience.

2dly, Civil good works, which are the duties of men's station, in the common affairs of this life; such as the management of family affairs, the duties of service, of a man's lawful trade or employment. These are good works on the matter, being commanded of God, and in which one is to walk with God, 1 Cor. vii. 24; and therein one may be accepted, Eccl. ix. 7, or rejected, Prov. xxi. 4. Here again men may be convicted of,

(1.) Regardlessness of God's acceptance, Luke xvii. 28. These things mostly are managed without any eye to God, or to be accepted of him in them. His command and call by his providence unto them is not waited for; or if men have it, yet they do not regard it, to go about their business under a sense of God's command, Eph. vi. 7. The Lord is not looked to for direction, but men trust themselves for conduct in these matters, Prov. iii. 5, 6. He is not depended on for success, but men are either flushed with presumptuous confidence, or tormenting anxiety as to events, Psalm cxxvii. 1. And not God's word is the rule they act by in them, but their own worldly interest or ease.

(2.) Dishonouring God in them. As by pride, passion, and selfishness, which are to be found in people's managing of their family affairs; if they get their business done, there is no concern how their families should serve the Lord. He is dishonoured by the unfaithfulness, dishonesty, eye-service, and perverseness of servants; and dishonoured by the lying, cheating, and injustice used by men in their dealings in their several employments.

These things are but time things either; and all the hurry of worldly business will be hushed ere long; and death will draw the busiest man out of the throng, as clean as if he had never been in it, Eccl. ix. 6. It will be your interest to seek to be accepted of God in them; otherwise ye will lay up bitterness from them, that will be lasting when they are gone for ever.

3*dly*, Religious good works, the duties whether of the first or second table, which are duties of our Christian calling, such as prayer, giving alms, &c. In them also men may here be convicted of,

(1.) Regardlessness of God's acceptance in them. Men proclaim this by their rash approaching to them, without considering what they are to be about, Eccl. v. 1; by their formality in them, satisfying themselves with the doing of the thing, without any anxiety to get their hearts up to the duty, to do it in a right manner, which is mere bodily exercise, 1 Tim. iv. 8; and their carelessness after them, unconcernedness as to their success, when once the task is off their hand, Psalm v. 3.

(2.) Making other things our main concern in them: As, [1.] A name for religion, Matth. vi. 2. An unholy heart, that is an enemy to religion at bottom, may be very fond of a name for it. And to advance this empty name, many times good gifts are prostituted, and enlargements in duty, and great performances for God; all of them running in that channel of ambition, to be highly esteemed of men as religious. [2.] Some worldly interest, John vi. 26, 27. So it was with Jehu. They will please men for their carnal interest, and do religious duties to please men. Often doth the fear of men go deeper here than the fear of God; and the loss of some worldly interest deeper than the loss of the soul. [3.] Peace in their own minds. There is a conscience within men that will drive to duty, when there is no love to God drawing; so men by such duties rather seek to please themselves than to please God. And, (1.) To keep conscience quiet, while it is quiet; so duties are made a bribe to cause conscience hold its tongue. And certain it is, that many could not live so quietly in their sins as they do, were it not for their duties, as appears from the case of the adulterous whore, Prov. vii. 14, 15. This is the reason that publicans and harlots enter into the kingdom of heaven before Pharisees; and Laodicea's case was the most hopeless of all the seven churches. (2.) To still it again when it is roused, Psalm lxxviii. 34. Men may be very anxious for comfort by duty, that have no concern for sanctification thereby. [4.] Salvation from hell and wrath, Matth. xix. 16–20. One may follow duties on this account, without any love to God, as appears ver. 22, "But when the young man heard that saying, he went away sorrowful: for he had great possessions." Self is a strong motive, and heaven and hell are strong arguments for duty; but the misery is, they seek not God for himself, but for themselves, and so are rejected, 2 Tim. i. 7.

In these duties we are now on our trials for heaven; in a little the sentence will be passed, according to our works. And those who are not now accepted of God in their duties, will then be rejected of God for ever.

Use II. Let it be your main concern in your works, that they may be accepted of God; whether they be natural, civil, or religious. For motives, consider,

1. This is a distinguishing character of one's state, whereby ye will prove yourselves either gracious or graceless. It is a native result of justification and acceptance of one's person with God, to be mainly concerned for God's acceptance of them in their work, 2 Cor. v. 9. So Noah's integrity and uprightness is traced to his justification as the source, Gen. vi. 9. For so the love of Christ constrains. Whereas the soul being in a state of enmity with God, natively issues in no concern to please him.

2. God is a great God and King, infinitely above the greatest on earth; he cannot be profited by our services, but requires us to labour to please him in them, Mal. i. 14. He gave us our being, and hath put each of us in our station, and carved out our work for us; whence it necessarily follows,

that it should be our main concern to please him, 2 Tim. ii. 4. And would men more narrowly consider this, that it is God that has set them their business and station, and consequently, that he will call for the account of our work, it would stir them up to make it their main care in their works, that they may be accepted of him.

3. There is a costly provision of an altar on which our sacrifices of praise may be accepted, Heb. xiii. 10, 15. There was nothing a sinner could have done, that could have been accepted, had there not been an altar to sanctify the gift. Now it is provided, a crucified Christ is that altar; he by his death has become a proper intercessor for acceptance, both of our persons and our works. How heinous will our sin be, if we seek not to bring our gift to this altar, for acceptance with God?

4. Whatever good work, natural, civil, or religious, we do, may be accepted of God, as pleasing service to him through Christ, Heb. xiii. 15, 16. Men are hugely mistaken to think that it is only works strictly called religious, that God accepts as service to him; nay, whatever God calls for at thy hand, as to tend the sheep, as well as to attend his worship, if thou act in it to please him, and offer it to him for acceptance through Christ, it will be accepted, Col. iii. 23, 24. It is observable, that the apostle having given that general direction, ver. 17, "Whatsoever ye do in word or deed, do all in the name of the Lord Jesus," &c. falls immediately on relative duties, ver. 18, "Wives, submit yourselves unto your own husbands," &c.

5. The example of Christ may be very moving here, Rom. xv. 3, "For even Christ pleased not himself." His work was heavy work, but to please his Father he undertook it, set about it, and went through with it, John viii. 29, Psalm xl. and John iv. 34. And shall not we be concerned to please him in our imperfect works, to please whom Christ laid down his life?

6. If ye be mainly concerned for acceptance with God in your work, ye may expect help from the Lord in it. The waters and rivers run all to the sea, and so they are fed again by the sea, that they never run dry. That work that has God's pleasure for its end will get God's hand to it for its help, Phil. ii. 12, 13, Prov. iii. 6. The man that slights God in his natural and civil actions, provokes God to leave him in them, Josh. ix. 14, and then his own understanding that he leaned to, proves folly. And he that slights God in his religions duties does the same, and his gifts prove a broken reed.

7. Whatever be the success of your work, ye will have solid peace, satisfaction, and comfort, in your having been

mainly concerned in your works for God's acceptance, Isa. xlix. 4. Men are great fools, to promise themselves success on their own wise management of their natural and civil actions. It has been a truth from the beginning, and will be to the end of the world, that "the race is not to the swift, nor the battle to the strong, neither yet bread to the wise, nor yet riches to men of understanding, nor yet favour to men of skill," Eccl. ix. 11. And it is equally foolish to expect the world's thanks for doing them a good turn; for ye will be fair to be disappointed, 2 Tim. iii. 1, 2, and look blunt on the disappointment. Nay, such an ill-natured world it is, that it is one to a thousand if they be not heavy on you for it. For, says Solomon, Eccl. iv. 4, "I considered all travel, and every right work, that for this a man is envied of his neighbour." But when this is one's main concern, he has what he looked for; 2 Cor. i. 12, "For our rejoicing is this, the testimony of our conscience, that in simplicity and godly sincerity, not with fleshly wisdom, but by the grace of God, we have had our conversation in the world, and more abundantly to you-wards."

8. If ye do not thus, your works will be lost; lost with God, and lost for eternity; and if that be, all that ye will find of them in the world, will be little worth, Matth. vi. 2. This is our sowing time, good works are the seed; will it not be sad to lose all, so as in the harvest ye have nothing to reap? So it will be, if in this your sowing time ye do not throw in the seeds of good works, and make it your principal concern to look for acceptance with God in them; all ye do will be lost for ever, ye will have nothing to reap in the harvest at the last day.

9. *Lastly*, If ye do not, your best works will be turned to sin, Prov. xv. 8, and ye will be surprised to find so many actions of yours that ye set down in the roll of good works, appear in God's book in the roll of sins; as cockle instead of barley. There is such a thing, Psalm cix. 7, "Let his prayer become sin."

For direction in this point, we proceed to

DOCTRINE III. Where there is a willing mind carrying out a man to do and serve the Lord, to his ability, what is so done is accepted of God.

Here I shall shew,

I. What sort of works they are that are accepted of God.
II. How or in what respect they are accepted.
III. Why they are so.

IV. *Lastly*, Apply.

I. I am to show what sort of works they are that are accepted of God.

FIRST, They are works done with a willing mind. Wherein we are to consider,

1. What this willingness relates to.
2. What it is.

First, Let us consider what this willingness relates to. This willingness of the soul respects the will of God, as that which the soul is willing to comply with. The will of God is contained in his commands, summed up in a word, 1 Thess. iv. 3, "This is the will of God, even your sanctification"; and it is the duty of all of us to be willing to that will of God, 1 Chron. xxviii. 9, and to say as Psalm xl. 8, "I delight to do thy will, O my God." Hence,

1. A work accepted of God is a commanded work, required of us by God himself, and not an unrequired work, Rev. xxii. 14, "Blessed are they that do his commandments." Matth. xv. 9, "In vain they do worship me, teaching for doctrines the commandments of men." Therefore,

(1.) Nothing in itself sinful can ever be accepted of God; though people may pretend they have no ill in their mind against God in doing it; yea though they may have a good intention in it to serve God by it, John xvi. 2. Yet how many do, on these pretences, lie without any check, and do other ill things? Prov. xxvi. 18, 19, "As a madman who casteth firebrands, arrows, and death; so is the man that deceiveth his neighbour, and saith, Am not I in sport?"

(2.) Nothing, that is not required of God, though it be not in itself sinful, can be accepted of him, Matth. xv. 9. For there can be no obedience, where there is not a command; these are relatives. If God command us not, we cannot be said to obey him, nor be accepted of him. Hence, [1.] Will-worship is false worship, and service to God just of men's own devising is not, nor can be accepted; Col. ii. 21–23, "Devised of one's own heart," is a brand of rejection fixed on a work, that is not in itself evil, 1 Kings xii. ult. And Saul lost the kingdom on such a work, 1 Sam. xv. 21. [2.] Doing a duty not the duty of one's station cannot be accepted, 1 Cor. vii. 24. It was a duty to sacrifice, and to burn incense; yet Saul provoked the Lord by his doing the one, and Uzziah was smitten with leprosy for doing the other; because though they were duties, yet they belonged not to their stations. In a well-ordered family, one servant must not take his neighbour's work and post.

2. The command of God requiring the work must be known to the doer; for otherwise men serve the Lord but at a venture, not knowing whether it be his will or no, which can never be accepted, Lev. xxvi. 21. The acceptable work must be done in faith, faith of the command of God, implying knowledge of it, Rom. xiv. ult.

The sum of the whole lies here. If ye would have your work accepted of God, ye must (1.) Know it to be a commanded duty. (2.) Commanded to you. The want of either will mar the acceptance, as a duty not proceeding from a willing mind.

Secondly, Let us consider what this willingness of mind is. It is twofold, habitual and actual.

1. Habitual; which is a disposition of the soul to comply with the will of God's commands, arising from the new nature given in regeneration or the saving change; Heb. viii. 10, "I will put my laws into their mind, and write them in their hearts." Psalm cx. 3, "Thy people shall be willing in the day of thy power, in the beauties of holiness from the womb of the morning." The carnal unrenewed mind is enmity against God and his law, Rom. viii. 7. And while that corrupt set abides on the heart predominant, as in all natural men, there can be no true willingness to comply with the will of God. Hence, that any work of ours may be accepted of God, we must be,

(1.) United to Christ by faith, John xv. 5. While we continue in our natural state, growing on the old stock of the first Adam, we can bring forth no fruit acceptable to God; for the whole nature is corrupt according to the stock, and so must the fruit be, Rom. vii. 5. Particularly there is a reigning refractoriness in the will, whereby the soul is as a bullock unaccustomed to the yoke of God's will. Whereas the soul being in Christ is changed, according to the nature of the new stock, and made willing, 2 Cor. v. 17, and gets his image, opposed to Adam's, 1 Cor. xv. 49.

(2.) We must be regenerated, and have our nature changed. The tree must be made good, before the fruit can be so, Ezek. xxxvi. 26, 27. How can there be a willing mind for duty, while the will is unrenewed? How can there be new obedience, while one is not partaker of the new nature? The dark mind, the perverse will, and disorderly affections, not rectified by regenerating grace, being all of them opposite to good, show the want of a willing mind.

(3.) We must have a predominant love to God, 1 Tim. i. 5. This disposeth the soul, by a constraining force, to fall in with whatsoever the Lord requires; and constitutes one's obedience labour of love. And where it is wanting, good things may indeed be done, for some by-ends, and from some by-principles; but there is not first a willing mind.

This is the habitual willing mind, whereby the soul being in Christ, regenerated, and having the love of God dwelling in it, is in such a disposition to fall in with the will of God, that getting a touch of a particular command, it readily complies therewith in obedience.

2. Actual; which is an actual compliance of the heart, with such and such a particular duty, laid before one at such a time and in such a place; and ariseth from the habitual disposition. The one looks to the whole law; the other to particular commands requiring such and such a particular duty, as of the Corinthians to help the poor saints of Judea. And it implies,

(1.) An approbation of the command of God for the duty. What the Lord by his word and providence requires of the man as duty, he has a love and liking of it from the heart, Rom. vii. 12. The carnal heart rises against this and the other command laying such a duty on the man; and he takes it on as a slave does his burden, because he cannot help it. But the willing mind has a liking of it, 1 John v. 3, as the little child has a liking of being bid do any little piece of service for his father.

(2.) A sincere resolution to set to the work in the season thereof, Josh. xxiv. 15; Psalm cxix. 106. The willing mind goes not about to seek how to shift obedience to the divine call; nor does it seek offputs and delays, till the season of the duty is away; nor does it muster up difficulties, saying, "There is a lion in the way," to palliate disobedience; but resolves to put to hand timely; Psalm cxix. 60," I made haste, and delayed not to keep thy commandments."

(3.) A compliance of the heart with the command to the duty, because it is God's command, Psalm cxix. 4. The authority of God has weight with the man's conscience; and the love of God inclines his heart to obey. So the will of God is the reason, as well as the rule, of his obedience. As he believes the promise, because God has said it; so he obeys the command, because God has bid it. So the man's great aim is to answer the call of God, and please him.

(4.) A delight and cheerfulness in the duty, Isa. lxiv. 5; 2 Cor. ix. 7. Love to the Lord oils the wheels of the soul, and the work goes on, not as of necessity, but as of choice, 1 John v. 3. The awfulness of the command is vailed with prevailing love; take off the threatening of wrath from the command, and the willing soul would not stop for all that; for the love of God in the heart is a law, and a powerful one too, Cant. viii. 6. Terror drives to duty, but weakens; love draws to duty, and strengthens, 2 Tim. i. 7. Terror will make men find their hands, but they lose heart; but love gives heart and hand too.

(5.) A design to honour God by the duty. The general direction is plain; 1 Cor. x. 31, "Whether ye eat or drink, or whatsoever ye do, do all to the glory of God"; and thereto the willing mind echoes back, "To me to live is Christ," Phil. i. 21. The willing mind is not obtained but by faith, whereby the conscience is made good, and the soul put in a state of salvation; hence natively follows the design of glorifying God by good works, and by them adorning the doctrine of God our Saviour, 1 Pet. ii. 9. The faith of Christ's salvation makes a powerful impression of gratitude on the soul, that it is glad of an occasion to glorify him, and express its love; Psalm cxvi. 12, "What shall I render unto the Lord, for all his benefits towards me?"

(6.) *Lastly*, A looking-out for promised help to the duty, by faith, Heb. xii. 1, 2. The willing mind is not blind to its own weakness, but sees that better than others. But what one is really willing and hearty for the doing of, he will use all means for reaching his end. Carnal men say they are willing but they cannot; in that they deceive themselves, for if they were really willing they would go to the fountain of strength for help. So do they with whom is first a willing mind, they set about the duty in the faith of the promise. Hence they will go forward on God's call, however difficult the work be, and get through too; as the women came to the sepulchre, though not knowing how the stone would be rolled away.

Secondly, They are works that from a willing mind are done to their ability. We may take up this in these four things.

1. They are works which people having ability for, are done; they are not merely wished and woulded to be done, as the sluggard uses to wish well with folded hands, Prov. xxi. 25. For where the heart is to a work, the hand will be put to it, so far as in them lies. Men do but deceive themselves, who please themselves with good desires and wishes, without endeavours backing them; Matth. vii. 21, "Not every one that saith unto me, Lord, Lord, shall enter into the kingdom of heaven; but he that doth the will of my Father which is in heaven." Jam. i. 22, "But be ye doers of the word, and not hearers only, deceiving your own selves."

2. They are done according to the ability they could get in. That is, not only according to the ability in hand, but the

man labours to get more ability for the work, whereby he may be fitted for it. We are naturally impotent for any good work; but there is a storehouse of strength opened to us in Christ, to be brought in by faith, Isa. xlv. 24. Wherefore they that are not concerned to fetch in strength for duty, but are unable for duty, and hold themselves so, will not be accepted; for there is no willing mind there.

3. They are not done quite below what they might have done, and was in the power of their hand, Isa. xxxii. 5. Where there is an utter disproportion betwixt one's ability and service, it cannot be accepted but that service brings a curse instead of a blessing, Prov. xi. 24. Hence a certain quantity of service may be accepted off one's hand that will not be accepted off another's, Luke xii. 48. Where God gives much, he requires the greater returns.

4. *Lastly*, They are works wherein the willingness of the mind carries out the hand to do, as far as it can reach, 2 Cor. viii. 3. The willing mind loves to serve the Lord, and to serve him liberally; and so carries a man to do to his power.

II. The next general head is to show how or in what respect such a work is accepted. God accepts such works,

1. As obedience to him and a doing of his will, Matth. xxv. 21. As the willing mind is peculiar to those within the covenant of grace, so it is the privilege of those in that covenant to have their works so done, accepted, though imperfect. There is not one piece of obedience they can do that is perfect, or could be sustained as obedience according to the covenant of works; but God in Christ, in virtue of the covenant of grace, accepts such imperfect works as obedience pleasing to him, Acts xiii. 22.

2. As a token of their love to God, Heb. vi. 10. A love-token is accepted, though not great, if according to the ability of the giver; especially with God, who looks more to the heart it is given with, than the gift. Some offered gold and precious stones for the service of the tabernacle; some but goats' hair and rams' skins; the latter as well as the former was accepted, where they gave according to their ability with willingness.

3. So as to be rewarded, 1 Cor. xv. ult. As believers' good works are tokens of their love to God, so God gives them tokens of his good pleasure with their works, not of debt, but of grace. To those that improve the abilities they have, he ofttimes gives more ability, "To him that hath shall be given." However, accepted good works are a seed that will never miss a rich harvest sooner or later.

III. I proceed to show why such works are accepted. It is not for their own worth; for the best works of the saints are attended with such sinfulness, that they could not be accepted in the eye of the law; but have in them more than sufficient matter of condemnation, Isa. lxiv. 6. But they are accepted through special privilege.

1. Being sanctified through the Spirit, Rom. xv. 16. Every work of ours is defiled by us, being in ourselves unclean creatures; but the Spirit works in believers, sanctifying them and their works. And he sanctifies their works, by influencing them to work, and in their work exciting them, giving gracious abilities; particularly working in them that approbation and liking of the command, that resolution to set about the work, that compliance of the heart with it, that delight and cheerfulness in the duty, that design to honour God by it, and that looking out for promised help, which I have spoken of before, and causing them to offer their works to God through Christ.

2. They are presented for acceptance, by the Mediator to the Father. Christ is the believers' resident in the court of heaven, managing all their matters there by his intercession, Heb. vii. 25. He takes their imperfect works, perfumes them with the merit of his obedience and death, and gains their acceptance with the Father, according to the covenant of grace, Rev. viii. 3, 4. The sum of the matter lies here; they are the work of his own Spirit in his children, presented for acceptance by the Son, and so they are accepted of the Father, Eph. ii. 18.

USE. From what is said, we may draw the two following inferences:—

1. See here of what concern it is to get the heart up to every duty, 1 Chron. xxviii. 9. The doing of the bare work is of small account with God; and where there is not a heart to it, God regards it not. A good work done grudgingly, whatever use it may be for among men, is an ill work in God's sight.

QUESTION. How may one get up his heart to every duty?

ANSWER (1.) Accept of Christ's free salvation by faith, that ye may be brought into a state of salvation. We have a spirit of slaves, a backwardness to good, derived from Adam. It is from Christ we must get the spirit of sons, and the willing mind, uniting with him by faith, John i. 16. Faith trusting on Christ for salvation to be received freely, works that willingness of mind.

(2.) Exercise faith for every duty anew. Believe the promise, [1.] Of assistance by the Spirit, Ezek. xxxvi. 26, 27. In the covenant of grace commands are turned to promises, as Deut. x. 16, "Circumcise the foreskin of your heart." Compare Deut. xxx. 6, "The Lord thy God will circumcise thine heart." Every call to duty implies a promise of assistance. The belief of this makes willing, Phil. ii. 12, 13. [2.] Of acceptance through Christ. The apostles' work was heavy, but that made them willing, 2 Cor. ii. 15, "For we are unto God a sweet savour of Christ, in them that are saved, and in them that perish." It is hard to be willing to a work, which one does not believe will be accepted.

2. See of what concern it is to put hand to every duty commanded us, and to do in it according to one's power; and not to content ourselves with lazy wishes as some do, and slack and scrimp performances as others, Eccl. ix. 10. Neither will to wish and do nothing be accepted; nor to do, but do niggardly. It is not in every case that God will accept the will for the deed.

1*st*, God will not accept the natural or unregenerate man's will for the deed, in any case. For such a one is under the covenant of works, and no less than works every way perfect can be accepted off his hand, Gal. iii. 10. But this is a privilege of the covenant of grace, which they are not under, not being in Christ. It is the privilege of sons, but they are but at best hired servants, working for hire, nay slaves, as under the curse. Their persons are not accepted; therefore nothing they are, have, or can do, can be accepted. Therefore deceive not yourselves, looking for this benefit, while ye are out of Christ.

2*dly*, God will accept no man's will for the deed,

(1.) When they content themselves with wishing only they could do a duty commanded them, but yet never essay it, nor put hand to it, Prov. xxi. 25. The sluggard unwilling to obey, makes a cover for his sloth, of the difficulty and his inability for duty, Prov. xxii. 13. But God will rend off that cover, and show them in their own, colours, Matth. xxv. 24–30. Men cannot deny but that such a thing is their duty, and they wish they could, but that is all.

(2.) When they do not what is really in their power to do, Rom. i. 20, 21. Men's power is indeed little, but their doing is far less. Men are not as stocks and stones, but there are many things acts of moral discipline, that they may and can do, but they will not. But they grasp at the principle, that they can do nothing, and so fold their hands, sitting down contented.

They cannot do all, therefore they will do nothing. But will that be accepted? No, Exod. xiv. 15. The women did not so, Mark xvi. 2, 4.

(3.) *Lastly,* When they do not by faith fetch in grace from the Lord Jesus to strengthen them to duty, 2 Tim. ii. 1, compared with John v. 40. Many a good work is laid by, because of inability, and marred because we can carry it no further; but God will take notice what course is taken for getting in strength for duty. There are full promises lying between us and the fall fountain, as the conduit-pipes at which faith is to suck and draw, Isa. xl. 29–31. Assure yourselves that the will will not be accepted for the deed, while this is neglected. And why should it? Is that man willing to pay his debt, who though he has nothing in hand, yet has a gift lying in a rich friend's hand, but he will not lift it? See the decision; Matth. xxv. 27, "Thou oughtest to have put my money to the exchangers, and then at my coming I should have received mine own with usury."

I shall now consider in a few words the last doctrine I offered from the text, viz.

DOCTRINE IV. Want of power to do more, shall not mar the acceptance of what is done from a willing mind according to power. In that case, God will accept of his people's will for the deed.

Here I shall shew,

I. In what particular cases God accepts his people's will for the deed.

II. Why he does so.

III. Apply.

I. I am to show in what particular cases God accepts his people's will for the deed.

1. Where there is a sincere will to serve him in a piece of work, requiring some external abilities which are wanting. If it be hindered only by such want, the will is accepted. The disciples would fain have watched more, but the weak body could not bear up with their mind; and Christ kindly takes notice of it; Matth. xxvi. 41, "Watch and pray, that ye enter not into temptation; the Spirit indeed is willing, but the flesh is weak." Sometimes Satan makes a rack here to God's children; such a duty they would do, but bodily strength will not answer, and hereupon they are disquieted; but that is from Satan, and their own weakness; for God does not require that

external duty from us, that we have no bodily strength for. That is a sweet word, 1 Cor. vi. 13, "The body is—for the Lord, and the Lord for the body." Peter would fain have given to the poor man, but had it not, and it was accepted in the will, Acts iii. 6.

2. When doing the best we can through grace, our work after all is attended with many blemishes; the Lord will not reject it for these blemishes, but accepts the will to do better for the deed, Cant. v. 1. There is a broad cover of Christ's righteousness cast over the believer's spots, that they appear not, Cant. iv. 7; and the Lord accepts of the will to that perfection they would be at.

3. Going as far as we have access in a work, but meeting with a providential stop, the will to complete it is accepted for the deed, as if it had been fully done, as in the case of Abraham's offering up Isaac, Heb. xi. 17. There is a great difference betwixt the stops men make in these, and those which God makes; the former argues an unwilling mind, but the latter not so.

4. Services that one really desires, and fain would perform for God, but have not opportunity; the will to them is accepted for the deed, as in the case of David's purposing to build a house for the Lord, 2 Chron. vi. 8; and the Philippians care about supplying Paul's wants, Philip. iv. 10. Some have opportunities of usefulness, but slight them; that is their sin; others may have a heart to be so and so useful, but they cannot have the opportunity; this God accepts.

5. *Lastly,* In services performed with a real desire of success for God's honour and men's good; the Lord accepts the good will to the success denied, as if it had succeeded according to their wish, Isa. xlix. 4; 2 Cor. ii. 15. The want of success may mar their present comfort, but neither the acceptance nor reward.

II. Why does God accept such will for the deed?

1. The sincere will to a work is present, which God mainly regards. The person sincerely aims at doing such a piece of service. for God, but not attaining what he really desires, his good will thereto being present before the Lord, it is accepted, as if the work had been done.

2. We have a merciful High Priest to present that will for acceptance, notwithstanding all the weaknesses, blemishes, providential hindrances, want of opportunity, and failure of success, that it may be attended with, Heb. iv. 15, 16.

3. We have a merciful Father to deal with, Psalm ciii. 13, 14, who pities the weaknesses and infirmities of his people, and graciously accepts of their upright designs to serve and honour him.

Use 1. If the Lord accepts the will for the deed in his own people, then men must answer for the ill they had a will to have done, as if they had done it, Numb. xiv. 42–45. A will and intention to do an evil action, though it be not actually done, is in God's account the same thing with doing it, and will be resented and punished accordingly.

2. God is a gracious master to his servants, taking kindly off their hands through Christ their sincere will to his service, giving them ample testimonies of his regard in all circumstances, and bestowing upon them the special comforts of his grace here, as pledges of the full reward laid up for them in glory hereafter.

VI. Jesus Christ the Beloved One, and Sinners Accepted of God Freely in Him[18]

His grace, wherein he hath made us accepted in the Beloved.
Ephesians i. 6

Before our works can be accepted, our persons must; and how that is attained is here declared.

The apostle taking a view of the state of salvation that believers are brought into, in the fulness of it, ver. 3; runs it up unto the prime author of it, the Father, *ib.* the eternal plan of it in the decree of election, ver. 4; whereof the great design to be accomplished on them, their true sanctification, *ib.* to be begun here, and perfected in glory; the reason of this design, that they were predestinated to adoption into his family, for it was inconsistent with the honour of a holy God, to have unholy children, ver. 5. In this verse are two things.

1. The great end of God's predestinating the elect to be his own children; "the praise of the glory of his grace." It was a display of his free grace that he aimed at. Grace is love and favour freely flowing, without anything in the object to draw it out. This grace shown to sinners is glorious grace, like a shining sun, casting such a lustre, as is most admirable and attractive. And it is to be praised by the sons of men; but they that do not see, and do not feel the glory of it, cannot praise it, more than the blind the light of the sun. But God purposed to bring the elect out of the devil's family, and make them his own children freely; that they seeing, tasting, and feeling this glorious grace, might raise a song of praise of it here, and joining voices in heaven, might carry it on in the highest strain

---

18 The substance of several sermons preached at Etterick in the year 1726.

there for ever, praising the glorious grace appearing in their adoption; opening the various folds of it, and admiring the glories of free grace, for ever and ever. It is dangerous then to cast a veil over it, doctrinally or practically.

2. A particular fruit of this glorious grace; "Wherein he hath made us accepted in the Beloved." Where we have,

(1.) The fruit itself, the acceptance of the persons of believers with God; "He hath made us accepted." The acceptor is the Father, vers. 3, 5. The accepted are us, believers, who are "blessed with all spiritual blessings in heavenly places in Christ," ver. 3. The acceptance is emphatically expressed. The word is, as if he had said, he hath graced us; and imports not only that he hath accepted us, but freely accepted us, without anything in us to render us acceptable; and bears not only free love and favour, but also all kinds of real benefits and favours flowing therefrom, Luke i. 28.

(2.) The way and manner of the acceptance. How can a sinner be accepted of a holy God? "In the Beloved," that is, Christ. It is not only for his sake, but God looking on the sinner in Christ, united to him, accepts him. He calls Christ here "the Beloved," to intimate that the accepting love and favour of God is first pitched on him, and then for his sake comes down on his members; so he is the Beloved by way of eminency. He saith not, "his Beloved," though doubtless Le mainly aims at that, but "the Beloved," that he might give a vent to that love to Christ that his heart swelled with on the mention of this; and so uses a general term, whereby Christ might be pointed out as the object whereon the loves of heaven and earth meet together.

(3.) The original spring and source of this acceptance, intimated by the relative wherein. It refers not only to the word grace, but to "the glory of his grace," *q. d.* From, through, and by which glorious grace and free favour, he hath freely accepted us undeserving and ill-deserving creatures; that glorious grace finding a way to accept the sinner, with the good leave of justice, in Christ.

From the text, thus explained, ariseth the following savoury points of doctrine.

DOCT. I. Jesus Christ is the beloved, the eminently beloved One.

DOCT. II. The way how a sinner comes to be accepted of God, is freely, in Christ.

DOCT. III. Glorious free grace shines forth in the acceptance of sinners in the beloved Jesus.

Doct. I. Jesus Christ is the beloved, the eminently beloved One.

In discoursing from this doctrine, I shall,
I. Show in what respects Christ is the eminently beloved One.
II. Make some improvement.

I. I am to show in what respects Christ is the eminently beloved One.

First, He is the beloved of the excellent ones of the earth. Who these are, ye may see, Psalm xvi. 3. They are "the saints." Him all the saints love with a love above all persons and all things, Luke xiv. 26. And,

1. They meet altogether in him in love, however they are scattered through the world; hence is he called, "the desire of all nations," Hag. ii. 7. So that lovers of Christ and saints are of equal latitude; Eph. vi. 24, "Grace be with all them that love our Lord Jesus Christ in sincerity." The American saints and the European saints take him all for their Beloved. As it is the same sun in the firmament that warms all their bodies, it is the same Sun of righteousness, Christ, that warms all their hearts in love. They differ vastly in their languages, customs, and particular dispositions; but they perfectly agree in their love of one beloved Jesus; Gen. xlix. 10, "Unto him shall the gathering of the people be." And so they are knit as one body, whereof Christ is the beloved head.

2. Each one of them loves him with a superlative and transcendent love; Psalm lxxiii. 25, "Whom have I in heaven but thee? and there is none upon earth that I desire besides thee." They have a general love to mankind, a special love to their respective countries, a more special love to their relations, but the most special and peculiar love, leaving all the rest behind, is to Christ, Luke xiv. 26. In the other they are divided, but in this they meet in one; their beloved ones are very different, but their beloved One is one and the same.

3. They love other persons and things for his sake, Rom. xv. 2, 3; Tit. iii. 3-5. When the soul is in its natural state, other persons and things have the man's love, but Christ has none of it; when Christ discovers himself in his glory to the soul, then the man hates all in comparison of him; but Christ regulates the soul's love to other things, and takes it not away, but makes it run in another channel, springing from himself. Now other things being loved for him, himself is the best beloved.

4. The liker any thing is to him, they love it the more. Hence the godly that bear his image, are therefore beloved by them; and the more godly they are, the more beloved are they, 1 John iii. 14. They love his ordinances, because they bear the impress of his authority, his law as the image of his nature; his way and example, because of the tread of his steps therein to be seen. All which bear him to be their eminently beloved. And,

1*st*, They love him with a love of good-will; and vent it in prayer and praise; Psalm lxxii. 15, "Prayer also shall be made for him continually, and daily shall he be praised." It is not in their power to profit him, and he needs nothing at the creature's hand, being completely happy in his Father; but they show good-will to him, in concern for his glory in the world, that his kingdom may prosper, his name spread far and wide, and be perpetuated to all generations.

2*dly*, They love him with a love of delight and complacency, 1 Pet. ii. 7, "Unto you which believe he is precious." His name and every letter of it is sweet to them, Cant. i. 3. They delight in him as a sister in a brother, a child in a father, and a spouse in a husband. Everything in Christ is sweet to a believer; therefore they are said to eat his flesh, and drink his blood: for as by eating one finds the sweetness of the meat, and every bit of it, so by faith the soul finds the sweetness of Christ and every thing in Christ. And,

(1.) They love him for what he is in himself, Cant. v. 10–16. The glorious excellencies of his person and natures, his attributes and perfections, make him the object of their love. Their hearts are framed to the love of God: so they love him for himself, they love him for that holiness and purity for which carnal men hate him, as the owl doth the sun, Psalm xxx. 4.

(2.) They love him for what he is to them, Cant. v. 16. And as he is best in himself, he is the best to them. They love him for all his offices; for what he has done for them, and for what be will do for them. They love him as the foundation of all their hopes, the scope of all their desires, and the spring of all their joys. And fitly does he go under the name, "the Beloved," even in respect of the saints: for,

[1.] They profess him to be the beloved of their souls; they are not ashamed of their choice. So the spouse calls him, Cant. *per tot*. See chap. iii. 3, "Saw ye him whom my soul loveth?" as if she would have all to know him by that name, "her Beloved"; supposing there is none so but he.

[2.] They show him to be so, by their life and actions before the world, Cant. viii. 6, 7. Where love to Christ is, it will discover itself by the soul's preferring Christ to all persons and things, so as to part with any thing when it comes in competition with him.

Secondly, Christ is the beloved of the glorious ones in heaven. All eyes are upon him there, for he is there the light of the pleasant land, Rev. xxi. 23, as the sun is in this world. And he is there,

1. The beloved of the glorified saints, who now love him in perfection, Rev. vii. 10. Their love to him is now perfected, and they love him with a pure and ardent love. They see him now no more through a glass, but face to face; they behold the glories of his person, the glories of his actings and sufferings for them; his eternal undertaking, his going through with his undertaking in his birth, life, and death; and the glory he now hath from his Father as the reward. So their love to him is in a continual flame.

2. The beloved of the holy angels, Rev. v. 11, 12. In the temple the cherubims were posted, looking towards the ark or mercy-seat, a type of Christ; which signified the angels looking to Jesus with love and admiration, 1 Pet. i. 12. They behold his glory, and cannot but love him. They love him as the brightness of the Father's glory, as the elder Brother of the family, the heir of all things, and their Lord, Heb. i. 6, as the Saviour of sinners, and the head of angels, by whom they and all things do consist, Eph. i. 10.

3. The Father's beloved, Matth. xvii. 5. And here we may consider Christ two ways, as God, and as Mediator.

1*st*, As God, equal and co-eternal with the Father and Holy Spirit. He was the beloved of the Father and the Spirit. The Scripture teacheth that "God is love," 1 John iv. 8, and that love must be eminently among the persons of the glorious Trinity one towards another. Thus, Prov. viii. 30, he is held out as the Creator's delight. See John i. 18, Heb. i. 2. But what our text mainly aims at, is,

2*dly*, As Mediator, God-man, having a common relation to God and sinners of mankind, as the representative of an elect world, and the bond of union and communion betwixt God and sinners, for the glory of God and the salvation of sinners.

(1.) As such he is the Father's beloved, his prime favourite, and most accepted, his "well Beloved," Mark xii. 6, in whom he is "well pleased"; Matth. iii. ult., the perpetual rest of his eyes and heart, 2 Chron. vii. 16. And he is his beloved,

[1.] In respect of his person; John i. 18. He "is in the bosom of the Father." For he is "the brightness of his Father's glory," Heb. i. 2. The glory of God shines forth in his face, 2 Cor. iv. 6. He is "the image of God" in a peculiar manner, ver. 4. Therefore says he, John xiv. 9, "He that hath seen me, hath seen the Father." See Col. ii. 9, and i. 19. So he is the most beautiful object in the eyes of God, in heaven or in earth; and accordingly has the highest place in his love, Heb. i. 13.

[2.] In respect of his office. The Father is well pleased with him in the character he took on. And,

(1.) He was well pleased with his undertaking for the great work of sinners' salvation. See with what satisfaction he speaks of it; Psalm lxxxix. 19, "I have laid help upon one that is mighty; I have exalted one chosen out of the people." He cordially accepted him as the sinners' surety, and took his single bond for all the elect's debt, and his security for the injured honour of his name. He was the Father's own choice, and he delighted in his choice, Isa. xlii. 1. He so loved the Undertaker, that,

[1.] He promised to be with him, and furnished him with all things necessary for the work, Isa. xlii. 6, and lxi. 1.

[2.] He bestowed eternal salvation on many, before the time the Saviour paid the ransom; he set them free, and gave them their discharge, before the death of Christ. He rested in the Beloved's engagement.

(2.) He was well pleased with and accepted him in his carrying on the work that he had undertaken.—With his birth, therefore the angels were employed to carry the tidings of it, and sung solemnly on that occasion.—With his entering on his public work at his baptism, testified by a voice from heaven, Matth. iii. ult., and all along, testified by his being always with him, John viii. 29.

(3.) He was well-pleased with his perfecting of the work, by his death and burial. He did in it the most acceptable piece of service to God that ever was done, John x. 17. His sacrifice of himself was of a sweet savour unto God. He so loved him for it, that he raised him up, and set him on his right hand for ever for it, Phil. ii. 8, 9, and accepts the worst of sinners in him, for his sake.

(2.) As such he is the rest of the Holy Spirit, Isa. xi. 2. The Spirit came on the prophets, but he rested on Jesus as the beloved, Matth. iii. 16. All the saints as beloved ones have the

Spirit in a measure; but he without measure as the Beloved, John iii. 34. The Spirit is in him as water in the fountain, to be communicated to others, Rev. iii. 1.

I shall conclude this point with a word of application.

Use. I. Hereby ye may try whether ye be saints or not, partakers of the divine nature. If so, Christ will be your Beloved, your eminently beloved One; for so he is to the saints, and so he is to God. And if he is your Beloved,

1. Ye will love him above all, Psalm lxxiii. 25, which will show itself in desiring him above all, prizing him beyond all, rejoicing most in his favour, and sorrowing most for the want of him; and in loving other persons and things for his sake.

2. Ye will hate sin above all things, because it is most contrary to him, his nature and will, Gen. iii. 15. Ye will hate it universally, constantly as to the habitual bent of your heart, and irreconcilably.

Use II. Of reproof to those who love him not eminently, above all. It is an evidence, that,

1. Ye know him not, John iv. 10. None can be let into a discovery of Christ in his glory but must love him, Matth. xiii. 44–46. It is to the blind world only there is no beauty in him for which he is to be desired.

2. That ye are in love with your sins and a vain world. For who would loath the physician but he that loves his disease and cannot part with it?

Use III. Let him be your Beloved then, and give him your heart.

1. He is best worth your love. None has done so much for sinners as Christ has, dying for them. None can do so much for you; he can satisfy the cravings of your souls, and make you happy.

2. If ye love him not, ye will be constructed haters of him, and enemies to him; 1 Cor. xvi. 22, "If any man love not the Lord Jesus Christ, let him be anathema, maranatha."

Doctrine II. *The way how a sinner comes to be accepted of God, is freely, in Christ.*

In handling this doctrine, I shall,
I. Show what is implied in it.
II. Consider the nature of a sinner's acceptance with God.
III. The way of it.
IV. Make some practical improvement.

I. I am to show what is implied in the doctrine. And there are these things implied in it.

First, A state of non-acceptance, or unacceptableness with God, that sinners are in, while they are not in Christ. And we may take up this in these following things.

1. They are offenders; they have sinned, and provoked him, Rom. iii. 23. Men's doing their duty, and men's misery, may make them unacceptable to men, yea, one may be unacceptable to another, who cannot show wherefore, only they cannot endure them. But nothing can make us unacceptable to God but sin. So the unacceptable to God are undoubtedly sinners, offenders against him.

(1.) They are sinners in Adam, Rom. v. 12. The root was corrupted, and all the branches withered and rotted in him. So his guilt lies on us by nature, we are deprived of righteousness of nature, and instead of that we have derived a corrupt nature from him; all which makes us unacceptable to God by nature.

(2) They are sinners in their own persons, who are capable of actual sinning, Gen. vi. 5. They imitate sinning Adam, as well as fall heirs to his offence. The debt left by him on their heads, they do not clear, but increase daily; they continue their rebellion while condemned for it. And so they are more and more unacceptable.

2. They are unpardoned offenders. All have sinned, but some are pardoned and accepted; but none are pardoned who are out of Christ, John iii. ult. The sentence of the broken law stands in force against all those who are not in him, who has fulfilled the law. He is "the end of the law for righteousness to every one that believeth," Rom. x. 4. And,

(1.) Their original guilt lies on them, unremoved, unforgiven, 1 Cor. xv. 22. God has never forgiven them their guilt of Adam's first sin, their want of original righteousness, and the corruption of their whole nature. The debt left on them by their father, they were never either able or willing to pay; and though they may have forgot it, God has neither forgiven nor forgot it, but it lies on them still, to all effects and purposes of a dreadful pursuit for it.

(2.) The guilt of all their actual sins lies on them, Gal. iii. 10. All the sins they have been guilty of, from the first sproutings of corruption in their childhood to this day, are hard and fast on them. None of all their sins of omission or commission, of heart, lip, or life, are forgotten by God, Amos viii. 7, but the accounts are closely kept, Deut. xxxii. 34; Hos. xiii. 12. They may have made a fashion of repenting, and begging pardon, for some of their grosser sins; but since they are not in Christ, there is not one of them blotted out; for "without shedding of blood is no remission," Heb. ix. 22, and there is no saving benefit of Christ's blood, but by being in him, chap. xii. 24.

3. God is not pleased with them; for his being pleased with any of mankind is in his son Jesus Christ, and without him he can be pleased with none of them, Matth. iii. ult.; Heb. xi. 5, 6. He is not pleased with their persons nor with any of their works; because they themselves are not in Christ; but yet in the old stock, Rom. viii. 8, and their works are not wrought in him, John xv. 5. So the apostle teacheth, that it was faith that made the difference between Abel's offering and Cain's, Heb. xi. 4.

4. He is highly displeased with them. There is a cloud of divine displeasure ever upon them, John iii. ult. Whatever case they be in, rejoicing or weeping; whatever they be doing, serving God in their way, or serving their lusts, his countenance is never towards them, because they are not in Christ, Isa. lxvi. 2, 3. There is a displeasure conceived against them on the justest grounds, not to be removed till they be in Christ.

5. He cannot endure them to have any communion or intercourse with them, farther than in the way of common providence, Psalm v. 5. He and they are at enmity, he legally, they really; so there can be no communion, Amos iii. 3. And they cannot have it till they come to Christ, John xiv. 6. God may lay common favours to their hand, health, wealth, &c.; as the condemned man is allowed his meat till the execution; but he grants them no special saving favours, no peace, pardon, &c. He may allow them to come, and call them into the outer court of ordinances, and make them offers of grace; but they cannot come into the inner court, nor partake of grace, not being in Christ, John x. 9.

6. He loaths them, his soul abhors them, as abominable. They are abominable in their persons unto God, as wholly corrupt and defiled, Tit. i. 15, 16. The whole herd of them is so, Psalm xiv. 3. Their works are abominable, even the best of them, like precious liquor in a filthy vessel, Prov. xv. 8. Sin is the abominable thing unto God, Jer. xliv. 4. And all their sins lie on them, and there is nothing on them to correct the abominable savour of the sinner by them. Sin is abominable in believers too; but the sacrifice of the sweet-smelling savour of Christ corrects it, and is a savour of rest, Gen. viii. 21.

7. *Lastly*, The wrath of God is upon them, and they lie under his curse, John iii. ult., Gal. iii. 10. They are "children of wrath," Eph. ii. 3. There is much wrath on them, and they are liable to more. There is wrath in God's heart against them, in his word, and in his providential dispensations. And if the thread of their life be cut while they are in that state of wrath, they are for ever undone without remedy.

Secondly, A way provided, how sinners may be accepted. The case is not hopeless, but he that is not, may be accepted. The acceptance of some with God is now secured, and cannot be lost. Believers on earth may fall under the frowns of a Father, but never out of the state of acceptance with him; being "accepted in the Beloved." The acceptance of the saints in glory is not liable to the least cloud. The acceptance of some, again, is absolutely hopeless. The fallen angels never can, nor could have been accepted: the damned sometimes might, but can no more now for ever be accepted; they sat their accepted time. But there is a way how sinners in life may be accepted.

1. God is ready to accept of them now, that will come to him in his own way; 2 Cor. v. 19. The Judge of all the earth is set down on a throne of grace, for receiving sinners into favour; and therefore we have now an "accepted time," and "day of salvation," chap. vi. 2.

2. There is ready for sinners what may procure them acceptance with a holy God, Matth. xxii. 4. There is a sacrifice slain and offered, that is of such a sweet-smelling savour, that the most loathsome sinner having the savour of it about him cannot miss to be accepted.

3. There is open proclamation made in the gospel, that all may have the benefit of that sacrifice, and be accepted of God, 2 Cor. v. 19, Matth. xxii. 4. Who they were whom the Father gave to the Son to be redeemed, is a secret; but the ransom is paid, the sacrifice is offered for you to lay hold on and be accepted by. And that is the voice of the gospel.

Thirdly, The sinner's bestirring himself for acceptance with God. There is a way to acceptance, but the sinner must take that way, else he will not get acceptance. He cannot sit still careless, and be accepted: he must be where he is not yet, that is, in Christ; otherwise he can have no acceptance. The sinner's bestirring himself in this matter, takes in these three things.

1. A conviction of unacceptableness to God, John xvi. 8. Men must be convinced of their being unacceptable to God, ere they will come to Christ. It is their not seeing their own

loathsomeness, that makes them slight the sacrifice of sweet savour; and think to be accepted of God, while yet they are not in Christ. And for that cause it is needful they get a sight of God's holiness and their own vileness.

2. A weighty concern and uneasiness about it. They must not go on to be easy, whether they be accepted of God or not. As long as a man can live contented without it, he will never be accepted. But the soul shall be brought to that, that all shall be sapless with out it.

3. Anxiety of heart for it, Acts ii. 37. There must be earnest; longings to be accepted of him, yea the soul must be brought to esteem and so prize it, as to be content with it upon any terms, Acts ix. 6. Not as if these were required to qualify us for acceptance with God; but that without them we will never come into Christ to be accepted in him.

II. The next general head is to consider the nature of a sinner's acceptance with God; and this I shall do, 1. In itself, and 2. In its effects and consequents.

FIRST, I shall consider the nature of a sinner's acceptance with God in itself. And in itself it is a great and unspeakable benefit, and implies these following things.

First, In general, it implies an acceptance of the sinner with God, as a righteous person. A righteous God cannot accept a son of Adam, but as righteous, that is, as being really righteous before him. And so a believer in Christ indeed is, and by faith pleading Christ's righteousness for his righteousness in the sight of God, he is accepted accordingly. The Lord reputes, accounts, and accepts him into favour as a righteous person, 2 Cor. v. 21, Rom. iv. 6, and v. 19. So it stands in two things.

1. God's owning and sustaining a righteousness upon the believer, as answering the demands of the law fully, Rom. iii. 22, and holding him a righteous person thereupon. The sinner standing before him in the Beloved, pleading the Mediator's righteousness, the plea is sustained, and God saith, "Deliver him from going down to the pit, I have found a ransom," Job xxxiii. 24. The law gives in its demands against him, of holiness of nature, righteousness of life, and satisfaction for sin. And it is found that all these demands are satisfied, and that the righteousness upon him fully answers them all, that the law has no more to crave. And so in the very eye of the law, he is through grace held righteous.

2. On the account of that righteousness he is accepted into favour with God, Rom. iii. 24, 25. It was the sinner's un-

righteousness that cast him out of God's favour, and held him out of it. Now that bar is taken away, and the righteousness upon him procures the favour of a righteous God, who loveth righteousness. God is perfectly pleased with that righteousness, as much as he ever was displeased with the party's sin; and he is so well pleased with it, that notwithstanding of all the sins the party ever committed, he accepts him into favour for its sake.

Secondly, More particularly, it implies,

1. The ceasing of wrath against the soul, Hos. xiv. 4. The wrath of God no more abides on the accepted person; that cloud clears. And it clears so, that that shower shall never come on again, nor one drop of it, of revenging wrath, for ever and ever, Isa. liv. 9. The small rain of fatherly anger may come on him for his after-miscarriages; but the great rain of his revenging wrath shall never return, Cant. ii. 10, 11.

2. The curse is removed, Gal. iii. 13. That is the sentence of the broken law, that lay on the sinner binding him over to revenging wrath; which seized all mankind in Adam, and which is fortified daily by actual sin, while the sinner is out of Christ. But being accepted in Christ, that is taken away, Rom. viii. 1. The sentence is reversed, ver. 33, 34, the cursed sinner is loosed from that dreadful stake to which he was tied as the mark for the arrows of God.

3. He is fully pardoned, Isa. xliii. 25. The accepted sinner gets the King of heaven's pardon, under his great seal; whereby his guilt of eternal wrath is for ever removed, as if he had never sinned. God takes the pen, dips it in the blood of the Beloved, and blots out his whole accounts. All his past and present sins are formally pardoned, and all his sins to come are secured not to be imputed to him, for guilt of revenging wrath, Rom. iv. 6-8.

4. He is reconciled to God, Rom. v. 1. The Lord lays down the legal enmity he bore against that person, never to take it up again; and he gives him peace through the Beloved, Eph. ii. 14. So that though all the world should be at red war with him, he has a firm peace with heaven, that he needs fear no hostilities from that quarter again for ever; which is enough to settle the heart amidst all troubles, Phil. iv. 7.

5. God is pleased with him, Heb. xi. 5. Still they are sinners indeed, and God can never be pleased with their sins; but their sins hinder not that he be pleased with their persons in Christ. The prodigal son returns to his father in rags, poverty, and want, with not a shoe on his foot; the father is not pleased

with the rags on his son, but natural affection embraces him notwithstanding of his rags, he being his own son. So God embraces the sinner in the Beloved, because he is in him.

6. He is highly pleased with him, Isa. xlii. 21. He is as much pleased with the believer's person, as ever he was displeased with him. He is pleased with him, as one is with his jewels, Mal. iii. 17; as if he saw no sin in them, Num. xxiii. 21; as if there were no spot on them, Cant. iv. 7. In a word, he is infinitely pleased with them, and can never cease to be so. For the only ground of his being pleased with them, is the Beloved in whom they are, his righteousness which is upon them; and he is infinitely pleased with the Beloved and his righteousness, and they are not liable to any alteration, John xvii. 21. Indeed, if their acceptance depended on what is wrought by them, or in them, it could not be so; but it is not set in such a slippery foundation. He is displeased with their sins, and they may smart for them; but the pleasedness with their persons in Christ is not alterable, Col. ii. 10.

7. He admits them into communion with him, 1 John i. 3. The person is let into the inner court, into the chambers of the King, Cant. i. 4. The Lord treats him as a friend, and not as a mere servant, John xv. 16. They are now agreed, and so walk together; and not only agreed, but received into special favour; and are made God's favourites, courtiers of heaven in the Beloved, in the court kept below, Isa. lvii. 15. He dwells and walks in them, 2 Cor. vi. 16; and they dwell in him; 1 John iv. 15; Psalm xc. 1.

8. *Lastly*, God hath a delight and complacency in them, Isa. lxii. 4. He looks on them in his own Son, and takes pleasure in them, as covered with his righteousness. As Isaac smelling the smell of the elder brother's garments on Jacob; so believers are to God a sweet savour of Christ, 2 Cor. ii. 15; and therefore he delights in them, whom before he loathed.

Secondly, Let us consider this acceptance in its effects and consequents. It is in these an unspeakable privilege. By means of it,

1. The springs of mercy are opened to the sinner, that rivers of compassion may flow towards him, Rom. v. 1, &c. Many look for mercy while unaccepted; but the unsatisfied law will draw a bar betwixt all saving mercy and them. But the believer being accepted, the law's mouth is stopt, and mercy may flow freely.

2. He is adjudged to eternal life, 2 Thess. i. 6, 7; Acts xxvi. 18. Life was promised in the first covenant, upon the fulfill-

ing of the law; now the believer being accepted of God as a righteous person, for whom the law is fulfilled, is accordingly adjudged to live for ever.

3. The channel of sanctification is cleared for him, and the dominion of sin is broken in him, Rom. vi. 14. While the sinner is unaccepted, and under the curse, communion with God is stopt, and death preys on his soul; for "the sting of death is sin, and the strength of sin is the law," 1 Cor. xv. 56. As long as the law has a cursing and condemning power over a man, sin reigns in him, like briers and thorns in the cursed ground; but these being removed, sin loseth its strength, and the blessing coming in their room makes him fruitful. So faith sanctifies.

4. He is privileged with peace of conscience. Peace with God makes peace within one's breast, Phil. iv. 7. While one is unaccepted of God, guilt lies on the conscience, which makes a foul and condemning one, that will gnaw like a worm, and blast all outward peace and prosperity; but being accepted, the conscience is cleansed, Heb. ix. 14, and turns a good conscience, that will make one rejoice in trouble, 2 Cor. i. 12.

5. Access to God with confidence, Eph. iii. 12; 1 John iii. 21. God allows them whom he accepts, access to him in duties, that they may come to him, as children to a father, with all their wants, complaints, &c. expecting all from him that is really good for them, Job xxxiii. 24, 26. They are privileged with the hearing of their prayers, communion with him in word and providences, receiving, by the means of grace, light in darkness, strength in weakness, health in sickness, &c.

6. Acceptance of their works, Prov. xv. 8. God accepting a man's person in Christ, does next accept his work, Gen. iv. 4. If it were never such a small work, a cup of cold water given one in name of a disciple, though attended with many imperfections, yet being fruit that grows on a branch ingrafted into Christ, it is accepted of God, as savouring of the stock.

7. The unstinging of afflictions and death, 1 Cor. xv. 55. It alters the very nature of these; afflictions are no more properly penal, but correctory and medicinal, Isa. xxvii. 9, and death perfects the cure. A bee-sting they may have, but the serpentine deadly sting is gone; for the curse is removed out of their crosses, and they are blessings.

8. *Lastly*, All things working for good, Rom. viii. 28. In a state of non-acceptance, all things work for evil to a man; his prosperity destroys him; the very gospel is a savour of death unto him, that he draws death out of what others get

life. But being accepted, the worst of things tend to his profit, God being for him, nothing can be eventually against him; but whether the wind blow on his back or face, it drives him to the harbour.

III. I proceed to show the way of a sinner's acceptance with God.

First, It is "freely." There is nothing in the sinner himself to procure it, or move God to it, Rom. iii. 24, but as the sun shines without hire on the dung-hill, so God accepts sinners of mere grace. It is done freely, in that,

1. It is without respect to any work done by the sinner, Tit. iii. 5. Grace and works are inconsistent in this matter. Men may render themselves acceptable to men, by some work of theirs, that is profitable or pleasant to them; but no work of ours can render us acceptable to God. It is natural for men to think to gain acceptance with God, by their doing better; and when they have set themselves to do and work for that end, they please themselves that they are accepted. But mistake it not, that way of acceptance is blocked up. For,

(1.) All works of ours are excluded from our justification, whereof our acceptance is a part, Rom. iii. 20, and faith and works are opposed in that matter, ver. 28; Gal. ii. 16.

(2.) Our best works are attended with sinful imperfections, Isa. lxiv. 6, and mixed with many evil works, Jam. iii. 2. So in them there is ground for God's loathing and condemning us; how then can we be accepted for what is in itself loathsome and condemnable?

(3.) We can do no good works before we be accepted, John ix. 31; Heb. xi. 6. The tree must be good, ere the fruit can be so. The person out of Christ can work no works, but dead works, John xv. 5, for he is, while so, in the gall of bitterness, and in the bond of iniquity. And what is all that the man can do before he believe and be accepted in Christ, but a parcel of hypocritical works?

2. It is without respect to any good qualification or disposition wrought in the sinner; Rom. iv. 5, "To him that worketh not, but believeth on him that justifieth the ungodly, his faith is counted for righteousness." Men may be accepted of men, if though they have done nothing, they yet are well qualified for doing, or are agreeable in their disposition; but that is not the way of a sinner's acceptance with God, though the bias of our nature lies that way to expect it. For,

(1.) The way of a sinner's acceptance with God excludes all boasting, Rom. iii. 27. And it is the design of the gospel to exclude it; but if there were a respect to any good qualities in the party accepted, there would be some ground for boasting.

(2.) What good qualities can there be in the sinner before he be accepted in Christ? Heb. xi. 6. It is true he, may be touched with a sense of his sin, may be filled with sorrow and remorse for it, and desiring to be delivered; but all these are but legal and selfish dispositions, whereof not God, but self is the end. It is by union with him that gracious qualities must be wrought in the soul, Acts xxvi. 18.

(3.) When the man comes to be endued with gracious qualities, as he is by that time already accepted, so if his acceptance depended on them, he would come short; for still they are imperfect, having a great mixture of the contrary ill qualities, that need to be covered another way. And how can one expect acceptance on that, for which he needs a pardon?

Secondly, It is in Christ the sinner is accepted. It implies,

1. The cause of a sinner's acceptance with God. It is for Christ's sake; Rom. iii. 24, 25, "Being justified freely by his grace, through the redemption that is in Jesus Christ: whom God hath set forth to be a propitiation, through faith in his blood, to declare his righteousness for the remission of sins." And v. 19—"By the obedience of one, shall many be made righteous." He is the Beloved of the Father, so highly acceptable to him, that sinners are accepted for his sake, Matth. iii. ult. The acceptance of the Mediator is so full, that like the oil on Aaron's head, it runs down to the skirts of his garments. He is the Mediator, that brings in the sinner to the throne of grace, mediates his peace, and procures his acceptance into favour with God. This is,

(1.) The sole cause of the sinner's acceptance with God, Rom. iii. 24. As in purchasing the sinner's acceptance, so in procuring it, he alone is the actor. No righteousness is mixed with his, no works with his works. God has an eye to none but him, and nothing but him, in accepting the sinner. Some are better than others indeed, before they are accepted, but both are absolutely free grace's debtors for acceptance.

(2.) The full cause, fully proportioned in its efficacy to the acceptance of the worst sinners, Heb. vii. 25. As there is nothing else that can procure our acceptance, so we need nothing else for that end. Corrupt nature reckons it is too great a venture, to lay our acceptance with God on Christ's righteousness alone; and therefore, to make sure work, requires such and such works to be done, and such and such good qualities the sinner is to be adorned with. But what needs wood, hay, and stubble, to be laid in with the Rock for a foundation.

2. The state of acceptableness of a sinner, wherein he may, and will be, and cannot but be accepted of God; it is being in Christ, united to him by faith. One must not think to be accepted for Christ's sake while out of Christ; no more than the branch of one tree can partake of the sap of another, while not ingrafted into it; or the slayer could be safe, while he was not yet got within the gates of the city of refuge. For,

(1.) Where there is no union with Christ, there can be no communion with him; John. xv. 6, "If a man abide not in me, he is cast forth as a branch, and is withered." Can a branch be nourished by the juice of a stock with which it is not knit? Neither can a man be accepted for the sake of Christ's righteousness, while he is not united to him. As it is the marriage with the woman that makes her portion the man's; so it is a spiritual marriage-union with Christ by faith that makes his righteousness actually ours, so as to be accepted for it.

(2.) Christ's salvation is in the event confined to his body, though in the offer it is extended to all. He is the Saviour of the world indeed, John iv. 42. But does he save all the world? No; thousands perish for all that, because they do not unite with him, are not in him. He is the Saviour of the body, Eph. v. 23. His body he actually saves, every member thereof, and none else. He is the Saviour of the world officially, of his body only eventually. An ark there was provided before the universal deluge, but none were saved that were not in it.

(3.) The Father's good pleasure with mankind-sinners goes not without him, Matth. iii. ult. As without the verge of the city of refuge the slayer could expect no protection; so without Christ there is nothing but the curse, wrath, and death. God cannot accept us as righteous, while he sees no righteousness on us; there can be no righteousness on us before God, but as we are in Christ, shaded with his righteousness, 2 Cor. v. 21. Therefore he cannot be pleased with a sinner out of Christ.

(4.) *Lastly*, The covenant of peace reaches not without him, Isa. xlix. 8. and there is no acceptance of a sinner but in it. He was the only party-contractor in it, and contracted only for his seed; and it is only by faith uniting with Christ that we are actually in it. Know then that the whole of your salvation lies here. Ye must be in Christ, or ye can have no saving benefit by him. For God will not accept you even for Christ's sake, if ye be not *in* him.

But in Christ the sinner is in a state of acceptableness to God. We take up this in these five things following:—

1. In Christ the sinner may be accepted of God; 2 Cor. v. 19, "God was in Christ, reconciling the world unto himself, not imputing their trespasses unto them." There God may, with safety of his honour, meet with the sinner, and receive him into favour. While the sinner is out of Christ, it is inconsistent with the honour of God to accept of him; where is the honour of his justice and holiness, and of his law, if that should be? But the sinner being in Christ, these bars are removed, Matth. xxii. 4.

REASON. Christ has fully satisfied the law, in the name and stead of all his, Rom. x. 4. The law can demand nothing of them, but what it has got of their Surety for them; so justice cannot hinder their acceptance. And it has got,

(1.) Holiness of nature. It is true, it is not in them in their own persons, in the eye of the law; but in Christ as a public person it is; for he was born perfectly holy, brought a holy spotless human nature into the world with him, which was never in the least stained, Luke i. 35; Heb. vii. 26.

(2.) Righteousness of life. They cannot pretend to it in their own persons; but Christ has furnished it for them; Phil. ii. 8, "He humbled himself, and became obedient unto death." All the ten commands had their due from him. His obedience was universal, constant without interruption, voluntary without constraint, and perfect without the least failure in degree or measure.

(3.) Satisfaction for sin. That is quite beyond their reach; but he has satisfied fully; Gal. iii. 13, "Christ hath redeemed us from the curse of the law, being made a curse for us." Death in all its shapes preyed on him. The forerunners of it met him, at his entrance into the world; it hung about him all his days; in end it came on him with all its joint forces, carried him to the dust of death, kept him in the prison of the grave, till the debt was declared to be completely paid.

2. In Christ the sinner will be accepted. Any, even the worst of sinners shall certainly be accepted in Christ; Acts xvi. 31, "Believe on the Lord Jesus Christ, and thou shalt be saved." Whosoever shall make their escape into this city of refuge shall be safe. Christ will refuse none that come to him; and God will reject none that are in Christ. Let this be secured, and all is safe.

REASON. The promise of the gospel ensures this. The truth of heaven is plighted for it, that sinners may have all encouragement to come to Christ; John iii. 16, "For God so loved the world, that he gave his only begotten Son, that whosoever believeth in him, should not perish, but have everlasting life." It is an unalterable statute, that "he that believeth shall be saved," Mark xvi. 16. The word is full of promises of this nature. See Isa. lv. 1, 2. So that as Christ's satisfaction shews it is in the power of a holy God, to accept sinners; the promise of the gospel ascertains it to be his will.

3. In Christ the sinner cannot but be accepted. It is impossible it should fail or miscarry; Heb. vi. 18, "That by two immutable, things, in which it was impossible for God to lie, we might have a strong consolation, who have fled for refuge to lay hold upon the hope set before us." Heaven and earth may pass away sooner than a sinner in Christ should not be received into favour with God.

REASON. There is a right of a third party in this matter, which it is impossible to be baulked. It is not only God and the sinner that are here concerned, but the Mediator Christ appears for his interest. In the covenant that passed from eternity betwixt him and the Father, it was promised him, that on condition of his fulfilling all his righteousness, sinners should be accepted in him; he has fulfilled the condition, and so demands it as his own right, to whom the promises were made, Tit. i. 2.

4. That moment a sinner is in Christ, he is accepted, Rom. viii. 1, "There is therefore now no condemnation to them which are in Christ Jesus." No sooner does the soul come into Christ by faith, but all is safe; the man is in a state of favour with God, the day is risen with him, and the long and black night of the state of wrath is at an end. For then,

(1.) Heaven's offer is accepted as it was made. In the gospel there is an offer of Christ and his righteousness made to the sinner, Rom. i. 17; and of acceptance in him, Acts xiii. 38. The soul by faith coming to Christ, accepts the offer; so the acceptance with God offered, becomes actually his.

(2.) Faith uniting the soul to Christ, upon that union with him follows a communion with him in his righteousness, yea, in his fulness; as in marriage there is a communion of goods, 1 John i. 3. So the soul wants nothing to commend it to God for acceptance, having all in its head Christ, 1 Cor. i. 30; Col. ii. 10. The holiness and purity of his birth is theirs; all the good works he did during his life are theirs; and all that he suffered in life and death is theirs. All fullness being united to all emptiness, the empty creature is filled, and rendered accepted;

the transcendent beauty of the Head casts a lustre on all the members.

(3.) The soul pleading Christ's righteousness, and Christ interceding for the soul on that ground, the imputation of it, and acceptance of the person upon it, must immediately ensue. Faith's plea is well bottomed, and cannot be refused: Christ's intercession is always effectual; so the righteousness that is theirs by faith, cannot miss to be reckoned theirs, and they accepted as righteous thereon, 2 Cor. v. 21.

5. *Lastly*, While they abide in Christ, they remain accepted; so their union with him being everlasting, the acceptance of their persons can never be interrupted; John x. 28, "I give unto them eternal life, and they shall never perish, neither shall any pluck them out of my hand"; Rom. viii. 1. It continues in their adversity, as well as prosperity, Job. xlii. 8. Their sins may bring them under heavy strokes, yet still their persons are accepted in Christ, Psalm lxxxix. 30–34. It continues in death, as well as in life, John xi. 11, and will continue through eternity, Heb. vii. 25, for that righteousness of Christ put on by faith will ever continue on them; their union with Christ can never be dissolved; and being in Christ, they can never be but accepted.

I come now to the improvement of this subject.

1. Then the door of acceptance with God is open to all; none are excluded, Isa. lv. 1, 2. What is given freely, one has access to, as well as another, whatever they have been. Not that God will accept of any who will continue in their sin, and will not come to Christ; but that none shall be refused, who will come for acceptance in the method God has laid down.

2. Seek then acceptance with God, that ye may find favour with him. This should be your main aim, 2 Cor. v. 9. Here your happiness lies in time and eternity; Psalm xxx. 5, "In his favour is life." The favour of the world is both insufficient and uncertain; it cannot satisfy in life, much less in death. God is the best friend, and the most terrible enemy; for he is an everlasting friend, and an everlasting enemy too.

3. Seek it freely, without pretending to anything in yourselves to recommend you to his acceptance or favour. Put no confidence in whole or in part, in your doings, sufferings, attainments, Phil. iii. 7, 8; otherwise ye do put a bar in your own way, and will meet with that, "Thy money perish with thyself." Mind that this may procure your rejection, and therefore not your acceptance.

4. Seek it through Jesus Christ only, that is, by faith in him, laying the whole stress of your acceptance on his righteousness. The Jews missed it, because they sought it not this way, Rom. ix. 32. No person nor thing else can procure you the favour of God; no righteousness else will cover you; nothing but the blood of the Redeemer can be a covert from revenging justice; nor will anything else purge the conscience. All other things will be but as a wall of dry boards betwixt you and the consuming fire.

5. *Lastly*, Therefore as ever ye would have acceptance or favour with God, seek to be in Christ; to be united to him. For as there is no acceptance with God, but for his sake; so there is no acceptance for his sake, but to those that are in him, Col. i. 27. There is salvation in Christ, but none partake of it that are not in him; a righteousness in him, but it covers none but the members of his body. And,

(1.) This is the only way to be safe in time; for it is the only way to be without the verge of wrath, John iii. ult. And they that are without it are safe, go times as they will, John xvi. ult. While the Lord is threatening a rousing stroke on the generation, the only safety will be in Christ, Micah v. 5; Isa. viii. 14; and xxvi. 20.

(2.) It is the only way to be safe in eternity, Phil. iii. 9. We must launch out of time into eternity, and there is no escaping the gulf of eternal wrath, but in him. They that are not in him must depart from him; and departing from him, they must go into everlasting fire.

QUEST. How may we then get into Christ.

ANSW. 1. The only way to get into him is by faith, Eph. iii. 17. And faith is the convinced soul's renouncing all confidence in itself, and trusting on him entirely for salvation from sin and wrath, upon the ground of the faithfulness of God in the promise of the gospel. Hereby the soul knits with Christ, hangs on him, depends on him, wholly to stand or fall, according as he shall deal with them.

2. The only way to get that faith, is by his Spirit in us, 2 Cor. iv. 13. Christ communicating his quickening Spirit unto the dead soul, it believes; and believing is united to Christ, and accepted in him. Wherefore breathe, pant, and long for the Spirit of Christ, Luke xi. 13.

I shall now drop a word very briefly to the last doctrine, and so conclude this subject.

DOCT. III. ult. Glorious free grace shines forth in the acceptance of sinners in the beloved Jesus.

We shall consider, wherein it shines there. It shines,

1. In his admitting a Surety to mediate for the acceptance of sinners, when he might have insisted that the soul that sinned should die, Rom. v. 8, "God commendeth his love towards us, in that while we were yet sinners, Christ died for us." The necks of all the elect were on the block, and it was in the hand of spotless justice to reach them the fatal stroke. But glorious free grace admits a surety in their room.

2. He provided the Surety, John iii. 16; as he did the ram to come instead of Isaac lying bound on the altar. All the beasts of the field could not have afforded a sacrifice sufficient for the sinner's acceptance; nor the angels in heaven a cautioner; but glorious grace gave God's own Son; Psalm lxxxix. 19, "I have laid help upon one that is mighty; I have exalted one chosen out of the people." So the righteousness is the righteousness of God, not only of one who is God, but provided by God.

3. He demands nothing of us, to render us acceptable in whole or in part; but the cause of his accepting sinners is wholly without them; Rom. iii. 24, "Being justified freely by his grace, through the redemption that is in Jesus Christ." To us it is in no wise, Give and get; but Take and have; Rom. iv. 16, "Therefore it is of faith, that it might be by grace; to the end the promise might be sure to all the seed." So nothing in us has any hand in it, but faith, as the hand whereby it is received.

4. The very hand of faith whereby it is received is God's free gift; Eph. ii. 8. "For by grace are ye saved through faith; and that not of yourselves; it is the gift of God." Philip. i. 29. That one believes while another doth not, is owing purely to free grace, which makes the difference; giving the quickening spirit to one, that is not communicated to another.

5. In its breaking over all impediments lying in its way, such as these in the case of the Corinthians, to whom the apostle says, "Know ye not that the unrighteous shall not inherit the kingdom of God? Be not deceived; neither fornicators, nor idolaters, nor adulterers, nor effeminate, nor abusers of themselves with mankind, nor thieves, nor covetous, nor drunkards, nor revilers, nor extortioners shall inherit the kingdom of God. And such were some of you: but ye are washed, but ye are sanctified, but ye are justified in the name of the Lord Jesus, and by the Spirit of our God," 1 Cor. vi.

9-11. In the best of sinners, there is that loathsomeness and unworthiness found, that proclaims a glory of grace in their acceptance; Jer. iii. 19, "I said, How shall I put thee among the children?" But in the worst of them there is nothing found but what glorious grace will break over, to accept them in Christ, as in Manasseh, Mary Magdalene, Paul, &c.

6. In the thoroughness of the acceptance; Isa. i. 18, "Come now, and let us reason together, saith the Lord; though your sins be as scarlet, they shall be as white as snow; though they be red like crimson, they shall be as wool." Acceptance among men is often coldrife,[19] and by halves, so as the heart is not freely toward the pardoned offender. But God's acceptance of sinners in Christ is perfect the first moment; they are perfectly beloved in him, John xvii. 21.

7. *Lastly*, In the perpetuity and constancy of it; sinners are so accepted in Christ that they shall never be cast out of God's favour again; John x. 28, 29, "And I give unto them eternal life, and they shall never perish, neither shall any pluck them out of my hand. My Father which gave them me is greater than all; and none is able to pluck them out of my Father's hand." They are not put on their good behaviour as to the acceptance of their persons with God, but it is secured unalterably in Christ. The smiles and frowns of a Father will indeed be as they carry.

USE 1. Let us loath Popery then, as the smoke of the bottomless pit darkening the glory of grace in the acceptance of sinners, by their merit of works, and other corrupt doctrines and practices, laying another foundation than Christ. It is evident we are in danger of it, and it will he our wisdom to be on our guard, that we be not catched napping, come what will.

2. Let all be encouraged to come to God through Christ for acceptance, assuring themselves they may have it through him, God being well pleased with him, and with every one who believes in him for life, pardon and acceptance.

---

19 Cold, chilling.

www.ingramcontent.com/pod-product-compliance
Lightning Source LLC
Chambersburg PA
CBHW011130070526
44583CB00023B/2973